PSYCHO-SOCIAL DYNAMICS OF BLIND STUDENTS

About the Author

Ranjita Dawn, Assistant Professor in the Department of Education at Loreto College, University of Calcutta has received her Doctorate from Jawaharlal Nehru University, New Delhi. She is one among the leading scholars working in the area of Disability Studies in India. Her association with various research organizations provided enormous scope to become acquainted with the underlying dynamics associated with research work. It was during her association with organization like Blind Relief Association and National Association for Blind, New Delhi that she discovered her zeal for addressing the cause of people with disabilities. She has authored many technical papers in this field and is working to bring their problems and issues to the forefront. Her experience of being an educationist encourages her at each moment to address the potential problems that people with disabilities come across in their daily lives. Dr. Dawn has been the recipient of various prestigious awards such as Indian Council for Social Science Research Doctoral Fellowship, National Scholarship Award and Dr. Neelu Sanghvi Sancheti Memorial Medal for Graduation.

PSYCHO-SOCIAL DYNAMICS OF BLIND STUDENTS

Dr. Ranjita Dawn
Assistant Professor, Department of Education
Loreto College, Kolkata

CONCEPT PUBLISHING COMPANY PVT. LTD.
NEW DELHI-110059

The publication was financially supported by the ICSSR. The responsibility for the facts stated, opinions expressed or conclusions reached is entirely that of the author and the ICSSR accepts no responsibility for them.

The work was evaluated by Professor Susheela Bhan, Director, Institute of Peace Research and Action (IPRA), Delhi on behalf of the ICSSR.

ISBN-13: 978-81-8069-781-4

First Published 2011

Published and Printed by

Concept Since 1974

Concept Publishing Company Pvt. Ltd.
Regd. Office:
A/15-16, Commercial Block, Mohan Garden
New Delhi-110059 (India)
Phones : 25351460, 25351794, *Fax* : 091-11-25357109
Email : publishing@conceptpub.com
website: www.conceptpub.com
Editorial Office:
H-13, Bali Nagar, New Delhi-110 015, India

Cataloging in Publication Data--*Courtesy:* D.K. Agencies (P) Ltd. <docinfo@dkagencies.com>

Dawn, Ranjita.

Psycho-social dynamics of blind students / Ranjita Dawn.

p. cm.

Originally presented as the author's thesis (Ph. D.)—Jawaharlal Nehru University.
Includes bibliographical references (p.) and index.
ISBN 9788180697814

1. Blind children—Education—Government policy—India— Delhi. 2. Blind children—India—Delhi—Psychology. 3. Adjustment (Psychology) in children—India—Delhi. 4. Blind children—India—Delhi—Social conditions. 5. Students with disabilities—India—Delhi—Social conditions. I. Title.

DDC 371.9110954

Preface

The study aimed at assessing and analyzing if the type of educational placement (integrated and non-integrated) produced any significant influence and differences among adolescent blind and sighted students in respect of their self-esteem, adjustment and academic achievement. The interaction pattern and self-perception of blind students at school has been looked into from the social constructivist perspective of disability to analyze if experiences of schooling for children with disability are mediated through school practices and processes rather than the physical impairment itself.

Significant effects of disability condition and school setting on self-esteem, adjustment and academic achievement were hypothesized. The two main effects were expected to have significant interaction. It was also hypothesized that academic achievement will have significant correlation with self-esteem and adjustment.

The sample consisted of four groups of students— blind students in integrated schools, blind students in non-integrated schools, sighted students in integrated schools and sighted students in non-integrated schools. Each group comprised of 40 male students within the age group of 14-17 years and from grades IX-XII. Ten students were selected from each of the age and grade levels (two sections each) for each group. In case of blind students, only totally and congenitally blind adolescents were selected. Those having any additional impairment were not included in the sample.

Data were collected using questionnaire technique, observational methods and school record sheets. A questionnaire was used to collect background information of the students. Students' self-esteem was measured using the translated and adapted version of Coopersmith Self-esteem Inventory, Adult For. The Adjustment Inventory for the School students by A. K. P. Sinha and R. P. Singh (Hindi) was used for assessing Emotional, Social and Educational adjustment. The academic achievement of students was assessed by using the percentage of marks obtained by them in their last school examination. Besides this, self-rating scales of students' own performance and teachers' ratings of students' performance were administered. An in-depth study of ecology of classrooms was done at the larger institutional level in the context of the schools and also in terms of interpersonal relations prevalent in the classrooms. Classroom observations and interviews were employed in order to observe the attitude and interaction of blind and sighted students and teachers in integrated schools.

The response of both blind and sighted students in integrated and non-integrated schools were scored and analyzed for each of the measures in the study. Mean and SD values were computed for each of the four groups of students. Correlations were found out to assess the degree of association among self-esteem, adjustment (emotional, social and educational) and academic achievement, students' self-rating of their performance and teachers' rating of students performance) for each group. 2 (Group) x 2 (School setting) x 4 (Grades) ANOVA were used to find out the main and interaction effects of each of the variables. Multiple regression analyses were done to identify different contributing factors of academic achievement.

The data obtained on the basis of questionnaires administered to blind and sighted students and the teachers was used for qualitative analysis. Detailed semi-structured interviews were also conducted for both the students and teachers. The recorded interviews were transcribed and subjected to content analysis. Case studies based on the response of selected students from each group were also used for further analysis. Ecological analysis of integrated school settings was also conducted.

Following were the findings of the study:

- Blind and sighted students irrespective of school setting did not differ in respect of their self-esteem, adjustment and academic achievement. The students were found to be confident, capable of shouldering responsibilities, adaptable and determined. Among the several factors, parents and teachers played a dominant role in shaping the behaviour of students.
- Blind students in integrated and non- integrated school settings did not differ in regard to their self-esteem, adjustment and academic achievement. Both groups of students were found to possess positive self-esteem and better adjustment. Though both groups maintained a positive view of their parents for being sensitive to their diverse needs, respecting them and providing assistance, love and affection, the attitude of other family members (relatives) was found to have adverse affect on their self-esteem, adjustment and academic achievement.
- Ecological analysis of integrated schools showed that the type of school setting failed to produce any significant difference among blind students. Though the process of integration was implemented in most schools, its impact was confined to mere physical placement of students than their complete integration into the mainstream educational structure. Architectural and instructional barriers such as lack of barrier free environment, adequate and appropriate study materials such as non-availability of Braille books, necessary support services, adequate transport services, lack of continuous funding, restrictions on the legislative measures undertaken for the empowerment of people with disabilities, lack of follow-up procedures for their implementation etc. emerged as some of the loopholes in implementation of educational programmes.
- No difference in self-esteem, adjustment and academic achievement was evident between blind and sighted

students in integrated schools as compared to the students in non-integrated schools. All the students showed positive self-esteem and adjustment. However, the interaction effects of student groups and settings was significant for academic achievement. The findings also failed to show that the process of integrating blind students into mainstream schools facilitated greater social interaction, peer and teacher support, better facilities of learning, etc.

- The interaction effect of school setting and grades on social adjustment was significant. The findings show that integrated school students showed better social adjustment in grades IX and XII as compared to their non-integrated counterparts. However, it was lower in grades X and XI. The students were more attentive, less withdrawn and had positive social interaction in grades IX and XII. However, the ever changing and widening social relationships and expectations in the higher grades had adverse affect on social competence of students from both settings.
- Family was found to produce significant influence on both groups of blind and sighted students irrespective of school setting. The home environment of blind students was found to be more protective than that of the sighted. The parents were found to be over-concerned about their children's safety and well-being and provided additional attention to them. Though the sighted students also preferred their home but they did not report of parental overattention or indulgence.
- Self-esteem was found to be one of the significant predictors of academic achievement for blind students in non-integrated schools and sighted students in integrated schools. The other variables were not found to produce any statistically significant effect for the same groups.
- Significant positive correlation was found to exist between teachers' rating of students' performance and

> students' self-rating of their own performance. The teachers were satisfied with academic as well as non-academic performance of both blind and sighted students in integrated and non-integrated school settings. This shows that teachers maintain positive attitude towards the integration of blind students in regular classrooms.

Thus, comparative analysis of blind and sighted adolescents with respect to self-esteem and adjustment (social, emotional and educational adjustment) and academic achievement showed no significant difference. Ecological analysis of school and classroom environment also showed that the type of school setting (integrated and non-integrated) did not have any significant effect on the self-esteem and adjustment and academic achievement of blind and sighted students. However, analysis of qualitative data revealed that irrespective of the school setting, home or family had a major role in affecting the behaviour and development of both blind and sighted students.

Some implications and limitations of the study have been discussed. It is suggested that longitudinal studies with a large sample can also be undertaken to look into the interactions between school setting and its impact on self-esteem, adjustment and academic achievement of blind students. Comparative studies can be undertaken to find out differences in self-esteem, adjustment and academic achievement between blind and individuals having other forms of handicap. Besides these, studies can be undertaken to find out differences in self-esteem, adjustment and academic achievement among individuals with various categories of visually impairment, i.e. blind, partially sighted and low vision and also among congenitally and adventitiously blind individuals.

Acknowledgment

At the very outset a special word of appreciation for my family members. There are no words sufficient enough to express love and gratitude for my family members my mother, my sister, my brother and my baby boy for their tremendous support. I would like to thank them for being there for me throughout my life and for everything they have done for me. This thesis would never have materialized without their love, presence and sacrifices.

I would like to extend my gratitude to my supervisor, Professor A. K. Mohanty, for his constant supervision, support and guidance. I also take this opportunity to extend my thanks to all the faculty members of the Zakir Husain Centre for Educational Studies, JNU, Nerw Delhi for their keen interest in my work and cooperation. My debt of gratitude to Dr. G. C. Pal for his valuable suggestions and opinions for qualitative improvement of the work. I appreciate the assistance provided by the non-teaching staff of Zakir Husain Centre for Educational Studies, Rajendra ji, Seema Ma'am and Ghani Sir.

My appreciation of life at the university would indeed be incomplete without appreciating the presence of great friends Roopa, Jayendu, Nandini, Arpana and Dola. They have been my support in good and bad times. No words are enough to express my gratitude to Tara. Rambabu and all my dear differently abled friends and colleagues for giving me an opportunity to become a part of their world and share their experiences.

I extend my sincere gratefulness to the Principals, teachers, students as well as the non-teaching staff of Government Co-education Senior Secondary School, R. K. Puram, Sector V, New Delhi, Upras School, Vasant Marg, Vasant Vihar, New Delhi, Tagore International School, Paschimi Marg, Vasant

Vihar, New Delhi and Blind Relief Association, Lodhi Road for their kind cooperation. Their assistance has been of immeasurable help and an experience to be cherished for life. Special word of thanks and admiration for my dear brother Jeetendra from National Association for the Blind, New Delhi whose innocence and love has opened up a new world for me.

My sincere gratitude to the library staff of Jawaharlal Nehru University, National Council for Educational Research and Training, National Institute of Educational Planning and Administration, Indian Council of Social Science Research, National Medical Library, Delhi University, Rehabilitation Council of India and National Library, Kolkata for their constant support. I extend my special thanksgiving to the staff of National Association for Blind, New Delhi and National Institute for the Visually Handicapped, Dehradun for their priceless guidance and consultation.

I also extend my sincere thanks to the Indian Council of Social Science Research, New Delhi for duly acknowledging by the my Doctoral work and consenting to provide financial assistance for its publication.A special mention of gratitude to Prof. Susheela Bhan, Director, Institute of Peace Research and Action (IPRA), Delhi for her valuable suggestions in the preparation of the book.

I also extend my utmost gratitude to Sister Christine Coutinho, Principal, Loreto College, Kolkata and all staff for their unconditional love, support and guidance. A special word of thanks for Sister Tina, Ex-Principal of Loreto College and Dr. Arundhati Ray, for their faith in me.

I also extend my gratitude to the Concept Publishing Company Private Ltd, New Delhi for undertaking the publication of the work.

Contents

APPENDICES

List of Abbreviations

AA	Academic Achievement
ANOVA	Analysis of Variance
CABE	Central Advisory Board of Education
DPEP	District Primary Education Programme
EDU	Educational Adjustment
EMO	Emotional Adjustment
IEDC	Integrated Education for the Disabled Children
ILO	International Labour Organization
NCPEDP	National Centre for Promotion of Employment for Disabled People
NGO	Non-Governmental Organization
NPE	National Policy of Education
PIED	Projected Integrated Education for the Disabled
PWD	Persons with Disabilities Act, 1995
SE	Self-esteem
SOC	Social Adjustment
SSR	Students' Self-Rating of Academic Performance
TR	Teachers' Rating of Students' Academic Performance
UN	United Nations
UNDP	United Nations Development Programme
UNESCO	United Nations Educational, Scientific and Cultural Organization
UNICEF	United Nations International Children's Education Fund
UPIAS	Union of the Physically Impaired Against Segregation
WHO	World Health Organization

List of Tables

List of Figures

1

Models of Disability

The broad domain of 'disability' encapsulates a diverse categorization to which the society further provides an additional hierarchical diversification. The term disability refers to any restriction or lack of ability or dysfunction to perform an activity within the range considered normal for a human being. However with passage of time, it has now come to be characterized by the use of a wide range of terminologies such as impairment, handicap, differentially able, etc. This includes people having numerous types of impairment among which those with sensory impairment particularly the blind constitutes focus of the present study. This work aimed at critically analyzing the attitude of society towards people with disabilities, various models of disability and the educational provisions to understand their effect on the self-esteem, adjustment and academic achievement of blind students. Social acceptance and psychological well-being as essential prerequisites for the successful rehabilitation of all individuals made it imperative to explore the traumas, dilemmas, challenges that people with disabilities experience. These have a significant influence on their self-view, adjustment pattern and acceptance into the mainstream society.

The issue of 'exceptionality' that adheres to the accepted pattern of isolating individuals who were considered exceptional or "different" and subjecting them to marginalization in income, education, employment, relationships, etc. has been in focus since time immemorial. In relation to this, disability also remains as a neglected category not only with regard to social policies but also in academic researches where class, race, gender, etc. were accepted as the criteria to delineate and bring the focus on to the 'excluded' sections of the society. Throughout history the disabled have been stigmatized, marginalized and discriminated in almost all societies (Karna, 1999; Hudson, 1988). The disabled have represented a segment of population that is most backward, least served and grossly neglected thus having been customarily denied their right to self-assertion, identity and development. Although it has been shown in literature that no two disabilities are similar in nature yet people with any form of disability continue to be treated as a separate category of people with characteristics similar to each other but different from the rest.

Though it is difficult to generalize the patterns of historical representations of disability in literary, artistic and visual media due to differentiations among cultures in giving meaning and form to it, a survey of disability representations helps us to visualize the extent to which human differences posed substantial conflicts for all communities. While for some like Nietzsche, the disabled were 'parasites' worthy of 'extermination', for others they were objects of humour. In societies where economic survival was difficult, elimination of such people was considered justified since they were regarded as weak and dependent members and hence a liability to the society. Throughout the records of ancient civilization such as Mesopotamia and Greece, disability was related to a metaphysical predicament. Within the texts of these societies, disability was regarded either as a punishment for sins and such people were subjected to the mysterious ways of divinities. Evidences of dehumanizing treatment towards people with disabilities were found in Ancient Sparta where children were considered to be properties of the State. Hence, newborn deformed infants were regarded as an indication of displeasure of the Gods and were disposed. In Ancient Rome also deformed children were reported of being drowned in the Tiber. Corbett

(1996) mentioned that children with disabilities were seen as less than human and were subsequently vulnerable to less than humane treatment. Apart from the traditional, cultural and religious underpinnings that influenced the extermination of people with disabilities, survival of the fittest became a rule rather than an exception.

In numerous situations people with disabilities were 'objectified' by cultural impairments. They were regarded as common representational objects which enabled artists to employ their uniqueness as an impetus for generating audience interest. Means of providing charities also became another medium of objectifying the disabled thereby highlighting on ways of filling the gaps left by unwillingness of statutory bodies to meet their obligations to disabled citizens. Epilepsy, restricted growth and sensory impairments together with figures of the crippled and leper were the common stock of cultural representations of disability having specific resonance and literary utility. The blind in particular were represented as harpists and singers on the wall carvings of Egyptian tombs. Even in European history between the fourteenth and sixteenth centuries, we witness an explosion of records about "fools" and "court jesters' highlighting on the decreased capacities of individuals with cognitive disabilities and deaf-mutes as well as the power often bequeathed to these individuals by rulers and other prominent members of the ruling regimes.

Barton (1995) exhibited that stereotyping and stigmatization through negative labelling have been a constant part of the experiences of disabled people. In countries like Kenya, there have been reports of families setting up their disadvantaged at street corners to appeal to public sympathy and provision for the survival of the people with visual impairment. They were referred to as 'wasiojiweja' meaning those unable to take care of themselves (Kiarie, 2004).

The emergence of Eugenic movement witnessed a shift in emphasis to the hereditary nature of defects resulting in wholesale incarceration and segregation. The rise in pathologizing designations during this period oversaw a proliferation of ways in which one could become "inferior". Developments such as Native American reservations, segregated systems of racial apartheid and widespread institutionalization efforts all shared an interest in sequestration practices as a response to reproductive fears of contamination. Techniques of sterilization and wider use of birth control became widely adopted measures.

During 19th century there was reappraisal in the attitude of people towards disability due to increasing importance of labour power and the need to segregate the disabled from those who did not wish to work. As an outcome of this people with disabilities were subjected to institutionalization.

Social representations as cultural products rooted in praxis are considered to play dominant role in the structuring of identities or self-representations. It is a common belief that people with disabilities analyze their experiences in light of the existing meanings and practices prevalent in society. Moreover-since a greater part of these systems are rooted in the medical connotations of disability hence becomes imperative to address these issues in the light of various models of disability.

Notions and Models of Disability

Various models and approaches have been advanced in the field of disability studies. The different views that have emerged can be broadly divided into the following categories—Individual approach and Social approach.

Individual Approach of Disability

The individual approach often referred to as 'personal tragedy theory' views the problems faced by disabled people as having directly emanated due to individual dysfunction. The individual approach encompasses two models within its broad framework—the medical model and the psychological model.

The *medical model* emanated from the disease model of medicine, which predisposes practitioners to think of a 'condition' that needs appropriate treatment. It is believed that the medical model appeared as a consequence of the WHO (1980) debate on usefulness of terms such as 'handicap', 'impairment' and 'disability'. According to it, disability came to be defined as the effect of impairment on everyday activities thereby reducing the origins of disability to individual pathology. This paradigm makes two fundamental assumptions— it locates the problem of disability within the individual and seeks the cause of the problem as stemming from functional limitations that arise from disability. The human being under such circumstances is viewed as flexible and alterable as compared to the fixed and unalterable society. Disability under this approach was not regarded as a defining state wherein disabling conditions such as 'mental retardation', 'blindness', etc. were taken into consideration along with other conditions that were not capable of causing disabilities. Emphasizing on individual pathology or biological determinism, the model holds that all differences can be wiped with prostheses, exercises, medical interventions and by stimulating disabled people to adapt to the norms.

The essence of the medical model which reduces identity of the disabled to that of deviants, damaged, dependent carriers of sick role and perpetuating labels subjecting them to continuous stigmatization and marginalization can be best summed up in the following lines —

> *"The injunction to be particular sort of person is always bound up with an act of division: to be what one is, one must be what one is not...... The vicissitudes of identification are not ontological but historical and technical."*
>
> —Rose, 1996, p. 309

The *psychological model* focused on the use of clinical diagnostic criteria like "standardized measures" for assessing, quantifying the problems, categorizing and labelling individuals. It negates the realization that disability emanates from social situation such as barriers of environment and attitude of an individual with an impairment or functional limitation. It upholds the assumption that all people with impairments are automatically handicapped or handicap their family and that the society has not been constructed to include disabled people and make provisions for this diversity.

Despite the numerous arguments, both medical and psychological models were subjected to severe criticism. Critiques of the medical model opined that it failed to take into account views of disabled people for whom disability emanates from the society's unwillingness to employ and alter necessary means rather than individual dysfunction. On the contrary, the medical model regarded them as objects without power and incapable of managing their own lives. It also failed to realize that although medical conditions restricted the functioning of people with disabilities which may or may not have required medical treatment, human knowledge, technology and collective resources did not prevent them from experiencing good lives.

The impositions of medically defined and adult imposed notions of difference and normality to the identity of disabled in terms of labels are also evident in both "special" and "mainstream" settings whereby children are expected to comply with the definition and status imposed on them. Stambolvic (1996) and Camilleri (1999) also criticized the medical model for portraying the needs of disabled people as special and different from others thereby reducing disability to personal tragedy, highlighting the inabilities, overlooking the latent abilities of disabled people and promoting human helplessness.

With marked emphasis on the use of clinical diagnostic criteria such as standardized measures of intelligence or self-concept to identify the nature of the problem, critiques maintained that the psychological model posed certain hindrances. Worthen and Spandel (1991) maintained that the tests used had little association with learning and low predictive value resulting in categorization and labelling of children. Llewellyn and Chung (1997) also questioned the authenticity of measures associated with identifying and segregating what is 'normal' in the sphere of disability research.

The individual approach to disability has been subjected to severe criticism for its narrow and reductionist nature and failure to consider the significance of psychological and sociological causes resulting in disabling conditions. Moreover, this approach was also found to play a dominant role in making individuals feel receptive, passive and compliant thus promoting human helplessness. The above arguments necessitated the need for a paradigm shift in the area of disability studies. This assumed a form with the formulation and acceptance of Social approach of disability.

Social Approach of Disability

The issue of disability has been historically conceptualized by different disciplines such as sociology and social policy using a range of theoretical approaches. Before critically analyzing the social approach of disability it is essential to look into the background that caused its foundation. Several sociological accounts have been shaped by the *Parsonian Paradigm* according to which people with disabilities authorize medical professionals to undertake the shaping of their lives thus alleviating them from their 'abhorrent and undesirable situation' (Parsons, 1951). Parsons (1951) adopted a functional approach to health and illness treating illness as a social role with precise expectations and limitations. According to him sickness exempted people with disabilities from the obligations and responsibilities that other members of society undertook thereby characterizing them in terms of 'incapacity' and 'deviance'. Parsons opined that conformity to 'normal' social roles facilitated in maintaining the integrity of social systems.

Early works in disability research based on the Parsonian perspective show that maintenance of social system being the prime focus made it imperative for all members of the society to execute their appropriate social roles.

Later a shift in paradigm subjected the Parsonian perspective to severe criticism. It was argued that although Parson's viewpoints were more suitable for impairments that were acute and transitory in nature its implication was not suitable on those which were permanent or chronic in nature. Some researchers further maintained that it was possible for the sick or impaired individuals to recover function or health within the context of their life position and resources since the meanings associated with them are conditioned by one's position and the social groups to which they belong (Kassebaum & Baumann, 1965; Gordon, 1973). Critically analyzing the Parsonian paradigm, Twaddle (1974) pointed out that while emphasizing on social and psychological reality of disease it failed to take into consideration the organic base of illness.

Another viewpoint that emerged regarding disability studies was the *Deviance approach*. The deviance theorists viewed people with disabilities as 'being deviant' from others. Goffman (1963) visualized the abnormal nature of people with disabilities as a source of stigma among the non-disabled which marked them as different and harmful. Friedson (1965) also visualized people with disabilities as social deviants. According to him, identification of factors that brings some people in conflict with society's morals and values facilitate the changes required for them to be accepted by the non-disabled. He thereby emphasized on deviance by using the term in the context of institution.

Later the deviance model was subjected to severe criticism. Haber and Smith (1971) rejected the model based on the argument that the key to the disabled role lay with legitimation whereby the external behaviour of disabled individuals were normalized through mechanisms that provided new social meanings and rules of interaction for persons with disabilities.

A marked change was observed in the field of disability research with the coming of the Social approach. Under this approach disability came to be conceptualized as an interaction between individual and society. It argued that whether a person was being labelled as disabled primarily depended on how the society arranged circumstances in order to compensate for the individual impairments.

The arguments of the social approach were well-reflected in the earlier works of UPIAS (Union of the Physically Impaired Against Segregation, 1976) which defined disability as 'the disadvantage or restriction of activities caused by contemporary social organizations and thus takes little or no account of people with physical impairment and thus excludes them from participating in the mainstream of social activities'. The earliest attempt to concretize the social approach was made by Mike Oliver with the view to reflect the growing distress and demands of people with disabilities and their allies for 'nothing more fundamental than a switch away from focusing on the physical limitations of particular individuals to the way the physical and social environments impose on certain groups or categories of people' (Oliver, 1983: 23).

According to Oliver, the Social approach does not deny the problem of disability but locates it within the society. Failure on the part of society to take into account the needs of people with disabilities and provide appropriate services to them rather than the individual limitations promotes the problem. Oliver (1996) opined that the 'impaired' or 'disabled' role makes individuals 'accept dependency', and make most of their abilities to achieve 'normality'. The oppression that people with disabilities face in the society results from institutional discrimination 'ranging from individual prejudice to institutional discrimination, from inaccessible public buildings to unusable transport system, from segregated education to excluding work arrangements and so on (Oliver 1996:33). According to him, lack of mobility is impairment, but lack of access to essential facilities was disability.

The Social approach also regarded as 'Social Oppression Theory' includes within it two perspectives on disability—*Social Constructivist* and *Social Creationist*. Besides these two broad perspectives, the social approach encompasses a number of other theoretical perspectives: Functionalism, Conflict, Interactionism and Post-modernism which would be critically discussed in the forthcoming section. The two other submodels that can be discussed within the framework of the Social approach of disability are the Systems model and the Transactional model.

The *Social Constructivists* view disability as a problem located within the minds of able-bodied people, whether individually (prejudice) or collectively, through the manifestation of hostile social attitudes and enactment of social policies based upon a tragic view of disability. This approach holds that individuals become a part of the existing world only when they learn and acquire socially anchored values and beliefs. The various meanings that people learn to attach to various activities have an impact on their ability to interact with the environment. Similarly, disability for them is defined by the meaning that we attach to different kinds of physical and mental deviations.

Researchers like Rose (1962) held that disability is only in a particular and narrowest sense a condition that a person has. The word disability (and the many sub-categories under the heading) does not simply symbolize a condition that is already there in advance, it makes possible the existence or appearance of the condition for it is part of the mechanism. Hence, they held that as a concept disability is a particular way of thinking, acting and reacting while the creation of disability concept, its application in specific settings and the effect it provokes is derived from and sustained in interaction. The most common means that are associated and results in segregation of disabled individuals from mainstream society are the effects of categorization, labelling and institutionalization. The labelling and categorization of an individual as 'disabled' puts the person in a category that is loaded with social meanings and preconceptions. The treatment that individuals receive from significant others in the society causes them to internalize the image inherent in labels. This in turn determines their behaviour pattern and affects their self-image.

Under the Social Constructivist approach, Soder (1989) outlined two other ways of viewing the relation between disability and environment— (a) Epidemiological approach and (b) Adaptability approach:

(a) The Epidemiological approach views disability as a disturbance within an individual with environment being treated as the potential cause of disturbances. This approach seeks to describe as well as interpret the distribution of disabilities within different substratas of a population and locate it in a geographical and social structure in causal terms.

(b) The Adaptability approach regards disability as an outcome of interaction between individual and environment rather than an intrinsic personal characteristic or abnormality within an individual. Hence, according to the Social Constructivists environment 'is seen as the creator of disability' (Soder, 1989).

The *Social Creationists* (Abberley, 1987; Oliver, 1992) perceived disability not as something that exists within the minds of individuals or groups or even society as a whole but in the institutionalized practices of the society. According to them, impairment is not an unavoidable 'fact of nature' but is primarily the consequence of social and political factors such as malnutrition, drug abuse, lack of medical treatment (Abberley, 1987). Abberley (1987) opined that besides emphasizing on the deplorable state of people with disabilities, there is the need to develop a more comprehensive theoretical approach which would facilitate masses to understand that perception of people with disabilities as 'disabled' are dialectically related to an ideology or a group of ideologies that further perpetuates the existing situation.

Among the other theoretical perspectives included within the social approach of disability are: *Functionalism, Conflict, Interactionism* and *Post-modernism*.

The earliest theory of *Functionalism* was evident in the sociological works of Emile Durkheim. Durkheim (1964) posited a fundamental difference between pre-industrial and industrial societies. According to him, social integration in the pre-industrial societies was based on similarities of roles in the social division of labour i.e. 'mechanical solidarity'. However, with the emergence of industrialization and its continuous emphasis on growing separateness and distinction of an individual from the group due to division of labour, a good society came to be recognized by its strong bonds of 'organic solidarity' that were constituted through the recognition of role of others in the complex division of society. The deprivation of such a role was referred to as deprivation of full societal membership.

The Functional perspective which explains the existence of a phenomenon or execution of an action in terms of its consequences thus contributing towards maintaining a stable whole laid emphasis on order, stability, consensus and maintenance of the *status quo*. Farber referred to the disabled and deviants as "the surplus population" i.e. a residual population from which recruitment could be made for various positions in the social organization. By addressing the disabled as a residual population, he regarded people with disabilities as deviants who are unable to adjust and meet the demands of the social setting in which they live and were hence subjected to classification, regulation and treatment. He held that placing them outside the larger society facilitated maintenance of order and stability in the society (cited in Tomlinson, 1984: 14). Such an objective necessitates the need to help children with special needs to adjust to the society by differentiating their needs and allocating them to segregated/separate settings. This was an essential prerequisite for maintenance of social order without the disabled people disturbing the regular educational system.

Emphasizing on the viewpoints of Durkheim, Topliss (1982) provided further support for the discrimination against people with disabilities. He maintained that although the type of impairment that disables a person from participating in the society may undergo a change, an inevitable line of distinction continues to remain between the disabled minority and the able bodied majority wherein the interests of the former are given less salience in the activities of the society. In addition to this, continuous emphasis on vigorous independence, competitive achievement in the occupational sphere further facilitates negative and stigmatizing view of the disabled. In view of the diverse values which underpins the varied spheres of society aiming to create desired categories of people, people with disabilities are subjected to further stigmatization and neglect resulting from the "disablement" which handicap them. Hence, according to Topliss, the inevitable disadvantage of the people with disabilities stems from general inability to meet standards of performance at work.

Emphasizing on social control, the *Conflict perspective* focuses on power and domination of one group over another. It views people with disabilities as a vulnerable group, oppressed and controlled by the larger population i.e. the so-called 'normal' people, who exclude them from the mainstream activities. According to this perspective, people with disabilities assert control over their lives by acting as a group to bring in changes in their disabling environment through laws and policies and altering the attitude of the people towards them through active participation in public life. This marked a shift in emphasis from the medical model which focused on functional impairment and the economic model which emphasized on vocational limitations to a political approach that helped to visualize the problems of people with disabilities resulting from a disabling environment rather than personal limitations. It also encouraged them to take control of the dysfunctional and interpretative processes with the aim of establishing their identities.

Within the context of the conflict perspective of disability mention can be made of the Human Rights Approach. Burgdorf (1980), Quinn (1995), Degener and Koster-Dreeser (1995) and Seighart (1985) were among the protagonists of this approach to disability. They were of the opinion that people with disabilities possess the same needs as the rest of humanity. The approach advocated for the formulation and implementation of legislation so as to provide leverage towards promoting mainstreaming of the disadvantaged individuals.

However, the critiques of the conflict perspective maintained that while the conflict perspective focused on the dimensions of conflict, coercion or the vested interests of the disabled in society, it failed to consider the implications and impact that social interaction and the construction of meanings have had on their lives.

Interaction with others holds the focus of arguments for the *Interactionist perspective*. The role of 'significant others' which Scott (1999) referred to as 'those people who have the greatest influence on an individual's evaluation of himself and who have the greatest impact on his acceptance and rejection of social norms', facilitates the manner in which people with disabilities give shape to their 'self'. Further support to the role of significant others in the formation of an identity of self was provided by Cooley (1902) and Mead (1934). Cooley (1902) maintained that an individual develops his conception of the self by way of imagining what others think of him by way of a "looking-glass" process. Later expanding upon Cooley's looking-glass self, Mead (1934) held that self-concept arises in social interaction as an outgrowth of an individual's concern about others, reaction to him or her. The need to anticipate others' reaction can cause an individual to behave accordingly thereby perceiving the world as the 'others'. Hence,

Mead (1934) also emphasized on the aspect of self being social and held that an individual comes to know about himself or herself by role playing.

However, the nature of interaction could extend from one of acceptance and compassion to labelling and stigmatization. Referring to the concept of stigma, Goffman (1969) maintained that the physically impaired, those with mental disorder, homosexuals and members of racial and religious minorities are viewed by the society as 'not quite human' but as deviants from the 'anticipated norms' (Vernon, 1999). The stigma attributed brings along with it certain negative connotation that prevents individuals with disabilities from being treated at par with their non-disabled counterparts. In the classroom situation also effective social interaction in terms of ability to reciprocate to others' actions affect the 'concept of self' of children. Labelling further results in self-fulfilling prophecy and prevents the child from realizing his or her potential.

The rise of *Post-modernism* challenged the existence of ultimate truth which could be discovered through reason and rationality. It also marked an end to the dominant beliefs of the Western culture for which world could be understood in terms of the underlying structures such as the economic structure as exemplified in the works of Marx and the psychic structures of Piaget and Freud. The tenets of post-modernism emphasize that there cannot be 'pure' measures of people's contexts and characteristics in order to inevitably arrive at 'purity' as they reflect the distorting practice of filtering out the normal social context of a person's life. According to them this can be of immense relevance for contemporary research in human behaviour.

The Post-modernist perspective was later applied to the study of disability as an attempt to develop a radical sociology of impairment. Post-modernists like Foucault (1973) attempted to study the power exercised by 'normal' people over people with disabilities. Modernity according to them had a pervasive capacity to produce strangers. The limits of tolerance and conformity provided the basis for constructing the aspects of strangeness, while modernity lends support to homogenize and annihilate the differences it invariably produces. The two major viewpoints existing in the generic construction of stranger in modernity regarding people with disabilities are the Anthropophagic (assimilationist) strategy by way of the segregationist policies and the Anthropoemic (exclusionary) strategy by way of community care. However, both the strategies were an outcome of powerful 'will to order', according to which impairment is constituted in terms of invalidation.

According to Foucault (1973) the stranger produced result due to categorization and normalization of the propensities of knowledge. For him the "gaze" manifests itself more in institutional forms of domination and regulation rather than the oppressiveness of intercorporal relationships. Self-surveillance by which people develop an awareness of how they are through the gaze of others and then modify their behaviour affects both disabled and non-disabled people. Under such circumstances people with disabilities are subjected to oppression wherein they internalize the prejudices and assumptions held by their non-disabled counterparts. Foucault (1971, 1976) held that medicine and psychoanalysis in addition to the penal system provide examples of disciplinary and regulatory control leading to the criterion of new norms. It is diffusion of the medical discourse that has enabled the medical model view of disability to become widespread at all levels of the society, affecting the manner in which institutions from the Government to industry treat disabled people (Chadwick, 1996). In this relation 'normal' people use the power of fixing which Sartre (1958) referred to as 'gaze' on the disabled people for not conforming to what they consider 'valid' behaviour.

Sartre (1958) was concerned with the dialectical play of power which manifests itself in the form of 'gaze' of others that subject one to objectification and internalization. The gaze for him was a 'constituent power' i.e. the power to fix an identity or to 'condemn' an individual identity wherein the absolute freedom of the solipsistic self is displaced by spatialisation and temporization. In other words, the experience of being looked at by others indicates denial of 'transcendence' and transformation into a 'degraded consciousness'. This is also applicable in case of the disabled where the 'steady and corrosive gaze' of the non-disabled others institutionalized in medicine highlights the corporeality of 'truth' and 'perfection' of normality subjects and stigmatizes the impaired for lack of wholeness, coherence and unity. Sartre (1982) referred to this gaze in the 'Critique of Dialectical Reason' as the 'praxis of oppression' which is socially constructed and through which the disabled people experience an act of 'invalidation', being reduced to status of an object itself and condemned to an 'identity'.

The concept of 'gaze' whereby the disabled are placed under constant surveillance of others was also emphasized by Allan (1998). He analyzed the formation of children's identities through three mechanisms of surveillance earlier identified by Foucault. He held that from the perspective of Hierarchical Observation one tends to see everything perfectly. According to him, children with special education needs are placed under constant surveillance of those who are entrusted with their supervision wherein the teachers, parents, head teachers and specialists are caught within the network of the gaze. This is chiefly based on the rationale that surveillance of pupils with special education need enable the professionals to show concern for the welfare of such children and acquire knowledge about their disability. At the same time, it also allows the aspect of power or control to remain inherent in the situation as they can enforce their perception of the situation on the children.

Among the other aspects that subject children with special needs to surveillance are the perspective of Normalising Judgements which separates children with special needs from the normal children and the perspective of Examination which tends to objectify the individual by classifying them and labelling them as cases who need to be 'trained or corrected, classified, normalized, excluded etc.' (Foucault, 1981). The completion of the assessment procedure ensures further subjection of the child and his or her parents to surveillance for the entire school life.

Expanding on the concept of gaze and its impact Fox (1993) maintained that it was clearly evident in institutional settings where bodies are disciplined. According to him, the body becomes a site of power or knowledge for the disabled people who are constantly under the surveillance of medical experts who use clinical gaze to identify deviance and disorder and to constitute them as patients.

Finkelstein (1980) based on his own experiences and those of other people with disabilities held that for centuries able bodied people have made decisions for the disabled ranging from deciding on appropriate behaviour pattern for them by means of rehabilitation programme to designing equipments for them with assumed expertise. This resulted in depriving people with disabilities the right to question the objectivity of the able bodied for making decisions on their behalf. He referred to this as the Social Barriers model of disability according to which disability results due to social and attitudinal barriers constructed by a world built for the able bodied. According to Finkelstein, the construction of boundaries among the able bodied and people with disabilities are also handicapped by discipline. Disability according to him failed to hold the focus as a subject or course of study other than remaining as an issue of discussion and a result of human malfunction.

French (1993, 1999, 2001) also emphasized on the role played by the society in disabling blind people using the prior social model of disability literature. She argued that conflicting discourse resulted due to sighted people definition of "acceptable" and "normal" behaviour for the visually disabled people and using them to "contest that person's identity".

Emphasizing on the lack of adequate academic attention to disability studies, Barnes (1999) held that current presentation of 'disability' in the Universities fosters the notion that disability is an individual or a family 'problem'. According to her, the absence of 'disabled voice' in the curriculum and shortage of disabled scholars and researchers within the universities largely accounted for inadequate interventions leading to the marginalization of 'disability' in humanities and liberal arts.

According to Finkelstein, the term 'disabled' or 'abnormal' denoted ownership of particular impairment and signified health problem of the able bodied whereby the disabled were regarded as able bodied victims of the inequities imprisoned in imperfect bodies. This ignorance about the nature of disability characterized the whole residential institutional approach. According to Finkelstein (1980), there have been three phases of development regarding the perception of people with disabilities. In phase one, the disabled people formed a part of a mainstream oppressed underclass. In phase two, the coming of industrialization, urbanization, regulation and externalization of working practices with the rise of capitalism prevented many people with disabilities from keeping pace with the new market economy. This resulted in them being redefined as passive and dependent and segregated from mainstream society to workhouses and asylums. In the third phase, introduction of new technology led to the belief that individual people would help people with impairments to reintegrate into the mainstream society and cause disability to disappear.

Michalko (1998), a post-modern sociologist deconstructed medical, psychological and societal ideas and practices around blindness. In his, "Mystery of the Eye and Shadow of Blindness" (1998) he critically analyzed blindness rehabilitation. He wrote 'Ophthalmology is recommending *agency* as an *actor* presented as qualified to speak about, and act upon, permanent blindness...". He criticized the authority assumed by the medical personnel in diagnosing blind individuals and referring them for rehabilitation. Such an approach suggests that blindness requires an agency and needs to be acted upon for rehabilitation for a "good life". In another book, "The Two in One: Walking with Smokie, Walking with Blindness", Michalko analyzed his own experience of vision loss and acquisition of a guide dog. He described his personal experience in the living world built by and for the sighted people by using post-colonial concepts of "home" and "exile". He also examined how the dog guide school created expectations about the behaviour of blind students and school environment based on sighted notions about blindness experience.

The Systems Model considers the society as a compound of different systems characterized by communication in contrast to the biological systems. It holds that behaviour of human beings can be understood within the perspective of these different systems that are distinct from one another. Bronfenbrenner (1979, 1989), Hayes (1994), Hornby (1994) and Mitchell (1986) were among the leading exponents of the Systems model. According to the systems model, disability is regarded as a phenomenon that cannot be analyzed other than in relation to the distinctive system/environment as individuals do not belong to a system but are a part of the environment. It refers to communication in functionally differentiated systems of the difference between impairment and no impairment. Each system indicates specific codification, whereby individuals are observed in different ways in different systems. The system ascribes a specific coordination to each individual thereby attaching a meaning to the particular individual's condition. All the other aspects of the person are ignored except those that fit the system-specific form of communication. Table 1.1 shows distinctions about handicap as used within different systems.

The basic theoretical underpinning of the approach that behaviour of people with disabilities cannot be considered independent of the social milieu is best demonstrated by the four levels of social systems as shown in Figure 1.1.

Table 1.1: Handicap as conceptualized within different systems

Perspectives	*Observation of Disability*
Medical system	Diseases, defects, malfunctions, impairments, treatment.
Economic system	Lack of economic resources, inability to pay, poverty.
Labour market system	Working disability, inability to engage in gainful activity.
Legal system	Legal incapacity, lack of rights/duties.
Rehabilitation system	Support/correction of functional incapacities.
Education system	Learning difficulties, low education level.
Art system	Ugliness, defective body.

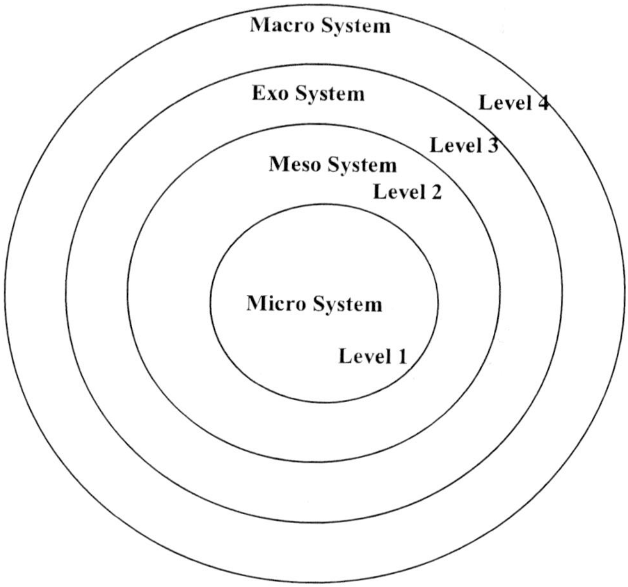

Fig 1.1: Four levels of social systems based on the Systems Model.

The four levels of social systems include—

- The micro system including the family and its various sub-systems.
- The meso system including extended family, friends and neighbours, associates, local agencies participative in delivering services to the disabled individuals.

- The meso sytem is in turn embedded in an exo system incorporated within which are health, employment, education, social welfare, recreation, voluntary societies and mass media systems, and
- The macro system comprises of the broad values and ideologies of the society.

In accordance with the systems approach, Bronfenbrenner (1979) maintained that the characteristics of a person at a given time in his or her life are a joint function of the characteristics of the person and the environment till his or her life up to the present time. It emphasized on the need to observe young people with physical disabilities in different contexts and environment at different points of time before making clinical or psychological judgement. Besides this, there is also the need to interpret the assessment of the competencies of any person with disability in the light of the culture or sub-culture in which he or she has been brought up.

In keeping with the above arguments, the advocates of the systems model maintain that the planning, management and evaluation of services for the people with disabilities and their families must address the changing developmental needs of such disadvantaged.

The Transactional model emphasized on the need to understand the environment as an interactive structure and view individuals as active synthesizers of information from the environment. This was considered to be imperative in understanding the impact that the perceptions of significant others have on the development of persons with disabilities.

Role of Culture and Media in Disability Studies: A Medium of Social Construction of Disability

Apart from the role of various social institutions, materialists and post-structuralists have explored and highlighted the importance of *culture* and *media* in justifying and maintaining exclusion of those defined as 'other' (Abberley, 1987; Barnes, 1991; Shakespeare, 1994). Barnes (1996) held that there is the need to see current social responses to impairment as cultural product of interaction between the means of production and Central societal values. The significance of use of cultural images as a medium to socially construct the unwelcome 'other' has been the focus of research among several theorists. Several works have criticized the use of negative imagery by general media and in literature which regards the differences as unacceptable, evil or a punishment from God (Barnes, 1991; Hafferty & Foster, 1994; Shakespeare, 1994). For instance, charity advertisers are shown to be especially fond of using images of people with impairments that are designed to evoke feelings of guilt, pity and sympathy in non-disabled people, as a means of persuading the mainstream population to make more donations (Hevey, 1992).

According to Libert (1975) two concepts can be related to the positive and negative attitudes toward disability- learning—observational learning and multiple modelling. He held that observational learning occurs through stages of exposure, acquisition and acceptance as a person observes the behaviour of another person and as this process of observation becomes more convincing it gives rise to the tendency to see less difference among individuals with the same disability, i.e. multiple modelling. Libert maintained that observational learning influences the three components of attitudes (cognitive, affective and behaviour) towards disability.

Television has been regarded a major medium addressing the issue of disability. However, the nature of its impact has been a debatable issue among disability activists. For some people television acted as a strong platform for voicing the needs of the "disadvantaged", while for others it subjected people with disabilities to greater stigmatization. On critical analyzing the frequencies of programmes depicting disability it was evident that majority of the programmes and feature films provided inaccurate and unrealistic portrayal thus creating a negative and misinformed image of persons with disabilities (Byrd & Allen, 1977; Byrd, McDaniel & Rhoden, 1981; Elliot & Byrd, 1982). The recurrence of such images contributes towards reinforcing cultural prejudice and paradoxical feelings of fear, pity, and guilt towards disabled people. Regarding this Barnes (1992) maintained that "They form the bedrock on which the attitudes toward, assumptions about, and expectations of disabled people are based".

Leonard (1978) urged that inappropriate portrayal of disability through television programmes tend to stigmatize people with disabilities by characterizing them as victims who possess undesirable social and personal qualities. Characteristics such as stress, trauma, overcompensation, character flaw or bizarre behavioural tendencies have constantly been associated with the disabled (Donaldson, 1981; Leonard, 1978). This was further affected by the nature of roles attributed to people with disabilities. Donaldson (1981) found lack of involvement of the disabled people in major or incidental roles.

Besides the nature, the focus of most of the programmes were found to be limited to specific forms of disabilities such as mental illness, drug addiction, emotional disturbance, etc. while severe physical disabilities failed to acquire adequate attention.

Apart from depiction of people with disabilities by the media, the use of stigmatizing language and metaphors by medical professionals was also found to have negative connotation for the disabled population (Peters, 1996; Swain & Cameron, 1999). Commenting on the usage of labels, Bogdan and Taylor (1982) maintained that labels create barriers in understanding handicapped individuals by encouraging the non-handicapped people to define them in terms of a single dimension, which in turn is used to generalize about the labelled person's character and ability. The process of labelling as applicable in the field of education of students with disabilities was found to have had little functional value other than giving a global indication of their educational placement. This in turn proved to be more detrimental by limiting the approach of providing them education in the least restrictive environment.

Criticism of the social approach of disability

The Social approach of disability has been subjected to certain criticisms. It is held by some researchers that disability exists only in the attitudes or as a function of the social power to coerce which is detrimental. According to them, complete acceptance of the belief that disability is a socially constructed phenomenon might result in regarding disability as 'unreal'. In addition to this misinterpretation of the social model by some disability activists have resulted in the belief that the model precludes discussions of impairments, importance of 'medical' treatments, ignores the question of gender, minority ethnic status, sexuality, class and so on.

Moreover, constant and increasing emphasis on 'post' theorizing has caused a marked shift in focus to personal narratives and experiences (Hughes & Paterson, 1997; Shakespeare, 1997) and analysis of role of impairment in the process of disablement. The diverse discourse on social model has diluted the meaning of 'disability' as perceived by people with disabilities themselves. The critiques also argued that increasing dependence on using euphemisms rather than labels to openly communicate about disabilities have come into use wherein denying disability have contributed towards limiting the numerous stigma and thwart prevention efforts.

Overall Analyses of Notions and Models of Disability

Overall analyses of the various approaches to disability brought certain essential issues to the forefront. It highlighted marked changes in paradigms for defining disability from the individual approach or more specifically the medical model to the social approach. Review of differing expressions and manifestations of the Individual approach or the 'personal tragedy theory' reveals that some of them were predominantly medical or biological while the others were concerned with identity or negotiation of social roles. Hence, they were more concerned with either the physical or psychological concomitants of impairment. As a result of this, they were found to marginalize the collective needs of people with disabilities for enhanced civil rights and removal of disabling barriers. This ushered in the need to incorporate a shift in paradigm to the social approach which was also found to encompass diverse viewpoints within it.

While some of the social approach theories were found to be more concerned with structural and material conditions, others laid emphasis on culture and representation. This diversity within the broad domain of social approach is evident in the works of various theorists. For instance, while Finkelstein (1980) emphasized on the need for sociological explanations of disability to accommodate 'social death' along with 'social barriers', Barnes (1996) maintained that the oppression of people with impairments can be explained with reference to material and cultural forces. Oliver (1990) opined that disability was a resultant of complex interaction of the 'mode of production and the Central values of the society concerned'. Similarly, while the modern materialists maintained that capitalism subjected people with disabilities to a specific and explicit form of exclusion and that social inclusion can be achieved only with the replacement of the exclusionary capitalist system, the Systems approach emphasized the need to observe the phenomenon of disability from different systems prevalent in the society as it would enable people to challenge and overcome the compulsory selectivity has been usually used to classify and describe people as objects in a functionally differentiated society. Despite differing perceptions and understanding of disability by various theorists, the social model continues to act as a philosophical base and catalyst for increasing the politicization or mobilization of the movement of people with disabilities.

2

Self-esteem and Adjustment of the Blind

Disability as a linguistic term is composite comprising of people with a large variety of unrelated characteristics. However, through the processes of separation and practices of defining society's responsibility they have been separated from the rest. It includes diverse categorization within itself, of which those having sensory disabilities particularly the blind constitutes focus of the present study.

Blindness comes under the broad category of visual impairment. It can be defined according to the purpose for which vision is required. There can be 'medical blindness', 'legal blindness', 'occupational blindness', and 'educational blindness'. Lowenfeld (1963) referred to blindness as Central visual acuity of 20/200 or if there is a field vision in which the peripheral field becomes contracted to such an extent that the widest diameter subtends to an angular distance no greater than 20 degrees. For educational purposes, individuals regarded as blind are so severely impaired that they must be taught to read by Braille or aural methods (Hallahan & Kauffman, 1991).

In India according to the Ministry of Human Resource Development, Government of India, blind are those who suffer from any of the following conditions:

- Total absence of sight; or
- Visual acuity not exceeding 6/60 or 20/200 (Snellen) in the better eye with correcting lenses; or

- Limitation of the field of vision subtending an angle of 20 degrees or worse.

On the basis of causative factors people having blindness can be categorized as— congenitally blind and adventitiously blind. Congenitally blind refers to those people who have never experienced sight and are unable to visualize visual concepts. Such people have to conceptualize ideas about objects and reality through any other means other than vision. Adventitiously blind are those who have developed blindness later in life. The loss of sight might be gradual or abrupt after experiencing the world through the medium of vision.

The effects of impairment of vision have been found to extend from both perceptual and non-perceptual domains of development resulting in fragmentation of learning in general and academic performance in particular. The unexpressed feeling of loss of sight is frequently associated with helplessness, inferiority, mobility related stress and anxiety, depression, loss of self-efficacy and poor performance (Meighan, 1970; Singh & Akhtar, 1971; Teare, 1985, Bhardwaj, 1995; Jindal-Snape, Kato & Maekawa, 1998; Rosenblum, 2000).

Since the desired outcome of life is preparation for independent living and to become a contributing member of the society, blind individuals are posed with several problems herein. Physical constraints lead to developmental delays in motor skills and physical competence thereby giving rise to feelings of helplessness and dependence. Due to such difficulties only a few blind people were considered to be successful in attaining full independence and full identity (Rice, 1984). Several researchers held that restricted mobility affects development of identity (Pollock et. al., 1997; Howard, 1996). From an interactionist perspective, identity development takes place in different interplay situations with peers (Mead, 1934). For those with restricted mobility, constant presence of adults or other support services can cause individuals to become more dependent. Most researches indicate that blind persons maintain negative or lower self-esteem.

Of the numerous problems experienced by visually challenged individuals, the influence that additional physical effort upon the alteration of feelings emerged as one of the dominant factors. Many regarded effort as a very important source of emotional disturbance and supported their belief with several examples and illustrations. It is held that disturbances occur when one has to abandon his own methods by which he or she can manipulate his or her visual environment conveniently and substitute it by the socially approved procedure of the sighted. Cutsforth (1951) while investigating schools for the blind to study the effect of over-supervision and overzealousness in training towards visual respectability found that many students were haunted constantly by the feeling that they were being watched and observed. This feeling followed them even in the privacy of their own rooms. (this is in conjunction with Sartre's concept of gaze). Kirk and Gallagher (1986) also reported that individuals with visual handicap were not markedly affected in terms of their intellectual abilities, their perception of other sense was not substantially different from that of the sighted persons, their language development was affected only in those areas where the meaning of words are dependent on visual concepts and their self-esteem and self-confidence were not distorted except when a peer group negatively influenced their attitude.

Among the diverse factors playing significant role in predicting psychosocial functioning of both people with and without disabilities, self-esteem and adjustment emerged as crucial variables. A strong relation was found to exist between self-esteem, adjustment (social, emotional and academic), stress and anxiety, classroom behaviour and behaviour problems. In this relation, it becomes important to explore the various theoretical perspectives on self-esteem. This also necessitated the need to explore the various dynamics involved in the process of development and maintenance of self-esteem and adjustment of blind individuals.

Self-esteem

The study of self-esteem constitutes one of the oldest and central focus of research in social sciences. Self-esteem is regarded as the evaluative component of self-concept and is commonly referred to as the extent to which one prizes, values and approves or likes himself. Many of the early theorists have posited the hierarchical models of self-concept that have implications for self-esteem. William James (1890) first referred to self-esteem as an "elementary endowment of human nature". According to him, one's feelings of worth were determined by the ratio of one's actual accomplishments to one's supposed potentialities. According to James, there were two distinct aspects of the self, presenting self-concept as hierarchical and multifaceted i.e. 'I' or Existential self and the Empirical self which was further classified as spiritual self, material self, social structural perspective self and the bodily self.

Structural Perspective

According to the (Coopersmith, 1967; Rosenberg, 1965, 1979) self-esteem is regarded as global positive or negative assessment, a personality trait characterized by considerable stability from one situation to the next. Rosenberg (1979) held that self-esteem implies self-acceptance, self-respect, and feelings of self-worth which influences the way by which people perceive themselves. According to him, self-esteem was affected by several factors such as Reflected Appraisals, Social Comparisons, Self-attributions and Psychological Centrality. On the one hand, Reflected Appraisals included direct reflections indicating how others directly respond to us and perceived selves, that is, how we think others perceive us while Social Comparisons emphasized on the meanings that people use to make self-evaluations by comparing themselves with others. On the other hand, Self-attributions denoted people's observations in various situations and maintaining self-regard by inferring causes of their behaviour to such situations, while Psychological Centrality maintained that different people assign different importance to various aspects of life wherein the same situation may have an enhancing impact on one and deteriorating impact on others depending on their differential psychological centrality.

Symbolic Interactionism

The precursors of symbolic interactionism laid emphasis on self as a product and reflection of social life (Pierce, 1868; James, 1890; Baldwin, 1897; Gordon & Gergen, 1968; Ziller, 1973). Emphasizing on the importance of 'reflected appraisals' or 'looking-glass self' in the development of self-concept, various researchers maintained that self-concept developed through interaction with others and was a reflection of others' appraisals of an individual (Cooley, 1902; Mead, 1934; Shrauger & Shoeneman, 1979). According to them others whose views individual learns to incorporate as a part of their own self-concept may include either specific individuals with whom they interact or a "generalized other" in their socio-cultural environment.

Cooley (1902) generally credited as the first interactionist while describing his notion of the looking-glass self posited that the self is inseparable from social life and necessarily involved some reference to others. According to him, three components play a major role in construction of a reflected self-imagination of our appearance to the other person, imagination of his judgement of that appearance and some sort of self-feeling such as pride or mortification. He held that from early childhood our concept of selfdevelops by seeing how others respond to us. Mead (1934) later amplified and expanded the view of self as a product of social interactionism based upon Cooley's 'looking-glass self'. She noted that self-concept arises through social interaction and is an outgrowth of an individual's concern of other's reaction towards himself or herself. In this process, the individual acquires a source of internal regulation that serves him to guide and stabilize his behaviour in the absence of external pressures by incorporating estimates of how the "generalized other" respond to certain actions.

From perspective of the "looking-glass self", members of the stigmatized and oppressed groups who are aware that others regard them negatively tend to incorporate those negative attitudes into their self-concept and consequently have lower self-esteem. The negative stereotypes and discrimination resulting from negative self-evaluations may develop through interaction with various sources such as attitudes of specific individuals with whom they interact (parents, teachers, peers) or their devalued projection in the wider culture as portrayed in media, books, etc.

Social Comparison Theory

The context of people's self-esteem being affected by judgement of others, relates it to the principle of Social Comparison theory (Festinger, 1954) and the Social Identity theory (Tajfel, 1981, 1982; Turner, 1987). Social Comparison is regarded to be at the core of the social evaluation process where individuals can gather positive, neutral or negative self-ratings and in the process learn things about themselves by comparing themselves with others. Festinger (1954) in his theory of Social Comparison theory held that individuals often compare their own attributes with those individuals whom they perceive as the "significant other" in order to evaluate the adequacy of their ideas or characteristics. However, the appraisal or comparison may itself alter the salience of the "significant other". In his theory of Cognitive Dissonance Festinger (1957) argued that if the significant other's attributes appear much more favourable or sharply different from one's own, it may cause an individual to devalue the salience of this person with the view to avoid loss of self-esteem.

According to the advocates of Social Comparison theory the process of comparison can operate in various forms. In the Theory of Downward Comparison, Wills (1981, 1987) argued that people with low self-esteem make more self-enhancing comparisons because of their greater need for self-enhancement. In such a case, people tend to compare themselves with others who are worse off in order to arouse positive feelings and raise their self-esteem—contrast effect. However, they can also compare with others to whom they relate to raise their self-esteem—the assimilation effect (Brown et.al.,1992).

With reference to members of stigmatized groups it is held that they may indulge in diverse forms of social comparisons (parallel, downward and upward) for their optimal functioning and subjective well-being (Festinger, 1954). Gecas (1986) also maintained that since selective comparison can be gratifying especially for the stigmatized groups, they may prefer to use selective downward comparison on certain occasions as they perceive downward comparison as less threatening and a means to enhance their self-esteem.

Social Identity Theory

The Social Identity Theory is based on the assumption that people have a desire to maintain a favourable view of themselves which is partly determined by how they value the social groups in which they hold membership relative to other groups. Tajfel and Turner (1979) held that individuals discriminate in favour of their group relative to other groups so as to increase the perceived value of their own group relative to other groups and achieve a more positive social identity and higher self-esteem.

Referring to the various ways that members of stigmatized groups use to maintain positive social identity in an intergroup context, Tajfel and Turner (1979) proposed the concept of 'social creativity' and identified three ways adopted by them to guard against in-group devaluation— change the target of social comparison, attach a new, positive meaning to the group attribute that was originally stigmatized and seek a new dimension through which the in-group can distinguish itself in a positive way. Hence, they advocated that there would always be higher cognitive preference for intra-personal similarities and interpersonal differences which help to enhance psychological distinctiveness of individuals.

Bandura's Self-efficacy Theory

In addition to the above theories mention can be made of Bandura's Self-efficacy Theory that influences the manner in which an individual perceives his or her self. According to Bandura (1997), Self-efficacy beliefs affect every aspect of people's lives their ability to think productively, pessimistically or optimistically; to motivate themselves and persevere in the face of adversities; make life choices, etc. Self-efficacy can be formed by interpreting information primarily from four sources. The most influential source is the interpreted result that emerges out of one's previous performance, or mastery experience. In such situations individuals engage in tasks and activities, interpret results of the actions, use interpretations to develop beliefs about their capabilities to engage in subsequent or related tasks or activities and act in accordance with the beliefs created. Self-efficacy is positively affected or raised if outcomes interpreted as successful while failures tend to lower it.

People form their Self-efficacy beliefs through the vicarious experience of observing others perform tasks wherein modelling plays a dominant role. The extent of similarity or divergence and success or failure of the attributes of the "significant model" and their own capabilities largely affects the beliefs formed. Social Persuasions in the form of verbal judgements can play an important part in the development of an individual's self-beliefs. Somatic and emotional states can also provide information about efficacy beliefs. The emotional state that accompanies execution of an action affects the degree of confidence. The affective reaction that accompanies the apprehensions about one's own capabilities can lower self-efficacy perceptions.

Self-efficacy beliefs can enhance human accomplishment and well-being in countless ways. They influence the choices made and course of action taken by people make. Individuals tend to select tasks and activities in which they feel competent and confident and avoid those in which they do not. Self-efficacy beliefs also influence thought patterns and emotional reactions of people. High Self-efficacy helps in creating feelings of serenity in approaching difficult tasks and activities. Conversely, people with low Self-efficacy may believe that things are tougher than they really are, thus fostering anxiety, stress, depression, and a narrow vision of how best to solve a problem. As a consequence, Self-efficacy beliefs can powerfully influence the level of accomplishment that one ultimately achieves. With such significant influence self-beliefs can act as a self-fulfilling prophecy affecting the accomplishments of people.

Efficacy-based View of Self-esteem

The efficacy-based view of self-esteem (Gecas & Schwalbe, 1983; White, 1959) appears to be in conjunction with Bandura's approach. The efficacy-based view of self-esteem holds that self-concept develops through efficacious interaction with environment. Self-esteem, according to this perspective is not passively acquired, but is 'earned through one's own competent actions' (Frank & Marolla, 1976). By learning that one can control and manipulate one's environment, one acquires a view of self as competent, successful and able and consequently one has high self-esteem. Therefore, it is suggested that members of stigmatized groups have lower self-esteem than non-stigmatized groups because of limitations in their opportunities to control and manipulate their environment.

Gecas and Schwalbe (1883) held that the limitations can be in terms of socio-structural conditions, such as segregation or discrimination against members of stigmatized or oppressed groups thus limiting their access to resources that are necessary for producing intended effects. According to them, such limitations causes them to possess lower self-esteem than members of more advantaged groups.

This perspective of the efficacy-based self-esteem view is consistent with the looking-glass self and self-fulfilling prophecy. In addition to this, the Equity Theory (Walster & Berscheid, 1978), Social Exchange Theory (Thibaut & Kelley, 1959), Social Comparison Theory (Festinger, 1954) and Social Identity Theory are also compatible with the prediction that social stigma has negative effects on self-esteem.

Several mechanisms have been found to be used by members of stigmatized groups to maintain their self-esteem. One of the prominent tendency of people is to make in-group social comparisons. In this context, it is held that members of stigmatized groups tend to compare themselves with similarly stigmatized groups whose outcomes are relatively poor. Referring to this Crocker and Major (1989) held that the stigmatized individuals compare themselves with others who share a common fate due to three reasons— as a consequence of segregated environments (a proximity effect) i.e. the in-group members are available for social comparison purpose on a larger basis because they tend to be more prevalent in the immediate environment; to obtain accurate self-evaluation (a similarity affect) i.e. they tend to make in-group comparisons because they share more similarities to the self on relevant attributes and to avoid unpleasant or painful social comparisons (a self-protective effect) i.e. avoid comparison with advantaged groups which may result in painful consequences for self-esteem.

Referring to the other mechanisms adopted by the stigmatized groups to maintain a positive view of self, Goffman (1963) noted that on certain occasions stigmatized groups attribute the negative feedback or outcomes to the prejudiced attitude of others. The use of this self-protective attribution function of social stigma has been found to be beneficial because attributing negative outcomes to external causes helps to protect self-esteem as compared to the internal, stable and global causes that results in lowered self-esteem.

Several explanations have been provided emphasizing the need for construction and maintenance of a positive self- ranging from the role it plays in organizing, interpreting and giving meaning to experience, regulating and motivating action, enhancing personal adjustment, promoting physical health to bringing about of self-improvement. It is important to note in this regard that although the mechanisms involved in achieving healthy and positive self-view can vary from one mechanism to another, the ultimate goal remains the same i.e. to achieve a healthy psychological well-being. This is applicable to all individuals including people with disabilities.

Self-esteem, Adjustment and Disability

Self-concept is an image that an individual has of himself or herself which is formed by a conceptualization process requiring experiences for information. Self-esteem being one of the components of self-concept also depends on experiences to develop and function. In view of this, physical ability is regarded as a crucial requisite facilitating conceptualization of information and is of paramount importance in the area of general mobility, maintaining body functions and enhancing the whole early learning process of social interaction, building up of self-esteem and achievement of life goals. It is also one of the prerequisites by which handicapped individuals learn about themselves (Cohen, 1977). In reference to this Adler maintained that one's sense of inferiority as a result of organ deficiency and bodily weaknesses acts as a major threat to self-esteem. Restricted mobility was largely found to affect development of identity because it is through different interplay situations with others that one develops a self-image/identity (Mead, 1934).

Harter (1981a, 1981b, 1990b) argued in her Competence Motivation Theory that positive experience of behaviour leads to development of positive self-concept with a subsequent positive effect on global self-worth. Emphasizing on the influence of physical perceptions upon self-esteem, Fox and Corbin (1989) reported in their Hierarchical Self-concept Model that Physical self-worth emerged as an important sub-component, a mediator among the four sub-domains of physical self-perceptions i.e. perceptions of sports competence, body attractiveness, physical strength and physical condition and self-esteem. The dominance of physical ability was also emphasized in the works of Uchida, Hashimoto and Lutz (2005) with regard to adults with physical disabilities.

Commenting on the significance of physical competence, Lowenfeld held that there are three major areas where blind people were at a disadvantage—the range and variety of experiences, which can affect their cognitive development, mobility that includes both orientation to the immediate surroundings and locomotion within those surroundings and interaction with the environment. The absence of sight imposes severe constrictions in their exploration and interaction with the environment. Several empirical studies on blind individuals have revealed that they experience developmental delays in area of movement, motor skills and physical competence, concept formation and learning of social conventions because of lack of opportunities to explore their environment (Dickinson, Perkins & Bilek, 1988; Hopkins, Gaeta & Hill, 1987; Kobberling, Leger & Jankowski, 1989; Shepard, 1990 etc.).

In addition to the limitations in movement inflicted by restricted mobility it also brings along with it certain social limitations. Limitations in mobility may necessitate the constant presence of adults or other support services thus causing the individuals to become more dependent and develop feelings of helplessness.

Besides the effect of physical self-worth on the self-esteem and adjustment of people with disabilities a strong relationship has been found between self-esteem and acceptance of disability regardless of age, disability and other characteristics (Linkowski, 1988). It is held that acceptance of disability is associated with better adjustment (Dembo, Leviton and Wright, 1956). Evidences of strong relationship were found to exist between acceptance of disability and self-esteem in deaf adolescents (Heinemann & Shontz, 1982), in teenagers with oral-clefts (Starr & Heiserman, 1977), in African Americans with a variety of disabilities (Belgrave, 1991) and in college students with physical disabilities (Linkowski & Dunn, 1974).

In the context of impairment related changes, each type of social comparison may be essential for the optimal functioning and subjective well-being of individuals. Upward comparisons with those more advanced in developmental growth or less constrained by impairment could motivate the person to strive for developmental growth. Downward comparison with those less advanced or more impaired on the other hand could help to protect self-esteem and motivate in spite of inevitable losses associated with the impairment and thus compensate for negative effects by secondary control. Keeping in view the devalued stereotypes of disability, people with disabilities adopt various mechanisms to safeguard their self-concept or self-esteem. Some attempt to preserve their self-esteem by identifying with the non-disabled others (Oliver, 1986; Jahoda et. al., 1988), while others have group tighter to form new organizations in order to combat negative stereotypes by creating positive images, developing self-empowerment and bringing about social change (Finkelstein, 1993). Others may adopt the stigma of disability which may lower their self-esteem (Szivos-Bach, 1993) or can avoid friendships with more 'able' people for reasons connected with self-esteem maintenance.

To develop self-acceptance and self-esteem people with disabilities not only have to consider their own attitude but also have to deal with the attitudes of others (Huebert, 1990; Tuttle, 1994). Tuttle (1984) regarded sense of self-confidence and perception of others as important factors affecting self-concept of an individual. He maintained that although all individuals are susceptible to certain threats in the development of positive self-concept, individuals with visual impairment are at a greater risk of being negatively perceived by others. Goffman and Sussman (1963) held that handicapped people might learn to regard themselves with the negative connotation that society attributes to their handicaps. This is more in case of blind individuals because blindness makes it difficult for individuals to incidentally learn the essential social skills by observing appropriate model behaviour.

Empirical evidences have shown that when compared with non-disabled people the quality of social experiences that the disabled have was poor. Generally, they had fewer friends without disability, receive less social and interpersonal experiences, less responsibility, have more unstable conflicting, uncooperative and non-emotional relationships and lower self-esteem (Alper & Ryndak, 1992; Kishi & Meyer, 1994; Santich & Kavangh, 1997; Yude et.al., 1998).

Adjustment for every living organism is a continuous process. Every change in the physical environment evokes the need for adjustment. Hence, the process adjustment of people with disabilities has also been a subject of enquiry. It has often being conceptualized as a staged process. Livneh (1991) in his unified theory of adaptation identified five stages: initial impact, defence mobilization, initial realization, retaliation and reintegration. According to this theory adjustment is characterized by confidence, contentment and satisfaction. The viewpoints regarding the adjustment of people with disabilities have been wide ranging from 'resolution of conflicts and establishment of a healthy new identity' (Shontz, 1991) to "lifelong process during which one's disability is gradually and incrementally incorporated into the overall perception of self that includes both roles and life situation" (Sidel, 1997).

However, most of the existing models of adjustment tend to be based on some model of bereavement and loss (Pitts,

1991). Hull (1990) in his autobiography outlined four distinct stages of his own adjustment to sight loss. He referred to the first as a period of hope which lasted from one year and eighteen months during which the finality of the loss had not been accepted. In the next phase he witnessed the appearance of what on the surface appeared to be quite a positive behaviour, the search for alternative techniques but this phase was replaced by a period of despair characterized by sleeplessness and depression. The final stage was marked by feeling of overcoming the despair, a realization that there was much inner strength although the process of adjustment was by no means over.

Werner (1959/1978), Piaget (1947) and Vygotsky (1927/1993) were some of the precursors of the developmental approach to adjustment in psychology and applied the findings to children with disabilities. However, the three differed in their approach. Werner and Piaget were primarily organicists while Vygotsky was primarily a contextualist. Piaget emphasized on the "wholeness" of development in children with retardation whereby they developed through specific sequences and stages. Inhelder (1943/1968), on the other hand emphasized on horizontally organized stages of development wherein while the children developed in accord with the usual sequences of development they more often demonstrated oscillation of depression and unstable functioning as compared to children having no retardation.

Werner (1959/1978) also reported that development of children with disabilities often occurred in sequences similar to their non-disabled counterparts. Vygotsky (1927/1993) being primarily a developmentalist was concerned with the interaction between children with disabilities and environment. Vygotsky in his writings on disability laid emphasis on interventions advocating for instruction in Braille for children who were blind, etc. He laid emphasis on special educators to reach out to the children. He was interested in the social effects of disability and need for adaptation and compensation. He criticized the theoretical measures of complete development and classification and regarded the measures such as IQ tests etc. as static means, a system powerless to solve the questions of origin, development and growth. He held that disability was a social problem and becomes troublesome only when children are made to feel inferior by others.

Social support has also been found to be one of the significant factors affecting the process of adjusting to disability (Belgrave, 1991). Li and Moore (1998) in their study examined the relationship between acceptance of disability and demographic characteristics, disability conditions (disability onset, multiple disabilities etc.) and other psychological factors (self-esteem, emotional support, perceived discrimination and hostility). Self-esteem and emotional support from family and friends, perceived discrimination and disability conditions played important roles in participants' adjustment to disability.

An overview of development and maintenance of self-esteem and adjustment of people with disabilities highlights the intervention of several factors. Physical ability was found to be the dominant factor that laid the foundation for an individual to develop a unique and separate identity. Restrictions in movement were found to reduce the opportunities for interaction as well as stimulation for cognitive growth and personal development. Therefore, whether a person with disability formed a positive self-view largely depended on the extent to which he/she perceived his/her physical competence.

Besides physical competence, acceptance of disability condition was associated with better adjustment. The extent of acceptance of disability was found to be associated with the degree that a person de-emphasizes those aspects of physical ability and appearance that contradicts his or her disabling condition, recognizes values other than those that are in direct conflict with the disability, does not extend his or her handicap beyond actual physical impairment to other aspects of the functioning self and does not compare himself or herself to others in the areas of limitations but instead emphasizes his or her own assets and abilities.

Social support has also been found to be one of the significant elements in the process of adjusting to disability. Self-esteem and emotional support from family and friends, perceived discrimination and disability conditions were found to play important role in peoples' adjustment to disability. This was essential because in order to develop self-acceptance, people with disabilities not only have to consider their own attitude but also have to deal with others, attitudes and learn to regard themselves with the negative connotation that society attributes to their handicaps. In the context of impairment related changes, various mechanisms of social comparison emerged as essential medium to maintain optimal functioning and subjective well-being.

In keeping with the above viewpoint it is held that disability is created the moment a person with a pathological condition or an injury interacts with an environment that does not support his or her performance in a desired activity. There has been a recent shift in the world and U.S. policy which reflects an understanding of the role that environment plays in the performance of persons with reduced capacity. In the second draft of their classification of disability, the WHO attempted to record not only the cellular and structural elements that contribute to their disability but also address the role that context plays in preventing or creating excess disability (WHO, 1999). New models developed by the WHO and others including the Institute of Medicine (IOM) (Pope & Tarlov, 1997) recognize that disability can be directly attributed to the society or context within which a person performs.

Keeping in view that self-esteem and adjustment emerged as crucial variables playing significant role in predicting psychosocial functioning of both people with and without disabilities, it becomes interesting and necessary to explore indepth as to how they influence the blind and the sighted individuals as well as the blind in comparison to people with other forms of disabilities.

Comparative Overview of Self-esteem and Adjustment of Blind and Sighted Individuals

Physical ability is considered to play an essential role in determining the self-image of a person. Physical activities offer many opportunities for individuals to compare their skills and competence. Since children have an early interest in these skills, a high level of physical ability reinforces positive evaluation of physical self and global self-evaluation.

Researchers have emphasized that the stigmatization process of registration itself constitutes one of the major causes resulting in feelings of inferiority, hopelessness and depression (Goffman, 1963). Therefore, inadequate information about the nature of orientation and mobility services combined with a sense of isolation was found to be a major source of stress and anxiety among blind individuals (Seybold, 1993). Morris and Whiting (1971) and Fraiberg (1977) held that blindness influences the development of motor learning since it limits not only possibilities, but also the awareness and organization of spatial information. Highlighting on the negative effects of visual handicap on development of spatial concepts among early and late adolescents, Hartlage (1967) and Morrongiello (1995) revealed that the performance of blind students was found to be inferior as compared to their sighted counterparts on spatial as well as non-spatial questions at all grade levels.

Exploring the effects of orientation and mobility on the lives of fifteen participants (aged six to fifty, four years) who were either blind or parents of blind children from transcribed interviews, Higgins (1999) showed that even the participants attached considerable significance to orientation and mobility. White cane and dependence were stigmatizing while restrictions on movement and lack of orientation and mobility instructions were found to be disabling.

However, several researchers contradicted the above argument. According to them, use of various interventions such as the assistance animals or instrumental assistance helped to normalize the lives of blind individuals such as guide dogs provide sightless people with increased mobility, etc. In addition to assistance they also assist in eliminating social barriers by enhancing how people are socially perceived (Lockward, 1983) and facilitating conversations (Messent, 1984).

Physical ability was also found to play an important role in the formation and further development of self-evaluation and image of sighted children. Numerous studies emphasized on a significant relation between self-esteem, pubertal timing and body image (Allgood-Merten, Lewinson & Hop, 1999; Williams & Currie, 2000). The findings revealed that self-esteem and body image accounted for gender differences in depression and that early maturation and lower ratings of body image (body size and perceived appearance) were associated with lower levels of self-esteem.

Age of onset and cause of blindness played a dominant role in affecting the adjustment patterns among blind individuals. Emphasizing upon the age of onset, a significant difference in adjustment patterns was found among the congenitally and adventitiously blind individuals. Several studies showed that congenital blindness did not preclude normal and affective ego development while adventitious blindness was related to disruption of ego functioning with severe affect manifestations (Robert, 1975; Kapoor, 1981). Verma (2000) reported that those who were congenitally blind or who lost their sight in the early years were better adjusted to their handicap as compared to those who lost their vision at adolescence or in the later years.

Elaborating on the impact of congenital blindness, McGuire and Meyers (1971) concluded that behaviour disturbances shown by these children have a psychogenic base and are 'a high risk of, but not inevitable to congenital blindness'. They ascribed the behaviour problems to the first year self-preoccupation that was an inevitable result of lack of vision and limitations in control over their physical and social environment. However, Pandey (1985) in his study of congenitally blind and post-natal blind found that at least 55 per cent of the children had adjustment problems.

Some researchers maintain that the nature of personality dynamics and adjustment of the visually handicapped could be understood through a study of their self-concept (Singh & Akhtar, 1971; Konarska, 2003). Comparative studies of blind and sighted individuals revealed statistically significant differences between the two groups. Teenagers with visual impairments demonstrated lack of confidence in conducting their life by themselves, lower self-esteem and social esteem, required professional help in solving their problems, inclination towards subordinating themselves to others, lack of eagerness to exert their will on others, etc. They also showed timidity in social contact as well as defensive attitude. The sighted individuals were found to be more energetic, self-confident, dominating and spontaneous in action. The researchers attributed the differences to sensory disability of the handicapped. Reddy (1997) in mapping the personality correlates of coping behaviour among physically handicapped students (visually/orthopaedically handicapped, hearing and speech impaired) showed that they manifested maximum negative personality tendencies such as insecurity, loneliness, depression, feelings of inferiority and emotional instability. Loneliness, depression, guilt-proneness and emotional stability were positively related to maladjustment.

Dash and Mohanty (1981) found blind individuals to be less aggressive, less moody, less gusty, withdrawn, less emotionally balanced, more rule abiding and have poorer self-concept and self-esteem in comparison to sighted children. Goel and Sen (1985) based on their studies on personality dimensions of visually handicapped students also concluded that they had poor self-concept and emotional stability, below average intelligence, physical dependence and possessed a sense of insecurity. The teachers also rated them as aggressive, un-inhibited, generally group dependent, sociable, predictable and emotionally maladjusted. However, the blind students showed less inter-individual variance in perceptual-motor skills. Bharadwaj (1995) in his attempt to differentiate the basic personality traits and orientation of handicapped (blind and celebral palsy) and non-handicapped children found that blind children manifested more behavioural disharmony.

It is widely held that positive self-esteem, good behavioural and emotional adjustment significantly enhances mood (Rosenberg, 1985; Taylor & Brown, 1988) and results in more adaptive learning strategies in classrooms (Covington, 1989). An inverse relationship was found to exist between self-esteem and stress. Several studies show a significant fall in self-esteem of adolescents with increase in the number of stressful life events (Cohen et al., 1987; Dumont & Provost, 1999; Kroger, 1980; Young et al., 1990). Negative shifts in global self-evaluation were found result due to negative events among low trait self-esteem students while positive affect resulted from positive events among high trait self-esteem students (Stake, Huff & Zand, 1995). Bachman and O'Malley (1977) and Wylie (1979) held that self-esteem tends to become more positive during adolescence and early adulthood.

Dubios, Bull, Sherman and Roberts (1998) while investigating global self-esteem and emotional, behavioural and academic adjustment of 213 young adolescents drawn from 7th through 9th grade students concluded that higher global self-esteem was significantly associated with fewer internalizing and externalizing problems (as rated by adolescents and parents), correlated with behavioural and emotional adjustment and academic achievement.

Although a number of studies were conducted on self-esteem of blind individuals, there is little evidence of consistently lower self-esteem than their sighted counterparts regardless of age (Obiakor, 1986; Obiakor & Stile, 1990). Blindness was not found to negatively affect the emotional and social development of individuals. Rather, a series of limitations rooted in the social image of blindness caused irreparable harm to people. Comparative studies on self-concept revealed no essential and consistent difference between visually handicapped and sighted adolescents (Jervis, 1959; Sunich & Ledwith, 1965; Williams, 1971; Sherill, Hinson, Gench, Kennedy & Low, 1990; Bissa, Singh & Helode, 1993). Elaborating on the nature of response, it was found that on certain occasions the blind subjects used either highly positive or negative statements than the sighted. Investigating on self-reported perceptions of blind and sighted individuals towards blindness, Hasan, Khan and Khan (1983) concluded that blind children did not rate their life anymore negative than their sighted counterparts. Kapoor and Sen (1988) in their study of the effect of congenital and adventitious blindness on some psychological variables concluded that no significant difference was found among blind and sighted individuals. However, the sighted showed slightly low score on emotional stability and social responsibility.

While examining the concept of adjustment and self-esteem from the cognitive point of view, Dodds, Ferguson, Ng, Flannigan, Hawes and Yates (1994) held that there was significant correlation between self-esteem and anxiety depression, attitude towards blindness, locus of control, disability acceptance, self-efficacy and attributions. All the subjects who were blind were found to have a positive attitude towards blindness, a feeling of internally being in control of their lives, acceptance of the present state of their disability, a feeling of being able to affect changes in their lives and felt responsible for their success but not failures. This was indicative of high sense of self-worth and well-being among blind individuals.

Numerous studies have been conducted relating self-esteem of blind individuals to diverse factors such as academic success, occupational self-efficacy, career belief, etc. Emphasizing on the relation between psychosocial adjustment and academic success of visually impaired children, Beaty (1994) reported of no significant difference in psychosocial adjustment between the visually impaired and sighted. On analysis, the visually impaired children were found to have scored slightly higher than the sighted in self-esteem and academic performance. Investigating on the difference between the visually impaired children and sighted children regarding occupational self-efficacy, career belief and self-esteem, Moore (1991) concluded that self-estimates of blind students on their ability to complete educational requirements for occupations did not differ from those of their sighted counterparts.

A significant relationship was found between the years of formal education, rehabilitation and their impact on the self-esteem of blind individuals. Beach, Robinet and Hakim-Larson (1995) identified a negative relationship between self-esteem and independent living skills of visually impaired. They held that people with higher self-esteem had significantly more formal education than those who had lower self-esteem thus highlighting the significance of higher education in the enhancement of self-esteem. Emphasizing on the significance of training for maintenance of positive self-esteem, Khalil (1993) based on his study of blind students at three levels of rehabilitation—access to computer training, no access to computer training and no rehabilitation training found statistically significant differences between the two rehabilitated groups and non-rehabilitated group in the perception of Internality, Powerful others, Chance control, General Self-efficacy and Self-esteem.

Social support from parents and friends is considered to play a dominant role in not only fostering self-esteem, self-assurance and feeling of self-worth but also sense of security and control over oneself and the environment (Nestmann & Hurrelmann, 1994). This was also found to be applicable both for people with and without disabilities. Most studies enquiring into the role of parents and "significant others" in lives of blind individuals have revealed that positive self-image and academic competence and a positive relationship with parents and friends classmates (Lopez-Justica et al., 1998; Huure, Komulainen & Aro, 1999) contributed to the enhancement of their self-esteem.

Adjustment being a dynamic process requires constant adaptation and it is widely held that disability can often create psychodynamic stress, conflict and also maladjustment which can manifest itself through various problems. Studies have shown that adolescents with visual impairments (those who are blind or have low vision) may be at a risk for psychological and social adjustment problems. Meighan (1971), Beaty (1992) and Obiakor and Stile (1989) held that visual impairment may cause adolescents to feel inadequate and inferior which reflect their lack of social acceptance, academic underachievement, physical incapability and social maladjustment.

Research evidence have shown varied patterns of maladjustments among blind individuals ranging from having no interest in curricular or co-curricular activities, being more reserved, emotionally unstable, shy, dependent, sentimental (Bhargava & Lavania, 1981) to differing significantly from the sighted with respect to parents' attitude, their adjustment to each other, subject's attitude towards home, school and other places, their interest in studies, liking for play, regularity in class attendance, being more disturbed in self-adjustment and health liabilities (Muhl, 1930; Brown, 1938, 1939; Morgan, 1944; Hubbard, 1945; Hasting, 1947; Qadari & Hussain, 1982; Sarita, 1985).

However, several researchers have contradicted the above viewpoint by arguing that the emotional problems exhibited blind individuals were not indicative of the need to engage in grief work which necessitates exploration of the unexpressed feelings of loss but rather an outcome of learned helplessness and associated concepts, such as self-efficacy (Seligman, 1975, 1981; Bandura, 1977; Seligman, Abramson, Semmel & Bayer, 1979), locus of control (Rotter, 1966), attribution style (Abramson, Seligman & Teasdale, 1978), and hopelessness-depression (Abramson, Metalsky & Alloy, 1989). Bauman (1950) in his study with an older group of blind, other handicapped and non-handicapped individuals concluded that the blind were more maladjusted. However, they held that the personality patterns of handicapped groups were largely based on the social and economic consequences of their handicap rather than the direct impact of physical deficit upon the personality. Vasudeva (1972) also concluded that though the visually impaired individuals indicated difficulty of adjustment, lack of sight was not found to be necessarily producing any personality changes.

Wright (1960) asserted that 'there is already sufficient research to establish the fact that there is but little relationship between adjustment and degree of disability and in no way assures better adjustment'. According to this perspective the manner in which an individual accepts his defect is conditioned principally by the attitudes of those around him, especially his parents. Several studies have emphasized on the perception of attitudes of acceptance and rejection by parent figures and its relation to the overall adjustment of blind adolescents (Barry & Marshall, 1953; Verillo, 1958; Underberg, 1958; Kekelis & Anderson, 1984). Substantial inability to maintain and restructure relationships emerging from such attitudes may have a negative effect on the psycho-social development of visually impaired adolescents. In this context, Sommers (1944) and Cutsforth (1930, 1933, 1939) laid emphasis upon the role of family, immediate environment, society and school. Regarding the family the reactions of parents were found to fall under five categories: genuine acceptance, denial that either the parents or the child is affected, over protectiveness and excessive pity, disguised rejection and overt rejection. She observed that parents' viewed their child's blindness as 'a symbol of punishment', as a personal disgrace. She found an extremely high correlation (0.81) between parental attitudes and general level of adjustment of blind individuals. Furthermore, she also found a significant correlation between parental overprotectiveness and overindulgence and the child's poor adjustment and concluded that maladjustment stems from social attitudes rather than from causes inherent in blindness and that social attitudes are most funnelled through parents.

On the basis of a comparative study of personality dynamics of blind and sighted students, Rai (1988) concluded that the blind subjects were less adjusted on the dimensions of family relationship, emotional stability, adjustment to reality, mood and conformity the adjustment of the blind students correlated with interaction with family members, interaction with the sighted, acceptance of blindness and setting of education. Similarly, while assessing the socio-psychological factors associated with mental retardation and blindness Ishtiaq and Kamal (1981) revealed that broken homes, neglect on the part of parents, malnutrition and infectious diseases affect the mental, emotional and physical growth and complicate the process of adjustment of the social climate in which they live.

Parental attitude was found to produce significant positive effect on the adjustment of blind individuals (Kef, 2004; Jackson & Lawson, 1995). Lata (1985) while enquiring into the difference of parental attitude towards handicapped and non-handicapped school students in the field of social, emotional and educational adjustment revealed that parental attitude did not differ but on the whole the handicapped students showed better adjustment than those non-handicapped. Several studies have highlighted no significant difference in adjustment patterns of both blind and sighted individuals due to parental attitudes (Cowen et al., 1961; Huure & Aro, 1998). In a qualitative study, Chien-Huey Chang and Schaller (2000) demonstrated that the visually impaired adolescents experienced various types of emotional, informational and tangible support from their parents and that majority was satisfied with the amount and the kind of parental support they received. However, the participants had problems in the domain of emotional and tangible support, which negatively affected their psycho-social development.

Alienation and lack of effective communication were found to be some of the other factors affecting the adjustment of blind individuals. In support of this Enrich (1981) maintained that more than blindness it is 'communication gap' that gives the blind a sense of deprivation. Similarly Sastry (1985) through his comparative study on alienation and adjustment of visually handicapped and non-handicapped males concluded that visually handicapped individuals differed significantly from their non-handicapped counterparts with regard to the degree of alienation but not in the area of adjustment. Rai (1988) in a comparative study of personality dynamics of blind and sighted students held that though the blind subjects were less adjusted on the dimensions of family relationship, emotional stability, adjustment to reality, mood and conformity their adjustment correlated with interaction with family members, interaction with the sighted, acceptance of blindness and setting of education. The students who had more interaction with the sighted and family members were found to be comparatively well-adjusted.

Besides the family, Friendship or peer relation also acted as another important support system having significant influence on psychological adjustment of individuals. It has been found that adolescents with visual impairments faced a number of peer related problems. In some cases visual impairment was found to interfere with the social activities of the individuals (Nemshick, Vernon & Ludman, 1986) and hence they were socially isolated with few friends and small networks than their sighted counterparts (Eagelstein, 1975 cited in Keilbaugh, 1997; Van Hasselt, 1983; Wesolowsk, 1987; Huure & Aro, 1998) and spend more time in passive activities (Wolffe & Sacks, 1997). In a study of the social adaptation of blind individuals, Davidson (1975) reached the conclusion that some teenagers were isolated from their sighted peers. On the other hand, Mulderji (1997) in a review article on peer relation and friendship in physical and sensory disabled children mentioned that these children experience higher level of social and emotional difficulties, like loneliness which was associated with negative patterns of self-perception and low self-esteem. Rosenblum (2000) conducted interviews with ten visually impaired adolescents and their best friends to find out the impact of visual impairment on their lives. He found that regardless of the age of onset, almost all the participants had negative feeling towards their own impairment and wished that they were sighted. Majority of them reported communication gap between them and their parents and received differential treatment as compared to their normal siblings. Adolescents who had visually impaired sibling found in him or her, a sense of comfort, a role model and a source of information. Many of them had problems in establishing friendships resulting in a complex psycho-social profile.

Within the broad domain of environment, school was another factor that affected the development of disabled individuals. The attitude of teachers in particular was found to play an important role in affecting the adjustment of students with visual impairments. An extensive survey of available literature on the attitudes of educators towards groups of exceptional children, particularly the blind indicate evidences of negative attitude (Murphy, 1960; Pastor & Jimenez, 1991; Buhrow, et al., 1998; Glaubman & Lifshitz, 2001). Tobin also found lack of interest in teaching visually impaired students on the part of teachers in sighted schools.

Emphasizing on the importance of familiarity with the diverse needs of blind individuals, researchers have pointed out that teachers who had constant contact with the students did not hold significantly negative attitude towards the students as compared those teachers who did not have had any contact with them (Kuhn, 1971; Pliner & Hannah, 1985).

In keeping with the importance of teachers in affecting the personal and social development of blind individuals Lowenfeld (1981) maintained that it is essential that the teachers of blind students should develop an attitude of acceptance of the child, not denying its influence but recognizing it and adapting their methods to it, not overprotecting the child but giving him experiences which he needs to prepare for an independent life.

Adolescence is a period with a myriad of physical, cognitive and affective changes directed towards independence, identity formation and value clarification. These changes can cause sighted adolescents to exhibit different types of behaviour patterns. A significant relationship was evident between negative life events and emotional and behavioural maladjustments among adolescents wherein negative events emerged as significant predictors of psychological functioning (Johnson, 1986; Cohen, Burt & Bjork, 1987).

The realization of being a valued part of the social network not only helps to foster self-esteem and self-assurance but also feelings of security and control over oneself and the environment (Heller, Swindle & Dusenbury, 1986). Failure in attaining acceptance results in stress, anxiety and a feeling of helplessness. Several studies have demonstrated significant affect of environment and social acceptance on the overall self-esteem of individuals. Simmons, Rosenberg and Rosenberg (1973) in a cross-sectional study concluded that environment had a strong effect in bringing about certain behavioural changes among adolescents rather than their age. The early adolescents exhibited heightened self-consciousness, slightly lower self-esteem and a less favourable view of the opinions held of them by significant others. On the other hand, students who entered junior high school appeared more disturbed on these dimensions than their age-peers in elementary school. Simmons, Blyth, Van Cleave and Bush (1979) also maintained that adolescents demonstrate depressed self-esteem if they experience multiple changes in the social environment.

Drawing from Cooley's (1902) conception of the 'looking-glass self', researchers have found that self-worth and depressed effects are influenced by one's perceptions of support from family members (Harter & Whitesell, 1996; Luster & McAdoo, 1995; Rubin et al., 1992). This was also evident in the self-enhancement and self-consistency theories which emphasized on independent and significant contribution of family and peer transactions to self-esteem of adolescents. In accordance with the self-consistency theory, a number of studies have shown that relations of family transactions to self-esteem were mediated in part by their associations with peer transactions and also strong linkages between qualitatively profiles of family and peer experiences (Roberts et al., 2000).

Numerous studies have highlighted a significant relationship between self-esteem and family and peer relations (Bartle, Anderson & Sabatelli, 1989; Anderson & Hughes, 1990; Nurmi & Pullianien, 1991; Hartup, 1995; Berndt, 1996; Fordham & Stevenson, Hinde 1999; Saad, 1999) and self-esteem and academic performance (Roger, 1978; Reitzes & Mutran, 1980; Dubois, Bull, Sherman & Roberts, 1998). This is essential because adolescence is a phase when various family process dimensions or parental behaviour serve as critical locus for the development of both self-esteem and engagement in the educational enterprise (Gecas & Schwalbe, 1986). The influence of perceived family support on psychological adjustment of adolescents has been issue of constant research. Consistent with the developmental theories of self-esteem, strong family relationships have been found to produce a positive effect on the self-esteem over time (Roberts & Bengston, 1996; Yabiku et al., 1999).

Critical analyses of the nature of parental control affecting adjustment pattern of adolescents provides us a mixed picture. On the one hand, studies have highlighted that children and adolescents who perceived congruent authoritative parenting and teaching styles accompanied by high parental involvement and a positive school atmosphere had the highest achievement outcomes and were more socially responsible, independent and instrumentally competent than their peers (Baumrin & Black, 1967; Paulson, Marchant & Rothlisberg, 1998). On the other hand, several studies have indicated that parents' attempt to control or overmanage the psychosocial development of their child may promote, rather than inhibit, undesirable adjustment problems and lead to diminished self-confidence (Nurmi & Pullianien, 1991; Harter & Whitesell, 1996; Herz & Gullone, 1999).

Adolescents with inadequate family support were reported to suffer from poor mental health, retarded social development and attenuated well-being overall (Barber & Olsen, 1997; Yoshikawa, 1994). Wenz-Gross, Siperstein and Untch (1997) while examining school stress, social support and adjustment among adolescents showed that higher academic stress and less emotional support from the family were related to lower academic self-concept while higher peer status and less companionship support from peers were associated with lower social self-concept. Cobb and Bowers (1999) regarded family, school and peer groups as instrumental mediums for learning and transfer of knowledge and developmental skills essential for self-definition.

Besides the family, peers were found to play an increasingly important role in the lives of adolescents (Savin-Williams & Berndt, 1990). At this stage friends and peers helped individuals to develop a sense of belongingness, cooperation, binding to the group, self-esteem and identification. Studies reveal that perceived friendship quality, peer support, or attachment to friends is positively associated with self-esteem (Newman & Newman, 1976; Armsden & Greenverg, 1987; Cauce, 1986; Dudow & Ullman, 1989; Hirsch & Rapkin, 1987; Keefe & Berndt, 1996; Ryan, Stiller & Lynch, 1994; Buhrmester & Yin, 1997; Fordham & Stevenson, 1999) and negatively associated with both depressive symptoms and psychosocial disturbance. Way and Chen (2000) and Berndt and Savin-Williams (1993) found that friendship support to be positively associated with self-esteem and negatively associated with depressed feelings. Greater satisfaction with their friends or peers have been found to be associated with feeling better about themselves than those who express less satisfaction with friends and peers. Berndt (1996) reported significant relationship between the quality of pre-adolescent friendship and indices of socio-emotional adjustment such as self-esteem.

Investigating about the association between self-concept and peer-group affiliations on the basis of arguments derived from ego-identity theory and symbolic interaction theories, Brown and Lohr (1987) concluded that crowd members as a whole exhibited higher self-esteem than the outsiders. Among crowd members, self-esteem was directly related to the position of one's crowd in the peer-group status hierarchy (based on both peer-rated and self-perceived crowd affiliation). Outsiders' self-esteem differed in relation to the accuracy of their reflected appraisal and the salience they attached to crowd affiliation.

Among the numerous social factors, school climate was also found to play a dominant role in significantly predicting psychological adjustment of sighted students (Bachman & O'Malley, 1986; Hoge et al., 1990; Kuperminc et al., 1997). Roeser et al., (1998) reported that perceptions of overall school climate and positive teacher regard by early adolescents resulted in positive emotional adjustment during the middle school years. Moreover, students who perceived their teachers as emotionally supportive were less likely to experience alienation in school or emotional distress. Epstein and Karweit (1983) also noted that those students who do not feel safe at school may experience isolation at school and may, consequently, report lower self-esteem and higher depressive symptoms than those who experience their school to be safer and more supportive.

Individuals making transition from an elementary school to a junior high school setting generally experience a rather abrupt change in both school environment and social status. This is marked by a shift from an environment characterized as protective and child-centred into one that is impersonal, subject-oriented and highly competitive. Studies investigating the effects of transition from elementary to junior high school on self-perceptions of early adolescents show disparate results. Several studies reported decline in self-esteem for both male and female students (Berndt & Hawkins, 1987; Simmons etal., 1973; Wigfield et al., 1991). These studies identified timing of transition and marked change in school environment as major contributing factors to the decline.

Contrary to the studies those focusing on self-esteem and perceived competence of early adolescents in the cognitive, social and physical domains across the transition from elementary school to junior high school found no significant change in their self-esteem (Hirsch & Rapkin, 1987; Nottelmenn, 1987; Hirsch & Dubois, 1991; Proctor & Choi, 1994). Based on findings of these studies it was concluded that in general, perceptions of self-esteem and competence of early adolescents were not adversely affected by the transition.

Overall analyses of available literature regarding the psycho-social development of blind individuals have brought certain issues into focus. One of the questions that arise is whether blind adolescents have a higher degree of social and emotional difficulties or are less satisfactorily 'adjusted' than the sighted population. However, this awaits any definite conclusion since the researchers have been unable to reach any specific decision as to whether these result from the regime of particular residential schools, influence of parental attitudes and public reaction or visual handicap itself. For adolescents with impairments the issues may be compounded as it is dependent to a large extent on how their impairment affect, who they are and what their role may be in a society that assigns negatively connotations for impairments (Hanna & Rogovsky, 1991; Morris, 1994; Thomson, 1997). However, based on general notion and observation it is largely maintained that loss of sight causes a person to undergo intense perceptual, behavioural, cognitive and emotional adjustments which may or may not be totally achieved without special forms of intervention.

Visual impairment was found to produce moderate-to-severe restrictions in the performance of social roles, work, schooling, leisure activities, family life and friendships which in turn threatens the quality and maintenance of relationships with friends and family members. However, considerable research evidence shows that perceived congruent authoritative parental, parental involvement and appropriate responsiveness and affection had positive impact on the psychological make up of visually impaired children, while broken homes, neglect or over-protectiveness had negative impact. Apart from the parents or family, "significant others" i.e. peers and teachers were also found to produce significant influence on the lives of visually impaired individuals.

Adolescence being a period of transition during which cognitive, physical, personality and social changes occur, necessitates the adoption and practice of several adult roles essential for the formation of personal identity (Haviland & Scarborough, 1981). Apart from adjusting to the varied biological changes that occur during this phase such as accepting and feeling comfortable with their body image, the adolescents also engage in evaluating themselves along several dimensions— academics, athletics, appearance, social relations and moral conduct. Hence, such a period may cause occasional discrepancies in reactions by which adolescents tend to characterize or describe themselves, such as shyness with friends, outgoing at home, etc. However, these discrepancies tend to decline in later years as adolescents form a more concrete view of themselves. Appropriate assistance and support from family or parents, peers and teachers were found to play a dominant role in the formation of self-view and adjustment of adolescents.

Comparative Analysis of Blind Individuals with Other Forms of Disability

Review of available research show that blind individuals demonstrate better self-esteem as compared to people having other forms of disabilities. Type of handicap and sex were found to produce significant effects on their overall self-esteem. William (1983) compared the adjustment of blind and deaf children using Pre-Adolescents Adjustment Scale (PAAS) by Udai Pareek. The findings show that both blind and deaf children possess good adjustment at home and with peers. Although the blind children demonstrated low level of adjustment with their teachers but they were better than the deaf children in areas of general adjustment.

Joiner, Lovett and Goodwin (1989) conducted a study on subjects from different disability categories— cardiovascular, spinal cord injury, neurologic, orthopaedic, visually impaired, hearing impaired, borderline educable, mentally retarded and substance users. The visually impaired were reported to be most assertive and significantly more accepting of their disability than the other disability groups.

Loeb and Sarigiani (1986) investigated the effects of sex, race, severity of handicap and age of onset on self-concept, self-esteem, locus of control, level of expectation and academics of 64 hearing-impaired, 74 visually-impaired and 112 non-impaired students. They used Nowicki-Strickland Children's Locus of Control Scale (Nowicki-Strikland, 1973), Piers-Harris Children's Self-Concept Scale (Piers-Harris, 1969), a Q-sort technique to assess self-concept and a Tower building Task to measure level of expectation. Parents' and teachers' ratings on personality and structural observational measures were also used. It was evident from the findings that children with hearing impairment were lower in self-esteem than their visually impaired and non-impaired counterparts. In a comparative study involving two hundred and twenty-nine blind and deaf students, Cambra (1996) (cited in Satapathy & Singhal, 2000) found the blind subjects to be more hardworking, attentive and confident than the deaf who were more reserved, solitary, significantly more nervous, unsure and impulsive.

Satapathy and Singhal (1999) based on comparative study of seventy-nine visually impaired and hearing-impaired students concluded that visually impaired students were significantly less stressed, were slightly better adjusted, had significantly fewer behaviour problems and better academic performance than the hearing impaired students.

Bala (1985) in a comparative study examined self-concept, mental make-up and adjustment of 500 physically handicapped (visually, hearing and orthopaedically handicapped) using High School Personality Questionnaire of Cattell, Allport-Vernon and Lindzey Inventory of Values, the Deo Personality Wordlist, Jalota General Mental Ability Test, Bhatia Battery of Performance Test and the Sinha and Singh Adjustment Inventory. The visually handicapped were found to be restrained, possess ideal, social and perceived self-concept and have poor home, health, emotional and educational adjustment in comparison to the two other categories of handicapped students. Both groups of handicapped (visually and hearing handicapped) significantly differed from the normal children in personality traits.

To study the correlation between social network, social support, friendships and adjustment, Wenz-Gross and Siperstein (1993) administered Hightower et al.'s Teacher-Child Rating Scale for Children's Adjustment to 106, 4th to 6th grade physically impaired (blind, deaf and crippled) and normal children. In both the measures students with impairments exhibited more problems than the normal group.

Emphasizing upon the role of family and its influence on self-esteem, Dote-Kwan and Hughes (1994) found the overall home environment of visually impaired individuals to be more favourable than those with other impairments regardless of socio-economic status of their families or visual activities.

Analysis of several studies comparing the self-esteem of blind individuals with those having other forms of disability show that blind individuals possess positive self-esteem and better adjustment. They also indicate that some of them have well-accepted their present state of disability and possess the confidence take control and affect change in their lives.

Overall Analyses of Literature

Available literature on blind indicates that there appears to be a strong and consistent relationship between self-esteem, adjustment patterns, classroom behaviour, behaviour problems and academic achievement. A desired outcome of life is preparation for independent living and to become a contributive member of the society. However, with regard to the visually challenged only a few people were successful in attaining full independence and full identity (Rice, 1984). Although positive self-esteem and adjustment are desirable feelings they frequently posited as an intervening construct. It is the general notion that loss of vision can induce low self-esteem resulting from feeling of disablement for people with visual impairment, which interactively retards their personal and social behaviour. Research studies indicate low self-esteem, inadequate adjustment and limited or poor achievement on part of individuals with visual impairment. Physical constraint has been found to be an important factor that results in developmental delays in motor skills and physical competence. The unexpressed feeling of loss of sight is frequently associated with helplessness, inferiority, mobility related stress and anxiety, depression, loss of self-efficacy, and poor performance. Blind individuals were mostly found to maintain low physical self-esteem but this is not so in other aspects of the self. In other domains of self, blind children were found to maintain positive self-esteem and not rate themselves and their life any more negatively than the sighted (for instance, Hasan, Khan & Khan, 1983; Beaty, 1994).

Besides physical competence, the extent of acceptance of disability was found to affect self-image and adjustment of blind individuals. A positive feeling towards one's condition largely affects an individual's attitude towards himself or herself. It enables people with disabilities to learn and de-emphasize their disabling condition, avoid subjecting themselves to comparison with others in their areas of limitations and instead emphasize on their own assets and abilities. Several studies have highlighted positive self-acceptance and better adjustment of blind individuals as compared to those having other forms of disability.

It is evident from literature that the type of educational setting and ongoing social relationships had strong influence on the self-esteem, adjustment and academic achievement of blind individuals. Even though debate regarding the most favourable educational placement for the all-round development of blind individuals awaits a definite conclusion, researchers have lent greater support to integration for ensuring greater gains in self-esteem, adjustment and degree of independence (Orkan-Lecka, 1980; Armstrong et al., 1992; French et al., 1996). It is evident from several studies that students in such settings tend to demonstrate strong feelings of independence, socialization and confidence. Moreover, within the type of school placement, besides the infrastructural facilities, curricula arrangements, teaching strategies, organization of materials, availability of adequate special supplies and equipments, attitude of peers and teachers towards the blind students also had immense impact on their self-evaluation. Several researches have portrayed negative feelings on the part of regular teachers towards blind students and their inclusion in regular classrooms. In certain cases they are associated in the presence of blind students in their classroom with trouble and additional work burden.

Overall analyses of literature allow focusing our attention on certain important issues as well as shortcomings existing in the area of research concerning visual impairment. Several studies have reported the possibility of a wide range of individual reactions to a specific disability emerging as a direct consequence of the operation of psychological factors in a person's immediate environment (Wright, 1960; Shanties, 1971; McDaniel, 1976). According to several researchers, greater anxiety, low self-esteem, poor adjustment emerged as the factors resulting in their academic failures. Positive self-esteem being regarded as the most desirable feeling was also frequently posited as an intervening construct facilitating other desirable outcomes as compared to impairment which induces a sense of worthlessness. Hence, there is a strong relationship between self-esteem and feeling of disablement which interactively produces significant effect on the personal and social adjustment of adolescents. This was also evident in case of visually impaired adolescents who experience the diverse effects of various psycho-social variables as compared to those not having any form of impairment. Such findings in turn highlights the need for undertaking more indepth understanding of the role played by each of these variables for assessing academic achievement of both blind and sighted adolescents thus facilitating their optimum development.

However, in India research on the visually impaired, particularly blind is limited. There is lack of sufficient empirical evidence on their behavioural and psycho-social development which further limits adequate understanding of their adjustment and educational problems. Therein also studies adequately failed to explain the extent to which psychological implications have impact on the sociological factors such as family acceptance, social integration, etc. Even though a few studies have attempted to focus on their academic achievement in comparison to sighted students, they failed to adequately address its relationship with other variables. In addition to this, most of the findings are based exclusively on self-ratings or teacher ratings or observation. This makes it difficult to obtain a holistic picture of the achievements of blind students based on such findings. In keeping view of these, the present study sought to address some of these issues.

3

Policies and Perspectives on the Education of People with Disabilities

In recent years there has been a paradigm shift ushering in a broader understanding of disability which recognizes that the circumstances and the discrimination that people with disabilities face are a socially created phenomena and have little to do with the impairments of people with disabilities. This critical reorientation of perspective has important implications for the manner in which law and policy in relation to disability needs to be developed. It is now been increasingly recognized that the problem does not reside in the person with a disability, but results from the structures, practices and attitudes that prevent that individual from exercising his or her capabilities. In this relation attempts have been made to investigate into the policy perspectives regarding the education of people with disabilities at the global level as well as in India in specific.

Education of the Disabled: International Scenario

While analyzing the nature and causes of educational exceptionality certain basic viewpoints have emerged. For instance, the Process of Dysfunction perspective places the locus of problem within the child and holds that there is either an expressed (example blindness) or implied (example minimal cerebral dysfunction) physiological basis. According to this viewpoint, the dysfunction itself is irremediable and must be bypassed or compensated for. The Experience Defect view, on the other hand regards the environmental factors and effect of adverse life experiences as causes producing educational handicaps. According to this conception 'undoing' the harm done by the experiences by suitable educational strategies can be the primary medium to remedy the defects. It holds that the lack of appropriate experiences results in a variety of educational handicap for the children ranging from grossly inadequate social behaviour to a severely limited vocabulary.

The movement for rights of the disabled gathered momentum from 1960s onward based on the Scandinavian concept about normalization of difference, the U.S. concept of the Least Restrictive Environment and the Warnock Report of 1978 in United Kingdom. These initiatives sensitized the masses and various international agencies about diverse issues of the disabled. This period witnessed the emergence of a number of programmes for the disabled in U.S. A massive programme called the Head Start was launched. It was a pre-school programme which made it mandatory for schools to enroll at least 10 per cent of the disabled children. This programme was soon followed by the Education for All Disabled Children Act in U.S. in 1975 to provide educational and other services to disabled children between ages 3 to 5. The thrust of the programmes was on normalization which aimed to make educational provisions for the disabled based on their needs in the community settings along with their non-disabled peers.

In consonance with this view, the Warnock Committee Report (1978) also made certain provisions for the education of the disabled. It took up the cause of integration and stated that—

> *'...Integration for the disabled means a thousand things. It means the absence of segregation. It means able to be treated like everybody else. It means the right to work, to go to cinemas, to enjoy outdoor sports, to have a family life and a social and a love life, contributing materially to the community, to have the usual choices of association, movement and activity,*

> *to go on holiday to the usual places, to be educated up to University level with one's non-handicapped peers, to travel without fuss on public transport..., this passage catches the part of changing attitudes to handicap in all its manifestations'.(J. Fish, 1981, p. 89).*

In ensuring equalization of benefits to the disabled, International agencies like United Nations through the 'UN Convention on the Rights of the Child' (1989), 'World Declamation on Education for All' (1990), 'The Standard Rules for Equalization of Opportunities for Persons with Disabilities' (1993) and World Conference on Special Needs Education (1994) emphasized on the need to provide equal educational opportunities to children with disabilities as their non-disabled counterparts. Some of the other international agencies working for the welfare of the disabled include UNESCO, UNICEF, UNFPA, UNDP and ILO.

Educators have emphasized on and suggested a variety of factors which needs to be considered while making placement decisions. Bishop (1990) proposed that the following areas should be considered in making educational arrangements: capabilities and needs of the students, receptivity of the school and classroom facilities, capabilities of the administrators and teachers, availability of support services, attitude and capabilities of families of the students and availability of community resources.

Later, the concept of Mainstreaming was adopted in view of the diverse educational needs of exceptional children. It was based on the philosophical framework that exceptional children should be educated with non-exceptional children and special classes or separate schooling should only occur when their needs cannot be satisfactorily met. More specifically it came to be referred to as the temporal, instructional and social integration of eligible exceptional children with normal peers based on an ongoing, individually determined, educational planning and programming process and required clarification of responsibility among regular and special education administrative, instructional and supportive personnel (Kauffman et al., 1975). This concept emphasized on three essential components—Integration, educational planning and programming and clarification of responsibilities.

Emphasizing on the context of equalization of educational opportunities, integration was adopted as the central theme for education of the disabled. Integration refers to non-categorical placement of handicapped children into heterogeneous groups with adequate scope for frequent and varied interaction between the handicapped and non-handicapped individuals. Vislie referred to integration —'an invitation to the handicapped to join the normal conditions of life and share whatever standards of quality this life may have and the focus of attention is turned upon the school system itself and normal conditions of teaching and learning.

The framework of integration can be visualized as a continuum ranging from complete segregation i.e., special school placement to full integration. From the organizational perspective, this continuum can be described as follows:

- Full time education in an ordinary class with any necessary help and support.
- Education in ordinary class or unit with periods of withdrawal to a special class or unit or other supporting base.
- Education in special class or unit with periods of attendance at an ordinary class and full tie involvement in the general community life and extra-curricular activities of the ordinary school.
- Full time education in special class or unit with social contact with the main school
- Education in special school, a day or residential with some shared lessons with a neighbouring ordinary

school.

- Full time education in a day special school with social contact with an ordinary school.
- Full time education in a residential school with social contact with an ordinary school.
- Short-term education in hospitals or other establishments.
- Long-term education in hospitals or other establishments.
- Home tuition.

From interactionist perspective the continuum is as follows:

- Locational integration, which involves the placement of children with special needs alongside their mainstream peers with joint utilization of resources.
- Social integration refers to psychologically meaningful integration whereby there is social exchanges and relationship among both the groups and understanding of the needs of each other.
- Functional integration subsumes physical integration thereby bringing both the groups into contact for specific activities.

The following years witnessed the enactment of legislation of integration for the disabled in several other countries such as Sweden, Norway, Italy, Canada, Germany, France and Denmark.

DISABILITY IN THE INDIAN CONTEXT

Legislation for People with Disabilities in India

Disability Rights movement is still in its infancy stage. There have been inadequate efforts made in the way of legislating sufficient legal intervention for persons with disabilities. Efforts started in 1971 when Mrs. Gandhi announced job reservations for the disabled. Though efforts were made by way of the National Action Plan (Government of India, 1981) for developing programmes, services and opportunities for the people with disabilities, the ideas failed to take practical shape. A Working Group was set up and a draft legislation titled the "Disabled Persons (Security and Rehabilitation) Bill, 1981 was prepared. The constitution of a committee under the Chairmanship of Member of Parliament Shri Bahrul Islam in 1987-88 made certain recommendations concerning various issues of rehabilitation such as prevention, early intervention, education, training, employment etc. However, these failed to be enacted into law.

By 1990, there was a marked rise of consciousness among various NGOs to create a barrier free environment for the disabled, to remove discrimination against them and allow for their rehabilitation thereby facilitating their integration in education and employment. This ushered in the issuing of a number of Bills such as The Blind and Other Physically Handicapped Persons (Rehabilitation, Employment and Welfare) Bill in 1993, conduction of serious workshops in early 1993 etc. However, nothing much followed.

Based on the guidelines of the 40th Session of Economic and Social Commission for Asia and the Pacific held at Beijing in 1992, the Indian Parliament enacted a law in respect of a subject of State List. The Commission had laid emphasis on enactment of legislation ensuring equal opportunities for people with disabilities, protection of their rights and prohibition of abuse and neglect of these persons and discrimination against them. Later, the Persons with Disabilities Act was enacted under Article 253 of the Constitution of India and came into effect from February, 1996. It laid emphasis on—

- state's responsibility towards prevention of impairments and protection of disabled peoples' rights in health, education, training, employment and rehabilitation.
- create a barrier-free environment.
- remove discrimination in the sharing of development benefits.

- lays down strategies for a comprehensive development of programmes and services for equalization of opportunities, and
- make provision for integration of the disabled people into the social mainstream.

However, one of the major limitations regarding enforcement of specified provisions has been the lack of follow-up procedures for their implementation. This diluted the entire process and curtailed the scope for people with disabilities who have limited resources and legal knowledge to take initiative on their personal front in the legal process.

Among the several other initiatives taken in the direction of legislation were the appointment of a Chief Commissioner for Persons with Disabilities and constitution of a National Coordination Committee. The Chief Commissioner is expected to act as a watchdog to safeguard the rights of persons with disabilities, monitor the utilization of funds, submit reports etc. The National Coordination Committee is expected to—

- review and coordinate the activities of all the departments of the Government of India and other Governmental and Non-Governmental Organizations concerned with matters related to the people with disabilities.
- develop a national policy to address issues faced by them.
- advise on the formulation of policies, programmes, legislation and projects.
- work in coordination with international agencies.
- look into funding policies of donor agencies.
- ensure barrier-free environment in public and work places, schools and other public institutions.

Policy Issues for Education of People with Disabilities in India

There is lack of adequate documentation about the educational needs of people with disabilities during the 19th century or the pre-independence era in India. There were sporadic interest in the education and training of the handicapped by way of *ad hoc* grants and voluntary efforts. The earliest attempt in this direction was made with the establishment of a school for the deaf in Bombay in 1883 and for the blind in Amritsar in 1887. The Central Advisory Board of Education (CABE) in 1944 emphasized that efforts should be made not to segregate the handicapped children from the normal children unless required. The years that followed witnessed the emergence of quite a number of schools and institutions for the blind. However, education in these institutions was confined only to the primary level and in most cases students were not admitted before the age of seven. It was only after independence that any major change was brought about in the educational scenario of disabled among educational professionals, voluntary agency administrators and Government officials.

After independence numerous policies addressed the cause of education for the disabled. The Kothari Commission (1964-66) maintained that 'experimentation with the integrated programme is urgently required and every attempt should be made to bring in as many children into the integrated programme as possible'. The two advantages underlined by the Commission were 'reduction of costs' and promoting mutual understanding between handicapped and non-handicapped children. As a means of implementation, the Ministry of Welfare launched the Integrated Education for the Disabled Children (IEDC) scheme in December, 1974. It aimed at providing educational opportunities to CWSN in regular schools, facilitating their retention in the school system, and placing children from special schools in common schools. The scheme also emphasized on pre-school, training, counselling for parents and special training in skills for all kinds of disabilities. In spite of all these facilities, the IEDC met with limited success.

The National Policy of Education (1986) was a turning point especially in the area of disability. It laid down certain guidelines to facilitate the welfare of people with disabilities such as inclusive education possibilities for children with mild disabilities in regular schools, provision for the training and education of children with severe disabilities in special schools and vocational training as being a part of the education for the disabled. It also recommended that reorientation of teachers training programmes were to include education of the disabled.

Later, there was a shift in strategy from a school based approach to a Composite Area Approach. With the objective of attaining universalization of primary education, the Ministry of Human Resource Development adopted the Projected Integrated Education for the Disabled (PIED) in 1987 and District Primary Education Programme (DPEP, 1994). The PIED primarily focusing on decentralization of education was tried out in selected blocks of various states. The scheme included two more categories — children with learning disabilities and children with severe disabilities. The project focused on placing disabled children in ordinary schools with the help of special teachers, aids and resources. It provided funds for training teachers, equipments, books and assessment facilities and also recommended that materials such as Braille and personnel such as itinerant teachers and consultants be consolidated in the Project Area Resource Centres. The project ensured not only a noticeable increase in enrolment but also in the retention rate among disabled children. It also brought about a greater awareness about the diverse needs of disabled children among educational professionals and teachers. The DPEP aimed at including education for all children with mild to moderate disabilities up to the primary level with suitable teacher preparation, infrastructural facilities, aids and appliances, community mobilization and resource support.

The Programme of Action (1992) also stressed upon the inclusion of educational needs of handicapped children in planning for Universal Elementary Education. It held that children whose educational needs can be met in common with others should not be placed in special schools and those placed in special schools should be integrated to general schools as soon as possible. The disability movement gathered momentum with the enactment of the Rehabilitation Council of India Act (1992) and the Persons with Disabilities (Equal Opportunities, Protection of Rights and Full Participation) Act, 1995. The PWD Act, 1995 assigned responsibility to the local Governments to ensure access to free education to each child till the age of eighteen years and proposed a variety of options including integrated education, special education, non-formal education and vocational training. Though it was envisaged through the 1995 Act that the quality of persons with disabilities could be improved by addressing certain issues such as education, literacy levels, employment, social security, assistive devices and barrier i.e. free environment, training of teachers, etc. but the implementation left much to be desired.

A Working Group for the Welfare and Development of the Disabled set up by the Ministry of Welfare in the IXth Plan. It made certain noteworthy recommendations—

- integration in all ongoing national and state level programmes under EFA including DPEP and adult education programmes, every district to have fully equipped resource centres to meet the challenges.
- 1200 special schools to be established during the plan period (1997-2002).
- five per cent of the total Budget allocation for education at the Centre and State levels to be earmarked for children with special needs.
- the State Government should assume appropriate responsibility.
- general teacher preparation programmes to include adequate input on special education in curriculum.
- vocational institutes for the handicapped in regional institutes of education, universities.

Role of NGOs in the education of people with disabilities in India

The bifurcation of the Ministry of Education that had been responsible for the education of the disabled in the 1960s witnessed the creation of Ministry of Social Welfare. The Ministry administered services to voluntary organizations by way of grant-in-aid schemes for the education, training and rehabilitation of people with disabilities. However, this failed to indicate any direct undertaking of responsibility by the Ministry for delivering services to the disabled but instead entrusted it to voluntary organizations. Recent survey of organizations working for the disabled in India indicates that more than 2,456 voluntary organizations are working in the area of disability and most of them are autonomous.

Four premier National Institutes were set up by the Ministry of Welfare in 1988 for specific disability areas such as An Artificial Limb Manufacturing Unit in Kanpur, District Rehabilitation Centres to facilitate comprehensive rehabilitation at district levels. The core objectives of these institutes were 'to develop models of services and care, conduct research, promote human resource development' (Government of India, 1993). By 'models of care', the emphasis was laid on training professionals to identify disability and refer them to appropriate agencies and rehabilitation in the form of manufacturing and distribution of aids and appliances, identification and referrals, manpower training, research and dissemination.

Barriers to education of the disabled in India

Even though several educational policies from the Kothari Commission (1966), NPE (1986) to the Programme of Action (1992) and Persons with Disabilities Act (1995) have laid down certain guidelines for education of children with disabilities within their policy framework, they failed to adequately address some of their basic concerns such as the issues of accessibility, education and employment (Nagarajan, 2001; A Reporter, 2000; Veedon, 1999). In regard to this mention can be made of the Projected Integrated Education for the Disabled (PIED) which has been subjected to a series of criticism. It is maintained that the expectations were not adequately met. The critiques of PIED hold that the scheme suffered from certain limitations such as there was lack of appropriate assessment tools due to which the categorization and selection of students was often reported to be arbitrary and incorrect. Due to this it was centrally focused on children with mild to moderate disabilities who are not identified while entering school and form substantial portion of the dropouts. As a result of this the due of pre-school support was also not adequately addressed (Karnath & Kaur, 1993). The magnitude of the problem was accounted for confinement of the scheme to limited categories of disability (Jangira, 1995). Lack of clarity on the status of special education teachers also resulted in confusion and professional competition (Seetharam, 1982) thereby diluting the purpose of various programmes. Moreover, there was also lack of specific prescribed curriculum and inadequate short-term orientation courses for providing sustained on-going support to classroom teachers (Seetharam, 1982; Nathan, 1991). Due to some of these factors the approach failed to attain materialization.

Despite various attempts to ensure integration of people with disabilities into the mainstream there is a dichotomy between intent and practice whereby although emphasis is being continuously laid by Governments on integration they are also accompanied by segregation policy at the parallel level. In a countrywide survey on the enrolment of disabled children in educational institutions in India, the National Centre for Promotion of Employment for Disabled People (NCPEDP) reveal that only a fraction of the disabled get admission into schools and colleges. The survey conducted in 119 universities report an enrolment of only 1,635 students and only 679 to 96 colleges. Further, the survey also revealed greater bias towards disabled in schools than colleges. Estimates indicate that only 382 students with disabilities were enrolled in 89 schools while 18 of them cited the existence of special schools to be the reason for not integrating them to regular schools.

There is lack of adequate community sensitization towards the disabled. The efforts of the Government in providing educational facilities remain minimal. Moreover, mandatory changes made in the educational systems and services do not suffice to adequately cater to the needs of people with disabilities. Even today separateness is confined not only within the purview of segregated classes but also in 'separate standards' used to evaluate the attainments of these students. Despite numerous attempts towards integration, the requirements of 'basics' of curricular aspects of such children such as facilities for reading, writing, field trips, standards of attendance, participation, etc. field to acquire adequate attention and implementation. In a recent attempt by the Government to evaluate the curricular issues in CBSE schools it was observed that not only there were difficulties related to the provision of barrier-free environment for such children but also lack of adequate and appropriate study materials such as rarity in availability of Braille books, necessary support services as well as adequate transport services.

Moreover, Government's conceptualization of the problem remains ingrained with the belief that education and management of disabled children relies on voluntary organizations. Though a number of special schools for blind, deaf, cerebral palsied, mentally handicapped and slow learners are maintained by NGOs, there are limitations to their functioning. Their functioning is limited only to the micro level, whereby the geographical logistics of the sub-continent, coupled with the expenditure act as barriers to frequent contact between the NGO groups hence resulting in fragmented and piecemeal services. This largely blurs the intention and efforts made towards mainstreaming. Moreover, much of the efforts are carried out at the micro level and the initiatives taken by the Governments and voluntary agencies suffer from lack of continuous funding and good infrastructural support. Besides these, the changing Governmental policies further limit the functioning of various agencies. Hence, it is imperative to depoliticize the field of special education by establishing a network of collaboration among the various bodies, Governmental policy, administrators, professionals, community, parents, etc.

An overview of numerous developments and trends in education of people with disabilities in light of different perspectives and approaches, policy perspectives, educational practices and problems have brought certain issues to the forefront. It is obvious that there has been marked shift in paradigms with regard to different educational policies and programmes for optimizing the development of people with disabilities by way of special education and integration and ensuring their incorporation into the mainstream society. At the same time, the various backlogs and barriers makes it imperative to undertake more focused and comprehensive efforts for deriving optimum benefits. It is within this perspective that the present work aims to look into the diverse trends and factors affecting the academic performance of blind individuals as well as their performance in relation to the sighted individuals. Attempt was also made to explore the effect of school setting on the self-esteem, adjustment and academic achievement of blind students.

Comparative Overview of Educational Achievement of Blind and Sighted Individuals

Research evidences show that individuals often seek to acquire social situations that facilitate them in expressing those characteristics and behaviours which are regarded as self-defining and provide self-verifying feedback (Neidenthal, Cantor & Kihlstrom, 1985; Swann, 1983). This is essential for the maintenance of stable and consistent views regarding themselves. This process entails a particular cognitive strategy which involves comparing one's own attributes with those of a typical person-in-situation and selection of a situation where the greatest self-to-prototype overlap (Neidenthal et al, 1985).

It is widely held in literature that visually impaired students tend to lag behind their sighted peers in academic achievement, particularly reading. Studies on academic performance of blind students mostly indicate poor academic performance and achievement. Meyer (1930) in a study of visually handicapped children found that about one-third of visually handicapped children were overage for their grade. Moreover, their educational retardation was also partially due to the inadequacies in teaching methods. Hayes (1941) in his 'Contributions to a Psychology of Blindness' reported that although blind and sighted children were in the same grade, their performance varied largely. The performance of the blind was poor due to their late entrance to school. Their rate of reading was also slow, wherein by the end of the elementary stage blind pupils read only 1/3rd as efficiently as the normal 5th graders. Moreover, no appreciable advance was reported to occur during the high school years. He maintained that although the visually impaired and sighted children of same age and grade performed at the same level on achievement tests, the visually impaired children were reported to be at least two years older than the sighted children. Moreover, due to dependence on Braille as the medium to acquire instruction their reading ability and vocabulary and language comprehension was reported to be slow and did not show much improvement in the high school years.

Commenting on the academic retardation of blind students, Lowenfeld (1955) emphasized on their over-age. Investigating the age grade status of 481 blind pupils in 3rd to 6th grades he noted the following degree of average over-ageness— 2.5 years for 3rd and 4th graders, 2.9 years for the 5th graders and 2.8 years for the 6th graders. While comparing age-grade difference between blind and sighted children Lowenfeld, Abel and Hatlen (1969) also found that fourth-grade Braille readers were 0.8 years older than sighted readers in local schools and 0.3 years older in residential schools.

Elaborating on low academic performance demonstrated by blind students, Brieland (1950) noted certain personality problems, excessive anxiety concerning family relationships and dissatisfaction with school achievement and activities. Some studies show that visual impairment may cause adolescents to feel inadequate and inferior-feelings that tend to reflect their lack of social acceptance, academic under-achievement, physical incapability and social maladjustment (Meighan, 1971; Obiakor & Stile, 1989; Beaty, 1992). Several reasons have been accounted by researchers for poor achievement of blind individuals. It is argued that since vision provides the vital foundation for learning, organizing and synthesizing information and incidental casual learning primarily comes from vision, the visually impaired individuals are at a disadvantage. Moreover in argument against the Piagetian perspective which holds that children construct knowledge through interaction with the physical and social environment, Lowenfeld (1963) argued that there are three major areas where blind people were at a disadvantage—the range and variety of experiences, which can affect their cognitive development, mobility that includes both orientation to the immediate surroundings and locomotion within those surroundings and interaction with the environment. Hence, absence of sight places severe constrictions in their exploration and interaction with the environment. These factors then cumulatively affect their performance. Besides these, lack of opportunities for making visual observations, slower Braille reading was also specified as some of the other factors limiting performance of the visually impaired.

Despite studies highlighting low level of academic competence among the visually impaired individuals, several studies have also focused on their better academic performance. Jangira (1987) reported that visually impaired children were neither isolated nor were they below average in achievement. Haider (1990) and Beaty (1994) found that sometimes visually impaired students performed better academically than their non-impaired counterparts. With increase in age, their language comprehension and memory became similar to the non-integrated group and performance remained intact. No significant difference was found in their psycho-social adjustment, self-esteem and level of stress. Beaty (1994) in studying the psycho-social adjustment and academic success of visually impaired children through Coopersmith Self-esteem Inventory, Social Provisions Scale and Student Information Questionnaire reported of no significant difference in psycho-social adjustment between the visually impaired and sighted. On the contrary, the visually impaired children were found to have scored slightly higher than the sighted in self-esteem and academic performance.

Erin, Corn and Wolffe (1993) while examining the learning and study skills of 106 high school students having visual impairments found differences in skills by the students' grade point averages and not by their preferred reading medium, type of school placement or plan to attend college. However, the strategies used by students having visual impairments were found to be similar to those of the sighted.

Research evidences indicate that the type of educational setting and ongoing social relationships in recurring social settings largely affect the psychological well-being of blind children. Attitude and interaction with the peers and teachers (Goldstein & Cisar, 1992; Pellegrini, 1984), availability of educational materials and characteristics of the physical setting (Burgess & Fordyce, 1989; Ladd & Price, 1993) were all found to play a significant role.

Marginalization of the disabled is evident in education where physical barriers, lack of infrastructural facilities and shortage of manpower limits the accessibility of disabled children to schools and other educational institutions. Studies reveal feelings of uncertainty and constraint among normally sighted peers in dealing with blind students (Erwin, 1991). Moreover within classroom situation while most of the sighted children gain access to information in their immediate environment through the use of vision, blind children have to learn them through alternative means and strategies. As a result they have difficulty in interpreting non-verbal messages and monitoring their own behaviour during social encounters (Scott, 1969; Ferell, 1986).

The attitude of teachers also affects the academic attainment of blind students. In a study conducted by Glaubman and Lifshitz (2001) to investigate the attitude of teachers in the independent educational system of Haredi community towards the inclusion of pupils with special needs in regular classroom they found unwillingness of teachers to include blind and deaf pupils in their classes. Similar negative attitudes were reflected through other studies where teachers associated the presence of blind students in their classroom with trouble (Murphy, 1960; Pastor & Jimenez, 1994), more work burden and a means leading to disparity of level between pupils that hindered pace of the course (Diamond, 1979; Bulloile & Rigg, 1980). The teachers rated the blind students lower in cooperation, academic competence and higher in problem behaviour than the sighted (Buhrow et al., 1998).

Research work on the academic achievement of sighted population indicates that there is a significant correlation between self-esteem and academic achievement and *vis-à-vis* (Renick & Harter, 1989; Hoge, Smith & Hanson 1990; Martinot & Monteil, 1995) school climate, evaluation and feedback from teachers were found to produce significant effects on self-esteem i.e. academic success furthers the development of a well structured academic self-concept. Findings show that high achieving participants tend to process self-related information more easily and possess very well structured academic self-concept whereas less achieving participants failed to process self-related information easily and their academic self-concept was not well structured. Moreover, individuals with low self-esteem tend to be unhappy, less sociable, more likely to use drugs and alcohol and are more vulnerable to depression which results in low academic achievement (Wiggins, 1994). Marsh, Smith and Barnes (1985) reported of no gender difference in academic self-esteem but found it to be positively associated with academic achievement.

Some theorists have argued that people with high self-esteem are more disposed to have positive affective orientations and effective relationships than those with low self-esteem. Smith and Perry (1995) indicated that even when undergoing negative moods people with high self-esteem tend to engage in counter-emotional thinking as a means of reducing their unpleasant feelings. As compared to individuals with low self-esteem, individuals with high self-esteem are less susceptible to emotional mood swings (Campbell, Chew & Scratchy, 1991), are less vulnerable to depression (Hokanson et al., 1989), prefer more challenging activities (Waschull & Kernis, 1996) and more receptive to favourable feedback from interaction partners (Swann et al., 1990). They are also more confident that their efforts will lead to success (Baumgardner, 1990) and are unlikely to experience negative affect when they perceive that others rank above them socially (Buunk et al., 1990).

Moeller (1994) maintained that self-esteem of college students is based or enforced by their academic success or achievements. Bray in his study to determine the effect of academic achievement of students' self-esteem with 64 college students by using the Rosenberg's Self-esteem Scale found a positive relationship between the two variables. Hence, the extent to which one's academic achievement lives up to one's academic expectations and desires is regarded as an important determinant of self-esteem.

Academic achievement may be associated with social functioning at both individual level and social level. The associations at the individual level may be derived from intrapersonal processes such as individual social-cognitive competence or specific family socialization experiences (Chen et al., 1997). The associations at the group level may indicate the significance of the group.

Contemporary theorists like Connell, Spencer, Deci, Ryan

and others concerned with motivation and development hold that academic engagement and achievement of adolescents is a resultant of a conjoint function of various aspects of their social world, demographic characteristics and personality and ability-related factors. Roger (1978) and Wylie (1979) showed that academic marks are highly correlated to self-esteem. Educational expectations and academic performance, background characteristics and expectations of significant others were found to influence academic performance through identity, self-esteem and self-concept (Patel, 1979; Reitzes & Multran, 1980; Watson-Tim et al., 1983). In examining the relation between parenting style and adolescent school performance, authoritative parenting was found to be positively correlated with adolescent school performance whereas negatively correlated with authoritarian and permissive parenting. Adolescents who described their parents as behaving more democratically, more warmly and more encouraging showed higher grades in school than their peers. (Dornbusch et al., 1987; Steinberg, Elmen & Mounts, 1989).

Social competence has been found to be a powerful predictor among several factors affecting academic achievement of students. Children who are well accepted by their peer or display prosocial and responsible forms of behaviour at school tend to be high achievers as compared to socially rejected and aggressive children who are at a risk for academic failure (Feldhusen & Benning, 1970; Lambert, 1972; Green, Forehand, Beck & Vosk, 1980; Vosk, Forehand, Parker & Rickard, 1982; Dishion, 1999). Sieber (1979) held that peer support can take the form of students providing mutual assistance by clarifying and interpreting their teacher's instructions, sharing various resources such as notes and books etc.

Though limited but important literature on school effects converge with the findings that perceiving a sense of belongingness or connectedness with one's school is positively related to academic, psychological and behavioural outcomes during adolescence. Most studies indicate that when students experience supportive environment in school they are more likely to experience positive outcomes. Battistich et al., (1997) demonstrated that the presence of a 'caring school community' is often associated with positive outcomes for students as improved social skills, motivation and achievement.

Emphasizing that students become actively engaged in educational activities to the extent classroom endeavours affirm their competencies and prove themselves to be interesting and relevant to the students' lives, the Self-determination theory seeks to foster in students an interest in learning, a valuing of education and a confidence in personal capabilities (Deci et al., 1991). The basic needs of competence and self-determination explain the motivational force underlying students' experiences of becoming interested in school and internalizing school related values. Both competence and self-determination represents energizing states which if nurtured facilitates interest, enjoyment, engagement and well-being (Ryan & Deci, 2000). Competence represents the need for seeking out optimal challenges and for perceiving oneself as efficacious in mastering those challenges and self-determination represents the need to experience choice in initiation and regulation of one's behaviour such that the student's choice rather than environmental events determine his or her actions (Deci & Ryan, 1985; Ryan & Deci, 2000). According to this theory, environment that support students' needs for competence and self-determination constitute autonomy-supportive environments, whereas those that neglect and frustrate these needs constitute controlling environments. These have wide implications on the academic performance of students. Thus to promote an interest in learning, to value education, an affirmation of capabilities, it is essential for educational climates to find ways to support students' needs for competence and self-determination as both environmental and personal factors contribute to students' motivation for achievement in school.

Students' perception of goals emphasized in schools was

found to be related to their personal achievement goals, feelings of academic efficacy, use of effective learning strategies and in school behaviour. It was maintained that constellation of educational practices and policies in the classrooms and schools such as public honour rolls for the highest achieving students, use of homogenous ability grouping, special privileges based upon academic standing, etc. gives rise to certain meanings or goals that define what constitutes success (Maehr & Midgley, 1991; Ames, 1992). Roeser, Midgley and Urdan (1996) examined the role of personal achievement goals and feelings of school belonging in mediating the relation between perceptions of the psychological environment at school and school related beliefs and affect and achievement. Findings show a significantly positive relation between perceiving a task goal and ability goal structure in middle school to academic self-efficacy and teacher student relationships to school related effect mediated through feelings of school belonging. Wentzel (1989) investigated the relationship between adolescent efforts to achieve a variety of classroom goals, standards for performance and academic achievement. Correlational results from 203 high school students suggested that achievement as indexed by GPA is positively related to efforts to be a successful student, be dependable and responsible, understand thing, do one's very best and get things done on time and negatively related to trying having fun. Student GPAs were also related to the number and uniqueness of the goals they try to achieve.

Classroom task structures, evaluation practices and group patterns partly determine performance information and thus affect students' achievement standards and ability perceptions (Marshall & Weinstein, 1984; Rosenholtz & Simpson, 1984a). Several studies indicate that general classroom environment is significantly related to student achievement. Classes perceived to have more cohesiveness, goal direction and organization (Rutter, 1983), authoritative, warmth, autonomy, supportive teaching behaviour (Moos, 1978; Ryan & Grolnick, 1986; Ryan, Stiller & Lynch, 1994) have yield higher achievement and be positively related to student motivation and feelings of academic competence. Rosenholtz and Simpson (1984a) argue that type of classrooms such as uni-dimensional i.e. high resolution classes whereby students use the same materials, have pre-decided and prefixed tasks to adhere to and are received as in definite ability groups makes it easy for students to compare their performance with classmates frequently and clearly perceive the inequalities in performance. Moreover, teachers in such classrooms assign grades frequently and students and teachers have higher consensus on students' relative academic rankings than those in multidimensional classrooms.

The nature of task structures also affects performance of students. Social-comparative performance information is found to be higher in classrooms where students are given undifferentiated task structures thereby reducing intra-individual variation in performance across time, makes the inequalities in performance more comparable, more public and more salient (Blumenfeld et al., 1982; Marshall & Weinstein, 1984; Rosenholtz & Simpson, 1984b).

Student outcomes were also found to be largely affected by ability grouping. Within classroom grouping has a greater advantage in contrast to between classroom whereby the former increases variance in achievement distribution of a class (Hallinan & Sorensen, 1983), serves as an important basis for social comparison and influences formation of friendships (Bossert, 1979; Hallinan & Sorensen, 1985).

Overall analyses of academic performance/achievement of visually impaired addresses diverse issues and attributes their low performance to numerous factors such as limited experience, limited cognitive abilities, over-age, etc. However, restrictions in the range and variety of available experiences, in mobility and interaction with the environment were found to be chief factors causing congenitally and totally blind individuals to face numerable difficulties. Delays in physical and motor development were found to lead to further lags in cognitive development (Gottesman, 1971; Tobin, 1972). Marked difference was evident in the manner by which blind and sighted individuals conceptualized object due to inadequate visual stimulation for observing, organizing and synthesizing sensory information.

Moreover, the blind students were found to be slightly older in age and also lag behind their sighted counterparts in academic achievement, particularly reading.

Though innumerable factors were found to affect the achievement of blind students as compared to their sighted counterparts, it is essential to note that there are certain limitations in undertaking a direct comparative study of school achievement of blind with that of sighted individuals. At the outset the problem lies regarding the medium of assessment. The method of Braille is not comparable to print. Moreover, the time limits in particular are also different. In spite of these, most authorities are of the opinion that if academic retardation exists among blind students it is closely related to slowness of the Braille reading than to their mental ability. In addition to this their academic achievement was also dependent on other environmental factors such as attitude of peers, teachers' attitude, teaching methods adopted, organization of materials, availability of adequate special supplies and equipments, etc. It is evident from literature that despite diverse problems and limitations the achievement of blind students did not differ significantly from their sighted counterparts.

School Climate along with parental involvement, attitude of peers and teachers were found to be dominant factors affecting the academic performance of sighted individuals. In accordance with the view that the school climate produces an important affect on the psychosocial development as well as academic achievement of individuals, it becomes essential to acquire an insight into the varied effects that the diverse school settings can have on the self-esteem, adjustment and academic achievement of blind students in particular.

Effect of School Setting on Self-esteem, Adjustment and Academic Achievement of Blind Students

Research has shown that school setting produces significant effect on the psycho-social development of people with disabilities. Two major schools of thought exist regarding their educational placement— integrated and segregated institutions. However, opinions regarding feasibility of the two have been a debatable issue since long. Those in support of integration regard it as the most favourable environment ensuring psycho-social well-being of blind students in terms of self-esteem and adjustment (Van, Vincent, Kazdin & Hersen, 1987; Armstrong, Rosenbaum & King, 1992; Dimigen et al., 1999; Murg & Wallander, 2002). According to them students in integrated schools showed lower levels of aggression and more positive view of themselves and the world as compared to those in segregated settings who demonstrated emotional difficulties such as loneliness and depression. Students who find their schools risky or isolating places tend to struggle on a daily basis and develop negative image of themselves.

With reference to blind students, Lukoff and Whiteman (1961) held that blind children in special schools showed a lower degree of independence than those in regular schools. Numerous studies show that self-esteem and level of adjustment to disability was much higher among students studying in integrated setting than those in special schools (McGuiness, 1970; Orkan-Lecka, 1980; Van, Vincent, Kazdin & Hersen, 1987; Jangira, 1987; Sharma, 1988; Armstrong, Rosenbaum & King, 1992; Martinez & Sewell, 1996).

Haider (1991) studied adjustment, social competency; aspiration and academic achievement of visually handicapped children in special and in integrated settings and also attempted to examine how personal and psychological characteristics influence educational achievement of students in these schools. The study comprised of 106 children from residential schools and 52 from integrated schools. Findings show that students from the integrated schools were better in all respects. Dimigen et al. (1999) undertook two case studies for determining the impact of integration (early and late) on blind students' self-evaluation. It was conducted over a period of six years on two blind subjects — Susan and Mark. Susan was integrated in a regular school at an early age whereas Mark at a later age. The findings revealed that Susan demonstrated strong feeling of independence, socialization and confidence as compared to Mark who was reported to be more dependent, reserved and less self-confident. Based on this, the researchers concluded that early integration was found to have positive affect on the general self-worth of blind students.

With regard to the structural and functional aspects of personal network, those in favour of integrated placement of blind students held that placement in such institutions ensured greater contact and interaction with the sighted as compared to special schools which provided homogeneous and categorical grouping with scope for little or no interaction among students except with those within the institution.

With reference to the special schools, researchers maintain that students with disability experienced greater gains in self-esteem and perception of ability in special classes than those in regular classes (Battle & Blowers, 1982; Coleman, 1983; Gurney, 1988; Bina, 1993). Increased attention and resources, specially trained teachers and the opportunity for children to make more realistic comparisons between their own achievements and those of their peers were held as some of the underlying factors. In support of special school placement, Eagelstein (1975) suggested that even though blind students find academic success in regular classes, they experience general rejection by the school and loss of prestige.

The supporters of special or non-integrated school settings held that blind students in special settings gained higher in adjustment and self-esteem. Das (1988) based on the study of psycho-social profiles of blind individuals showed that they had highly positive relationship with their family members, but lacked the intimacy they shared with their friends. They preferred to stay at school rather than at home and despite liking integration preferred special school.

As against integration the supporters of special placement maintain that integration often results in marginalization of the disabled in terms of physical barriers, lack of infrastructural facilities and shortage of manpower with further limits their accessibility to educational institutions. McConnell (1985) studied the problem of adjustment and self-worth of visually handicapped students in integrated industrial education classes and suggested that for successful placement certain issues have to be settled such as curriculum modification, safety provisions, attitude of teachers and students, orientation and mobility, etc.

Studies have also revealed feelings of uncertainty and constraint among sighted peers in dealing with blind students (Erwin, 1991). Moreover in classroom situations while most sighted children gain access to information in their immediate environment through the use of vision, blind children had to depend on alternative means and strategies. Due to this they faced difficulty in interpreting non-verbal messages and monitoring their own behaviour during social encounters (Scott, 1969; Parish, Baker, Arheart & Adamchak, 1980; Ferell, 1986).

Supporters of segregated or specialized schools further held that apart from the exorbitant cost of mainstreaming, integration failed to produce any positive impact upon the personality, self-esteem (Battle, 1982; Gurney, 1988; Lalkhen, 1990; Bear et al., 1991) and social and academic adjustment (Brinker, 1985; McConnell, 1985; Haider, 1990) of blind individuals. Havill (1972) in one of his studies stated that the estimated socio-metric status of blind children was inferior to that of their classmates in integrated classes. They were less well accepted and only above average achievement improved their status.

Some researchers maintain a neutral approach regarding

the impact of different educational settings on the psychological make-up of blind individuals. They found no significant difference between blind students in integrated and specialized schools with regard to their self-esteem, social behaviour and participation (Schindele, 1975; Erwin, 1993; Kielly, 1994; Gronmo & Augestad, 2000). On the basis of their findings they concluded that different types of school provisions were not crucial in explaining differences in physical competence, physical and social self-concept and global self-worth of blind youths. While examining the learning and study skills of 106 high school students having visual impairments, Erin, Corn and Wolffe (1993) found differences in skills by students' averages and not by their preferred reading medium, type of school placement, or plan to attend college.

Though the debate on effectiveness of both integrated and non-integrated or segregated schools on the psychological make-up of disabled individuals awaits a much definite conclusion, the current educational discourses still maintain that they constitute fundamentally different ecologies (Carta, Greenwood & Robinson, 1987, Odom, Peterson, McConnell & Ostrosky, 1990). On the one hand, certain researchers have highlighted the significance of integrated set up in terms of greater social interaction and peer and teacher support, better facilities of learning, etc., thereby regarding specialized schools as 'second class' inferior placements for students unable to meet their needs. On the other hand, those in favour of non-integrated schools maintain that although integrated classrooms may facilitate better social and emotional adjustment by providing more developmentally competent peers, smaller group size and specialized training of teachers in segregated classrooms results in higher level of physical, social and emotional development. According to the latter viewpoint characteristics of an individual may interact even in ill-defined ways with environmental factors to result in certain behaviour and overall functioning (Sontag, 1997).

4

Rationale, Objectives and Hypotheses

Review of available literature on visually impaired individuals, specifically the blind has been found to be limited. Research on blind people has been dominated by literature written from the perspective of medicine, psychology and rehabilitation. The focus of these studies has been disease and its effects, psychological aspects of blindness (loss, grief and eventual 'acceptance'), adaptation and coping strategies. Blindness was positioned absolutely on individual approach with little consideration of the societal context. This approach tends to assume blindness as solely a physiological event and not a social process. However, Scott's pioneering Social Constructionist approach to blindness and society was an exception to this pattern. Scott's work has been built upon in the past decade by interdisciplinary literature on blindness. They were strongly influenced by blind disability studies scholars (Michalko, 1998; Kleege, 1999; Kuldick, 2001; French, 1993, 1999, 2001).

Regarding the psychological development of blind individuals, it is important to note that though studies have focussed on various psycho-social factors (anxiety, depression, self-esteem) affecting their development there is dearth of adequate research emphasizing on the correlation between these variables. Further sufficient attention has not been focussed on assessing and analyzing the influence of these variables on educational performance of blind students especially in the Indian context. Due to these shortcomings it was difficult to deduce whether blind students' perception of positive feelings about themselves and academic achievement was affected by their loss of vision or the influence of psycho-social variables.

In addition to this the concern of most studies undertaken has primarily being focussed on young children with a few on adolescents and adults. This is essential because adolescence is a critical period of development marked by rapid changes such as transition to independence and finding one's own identity. The psychological well-being of both blind and sighted adolescents is dependent on several factors such as their social and economical background, gender, age, perceived social support and social and emotional maturity. Inability to adjust to the various physical, cognitive and affective changes may cause them to exhibit different types of behaviour problems.

Closely related to this, though studies have been undertaken to assess social adjustment and emotional development of the visually impaired, there is lack of sufficient attention on various types of school settings. Though the ongoing debate on maximum feasibility of an educational placement for blind students awaits any definite conclusion, it is evident from available research studies that blind students in integrated educational settings tend to possess higher self-esteem and better adjustment as compared to those in non-integrated schools (Orkan-Lecka, 1980; Armstrong et al.,1992; French et al., 1996). This difference was also reported to produce significant impact on their educational performance or achievement. However, it is essential to note that though most integration studies indicate difference among students with visual impairments regarding their psycho-social development and social interaction, there is lack of substantial attempt to describe the structural properties of diverse educational settings and its effect on their adjustment pattern and academic performance.

Regarding methodological aspects of research, findings of most studies were exclusively based on self-ratings or teacher ratings or observation. This limited the chances of obtaining a comprehensive picture.

In view of the above-mentioned limitations in the area of

disability studies, the present study attempted to address some of these issues. The study aimed to find out if the type of educational placement (integrated and non-integrated) produced any significant influence and differences among adolescent blind and sighted students in respect of their self-esteem, adjustment and academic achievement. The theories of Festinger (1954), Tajfel and Turner (1979) and Bandura (1977) which have been chiefly used to interpret the behavioural and psychological functioning of individuals having no impairment were used to explain the variations in psycho-social dynamics as well as academic achievement of blind students. The interaction theories of self-esteem development (Mead, 1934, Goffman, 1963) were also used to explain self-esteem and adjustment pattern of blind and sighted students.

Further since the interaction pattern and self-perception of blind students at school has been analyzed in most studies by adopting a psycho-medical approach rather than analyzing it as a socially constructed problem, the present study critically looked into these issues from the social constructivist perspective of disability. This was based on the assumption that experiences of schooling for children with disability are mediated through school practices and processes rather than the physical impairment itself (Finkelstein, 1980; Foucault, 1981; Allan, 1998). In this relation attempt was made to explore into the ecological aspects of the two school settings (integrated and non-integrated) and their impact on blind students. This was made through an in-depth study of the ecology of classrooms both at the institutional level in the context of schools and also in terms of interpersonal relations prevalent classrooms. Both rating and observation methods were used for obtaining holistic analysis.

Objectives of the Study

The primary objectives of the study were as follows:

- A comparative analysis of blind and sighted adolescents with respect to self-esteem and adjustment (social, emotional and educational adjustment) in two types of school settings (integrated and non-integrated).
- Exploring relation of the psycho-social variables with academic achievement for all the four groups of students.
- Ecological analysis of school and classroom environment in order to investigate and interpret the effect of type of school placement on self-esteem and adjustment (social, emotional and academic adjustment) and academic achievement of blind students.

Hypotheses

Keeping in view that formation of positive self-esteem and healthy adjustment both being dynamic processes requiring constant adaptation, it was found that disability often creates psychodynamic stress, conflict and also maladjustment which manifests itself through various problems. It is evident from research studies that adolescents with visual impairments (those who are blind or have low vision) may be at a risk for psychological and social adjustment problems (Muhl, 1930; Brown, 1938, 1939; Morgan, 1944; Hubbard, 1945; Hasting, 1947; Meighan, 1971; Qadari & Hussain, 1982; Sarita, 1985; Obiakor & Stile, 1989; Beaty, 1992; Konarska, 2003). Moreover, visual impairment may further result in moderate-to-severe restrictions in the performance of social roles related to work, schooling, leisure activities, family life and friendships which may further threaten the quality and maintenance of relationships. The sighted students were found to show positive self-view, social and emotional adjustment. The psychological well-being of both blind and sighted students was found to have significant effect on their academic achievement. Hence, on the basis of the findings it is assumed that positive self-esteem and better adjustment of sighted students may result in better academic achievement as compared to the blind students. Keeping these earlier findings in view, the following was hypothesized.

Hypothesis I

- There will be significant difference between blind and sighted students (integrated and non-integrated) in respect of self-esteem, adjustment and academic achievement.

On the basis of research evidences, blind students in integrated educational settings were found to possess higher self-esteem and better adjustment than the blind students in non-integrated schools (McGuiness, 1970; Orkan-Lecka, 1980; Van, Vincent, Kazdin & Hersen, 1987; Jangira, 1987; Sharma, 1988; Armstrong, Rosenbaum & King, 1992; Martinez & Sewell, 1996; Dimigen et al., 1999; Murg & Wallander, 2002). This appears to be in conjunction with the arguments that integration of blind students into mainstream schools ensures greater gains in self-esteem, adjustment and degree of independence. The students in such school settings demonstrate strong feelings of independence, socialization and confidence. Keeping these earlier findings in view, the following was hypothesized.

Hypothesis II

- Integrated and non-integrated school settings will have significant effect on self-esteem, adjustment and academic achievement of blind students.

The process of integrating blind students into mainstream schools was found to facilitate greater social interaction, peer and teacher support, better facilities of learning, etc. This in turn played significant role in ensuring psycho-social well-being of blind students in terms of self-esteem and adjustment (Haider,

1991; Dimigen et al., 1999). Lower levels of aggression and more positive view of self were evident among the blind students in integrated schools as compared to those in segregated settings who more likely demonstrated emotional difficulties such as loneliness and depression. The sighted students in both integrated and non-integrated schools showed positive self-esteem adjustment and good academic performance. Keeping these earlier findings in view, the following was hypothesized.

Hypothesis III

- The difference between blind and sighted students in self-esteem, adjustment and academic achievement will be less in integrated schools than blind and sighted students in non-integrated schools.

Academic achievement is an interactive function of many psycho-social variables wherein a number of psychological and environmental variables facilitate students' educational performance. School climate and social support (parents, peers and teachers) were found to play a dominant role in positively affecting the performance of students (Bachman & O'Malley, 1986; Hoge et al., 1990; Kuperminc et al., 1997; Roeser et al., 1998). Similarly, self-esteem and adjustment could play an important role in achievement because good adjustment was found to foster confidence, better concentration, less stress etc. (Roger, 1978; Reitzes & Mutran, 1980; Dubois, Bull, Sherman & Roberts, 1998). It may, therefore, be assumed that self-esteem and adjustment may relate to the academic achievement of both blind and sighted students. Keeping these earlier findings in view, the following was hypothesized.

Hypothesis IV

- Disability condition (blindness and sighted), school settings, self-esteem and adjustment will be significant predictors of academic achievement.

Variables

Self-esteem, adjustment (social, emotional and academic adjustment) and academic achievement were assessed in the study using the tools that have been mentioned in a separate section.

Operational definitions

Self-esteem

Coopersmith (1967) defined it as—"By self-esteem we refer to the evaluation which the individual makes and customarily maintains with regard to himself, it expresses an attitude of approval and disapproval, and indicates the extent to which individual believes himself to be capable, significant, successful and worthy. In short, self-esteem is a personal judgement of worthiness that is expressed in the attitudes the individual holds towards himself".

In this study, self-esteem was measured using the Coopersmith Self-esteem Inventory—Adult Form (translated and adapted), 1975.

Adjustment

In general, adjustment is defined as a process involving both mental and behavioural responses by which an individual strives to cope up successfully with inner needs, tensions, frustrations and conflicts and to affect a degree of harmony between those inner demands and those imposed on his or her objective world.

In the present study, the term 'adjustment' was used collectively to refer to both the pupil adjusting to the social, emotional and school context and peer group as well as the attempt of others (teachers) within the school to adjust to what they see and expect of the pupil. Therefore, adjustment was seen as a satisfactory relationship between the individual and his environment in respect of three areas — social, emotional and academic. It was measured by using the Adjustment Inventory for School Students by A. K. P. Sinha and R. P. Singh (1971).

Academic Achievement

Academic achievement refers to knowledge attained or skills developed through school curriculum and is usually measured and represented in terms of student's examination scores and teachers' assessment.

For the present study, academic achievement has been assessed through marks obtained by the students in their last examination, students' rating of their own performance and teachers' rating of students based on their classroom performance.

5

Method

Participants

Four groups of students were selected for the study—blind students in integrated schools, blind students in non-integrated schools, sighted students in integrated schools and sighted students in non-integrated schools. Each group comprised of 40 male students within the age group of 14-17 years and from grades IX-XII. Ten students were selected from each of the age and grade levels (two sections each) for each group as shown in the Table 5.1

Table 5.1: Sample size of the Students

Categories of Students	*Integrated School Setting*				*Non-Integrated School Setting*			
	Grades				*Grades*			
	IX	X	XI	XII	IX	X	XI	XII
Blind	10	10	10	10	10	10	10	10
Sighted	10	10	10	10	10	10	10	10

Care was taken in selecting the blind students from both integrated and non-integrated schools. Only totally and congenitally blind adolescents were selected. Those having any additional impairment were not included in the sample.

As an initial step towards selecting blind students from the integrated schools a list of institutions integrating students with disabilities, especially blind students was obtained. After a close scrutiny of the list, only those schools consisting of the required number of male students with the required age and grade levels were short-listed. Since it was difficult to select the total number of blind students within the specified age and grade levels for the integrated setting from any one school as they were less in numbers, therefore, the required number of students were selected from three schools and from two sections of each grade.

The schools from which the blind students were selected for the integrated setting were—Government Co-education Senior Secondary School, R. K. Puram, Sector V, New Delhi; Upras School, Vasant Marg, Vasant Vihar, New Delhi and Tagore International School, Paschimi Marg, Vasant Vihar, New Delhi.

Government Co-education Senior Secondary School is located in R. K. Puram, Sector V, New Delhi. It is a co-educational school from grades 1 to 12 accommodating approximately 2,500 students mainly from the middle and upper middle class. It is one of the Government institutions that integrate students with disabilities. Upras School located at Vasant Marg, Vasant Vihar, New Delhi is a co-educational school from grades 1 to 12. It accommodates more than 2,700 students and a well-trained staff of around 40. Tagore International School is also a co-educational institution. The institution excels in academic standards as well as in co-curricular activities. The school lays great emphasis on quality and standards of achievement. Located at Paschimi Marg, Vasant Vihar, New Delhi, with a well-trained staff of around 50 and a student body of 2,700, it engages in various educational as well as non-educational endeavours for the attainment of these goals.

Equal number of sighted students for the integrated group was also selected from each of the similar schools, grade levels and sections.

In selecting students from integrated settings care was also taken to ensure that they were selected from co-educational institutions so as to maintain uniformity in the selection pattern for all the students and reduce the effect of gender differences as far as possible that might have resulted in the process of selecting them from a combination of co-education and single sex schools.

The blind students in non-integrated setting were selected from a single residential institution—Blind Relief Association, Lodhi Road from the same age and grade levels. The Blind Relief Association at Lodhi Road is a residential institution for the visually impaired. Apart from imparting academic knowledge the institution aims at the all-round development of the personality of its students whereby special emphasis is also laid on vocational education and a unit is also maintained for the purpose in the institution. The institution also has the facility of a talk book library.

The sighted students for the regular school setting were selected from St. Mount Mary's School for the same age and grade levels. St. Mount Mary's School located at the Defence Colony is a boys' school. It accommodates students from middle socio-economic background and from diverse places in the country. It lays great emphasis on discipline and order besides academic excellence.

Detailed information about the socio-economic background of all students in terms of parents' education, parents' occupation, number of siblings were collected to find out if there would be any difference in socio-economic status of students belonging to different schools and find out if they can be used to interpret findings. In keeping view of this, the students were primarily selected from middle and upper middle (income range of Rs.5,000-8,000) socio-economic background so as to maintain uniformity and reduce the effect of class difference as far as possible.

Teachers were selected from each of the respective schools for the blind students in both school settings in order to obtain their rating of the students' performance based on classroom participation and achievement. Care was taken to confine the teachers to only the class teachers.

Tools used in the Study

1. An information schedule was prepared by the researcher in order to collect information about the background of students from different schools to determine if there will be any difference in their socio-economic status.

2. Coopersmith Self-esteem Inventory—Adult Form (translated and adapted).

3. Adjustment Inventory for the School students by. A. K. P. Sinha and R. P. Singh.

4. Aggregate marks obtained by the students in the last examination were converted into percentage and were used to assess their academic achievement. Besides this a self-rating report of students' performance and teachers' ratings of student's performance with reference to other students in the class were also used. The rating scales were developed by the researcher.

5. Classroom observations and interviews were employed in order to observe the attitude and interaction of blind and sighted students and teachers in integrated schools and among blind students and teachers in the non-integrated schools. An in-depth study of the ecology of classrooms was done at the larger institutional level in the context of the schools and also in terms of interpersonal relations prevalent in these classrooms.

A description of the specific tools used in the study is as follows:

Background Information

An information schedule was developed in order to obtain background information about the students. It included items to obtain varied information about each individual student such as name, age, type of residence, type of family (extended or nuclear), type of school attended, details about the parents' education and occupation, information about the siblings, etc. (See Appendix A). Effort was made to include the items in such a manner so as to obtain comprehensive information about the students. Moreover, in order to explore if family background had any impact on the self-esteem, adjustment and academic achievement of students (both blind and sighted) detailed information was collected about the families besides the type of schooling.

Coopersmith Self-esteem Inventory—Adult Form (1975)

The Coopersmith Self-esteem Inventory—Adult Form was adapted from the School Short Form for use with persons over fifteen years of age. It is usually self-administered. For the purpose of the present study, the scale was translated into Hindi for the convenience in administering it as majority of the students under study had Hindi as their mother tongue. The translation facilitated greater understanding of the items by the students as well as their response. In translating the scale care was taken to ensure that it did not affect or change the meaning of the items as far as possible. However, for certain items more colloquial and simple language was used in order to help the subjects related to them. At the end the Hindi version was back translated into English to determine the meaning of the items (See Appendix B1A).

The scoring procedure was similar to the English version. The scale was scored based on the general rules listed below:

Score negative items correct (e.g.) if they have been answered as "Unlike Me".
Score positive items correct (e.g.) if they have been answered as "Like Me".

Items scored correct when answered "Unlike Me"
2, 3, 6, 7, 10, 12, 13, 15, 16, 17, 18, 21, 22, 23, 24, 25

Items scored correct when answered "Like Me"
1, 4, 5. 8, 9, 11, 14, 19, 20

To arrive at a total Self-score the total raw score had to be multiplied by 4. This resulted in a maximum possible Total score of 100.

An interview schedule was developed based on the items included in the Coopersmith scale in order to obtain in-depth and more comprehensive information from the students (See Appendix B1B). Most of the questions were based on daily life situations and incidences.

Adjustment Inventory for School Students—A. K. P. Sinha and R. P. Singh (1971)

For assessing the adjustment of students, the Adjustment Inventory by A. K. P. Sinha and R. P. Singh was used. The adjustment inventory has been designed for use with the Hindi knowing school students of India. The inventory seeks to segregate well-adjusted secondary school students aged 14-18 years from poorly adjusted students in 3 areas of adjustment—Emotional, Social and Educational (See Appendix C1A).

Initially, the inventory had 100 items which was later reduced to 60 items. It was administered to a randomly selected representative sample of 1950 pupils from grades IX to XI in 40 schools. It is a self-administered inventory. The examiner should read the instructions given on the front page. There is no time limit answering them. Meaning of difficult words if any should be given by the examiner.

In the area of emotional adjustment high scores indicate unstable emotion. Students with low scores tend to be emotionally stable. In social adjustment individuals scoring high are submissive and retiring. Low scores indicate aggressive behaviour. In educational adjustment individuals scoring high are poorly adjusted with their curricular and co-curricular programmes. Persons with low scores are interested in school programmes.

The scale has a test retest reliability of 0.94 on emotional adjustment area, 0.93 on social adjustment and 0.96 on educational adjustment area.

The inventory can be scored by hand or by scoring stencil (See Appendix C1B). For the present study it was scored using the hand. For any answer indicative of adjustment zero is given, otherwise a score of one is awarded. Total score indicates total adjustment score.

Academic Achievement

The academic achievement of students was measured by using the percentage of marks obtained by them in their last school examination—Student rating scale and Teacher rating scale.

Marks obtained by students

The aggregate marks obtained by all the students in the last examination was obtained and converted into percentage to assess their academic achievement (See Appendices D1).

Student rating scale

To measure the academic achievement of students, a rating scale was developed to obtain students' self-rating of their own performance—academic, non-academic, social and emotional adjustment. All the items in the scale had to be rated on a five point scale—

1	2	3	4	5
Very Good	*Good*	*Average*	*Poor*	*Very Poor*

The items regarding the academic dimension were prepared with the view to obtain information from the students about their own individual performance as well as in comparison to other students in the class. Each student was asked to rate their performance on various dimensions such as regularity in the class, participation in classroom discussions, concentration on work, do independent work, etc.

Regarding social and emotional adjustment emphasis was laid on skills such as the student's ability to interact with the teachers and other students, behaviour in the classroom, self-confidence, etc.

Effort was made to keep the items in each of the dimension less in numbers and in as simple and direct language as far as possible. The scale was prepared in a tabular form for ease of administration and response. The items were accompanied by columns labelled 1 to 5 whereby the students were asked to put a tick mark in any of the boxes for the respective items in keeping with their performance. The rating scale was administered individually to the students.

An interview schedule was also developed in order to obtain detailed response of the students based on the feedback provided by them on the rating scale (See Appendices D2A & D2B).

Teacher rating scale

To measure the academic achievement of the students, a rating scale was developed to obtain teachers' ratings of each individual students—academic, non-academic, social and emotional adjustment. The items were prepared keeping in view the need to obtain as objective responses as possible. All the items have to be rated on a five point scale—

1	2	3	4	5
Very Good	Good	Average	Poor	Very Poor

The items regarding the academic dimension were prepared with the view to obtain information about the academic performance of the student both at the individual as well as the group level. The teachers were asked to rate each student keeping his individuality in view as well as was later ask to rate his performance in relation to other students in the classroom. Various dimensions were emphasized on such as regularity in the class, participation in classroom discussions, concentration on work, do independent work, etc.

Regarding social and emotional adjustment emphasis was laid on skills such as level of interaction with the teachers and other students, self-expression, time management, behaviour in the classroom, self-confidence, emotional responses appropriate for his age, etc.

Effort was made to keep the items in each of the dimension-less in numbers and in as simple and direct language as far as possible. The scale was prepared in a tabular form for ease of administration and response. The items were accompanied by columns labelled 1 to 5 whereby the teachers were asked to put a tick mark in any of the boxes for the respective items keeping the student in viewpoint. The teacher had to rate the student from amongst the forced choice rating categories. The rating scale was administered on an individual basis to only the respective class teacher of the student concerned.

An interview schedule was developed in order to obtain detailed response of the teachers based on the feedback provided by them on the rating scale (See Appendices D3A & D3B). The items included a number of follow-up questions to enquire into the teacher's perception of the students, their performance, attitude towards inclusion of the students with disabilities in the regular classroom, the problems faced by them, etc.

School Observation Checklist

Certain parameters were set by the researcher in order to prepare a checklist for the purpose of determining if the schools selected facilitated adequate integration of students with disabilities. The study of the ecology of the schools and classrooms was done at two levels—Institutional Level and Interpersonal Relations in the Classrooms (See Appendix E).

The following parameters were assessed at the institutional level—

School Climate/Organization.
Instructional Strategies and Adaptations.

School Climate has been further sub-divided into (a) Outdoor Orientation and Mobility, and (b) Indoor Orientation and Mobility such as physical and social organization of space that is inclusion in school functions, sports, seating arrangements for the purpose of detailed and comprehensive observation and recording.

Instructional Strategies and Adaptations was used to monitor the various methods/strategies undertaken to offer instructions to the students such as lecture method, demonstration, use of audio visual aids. Adaptations undertaken in teaching procedures if any were also taken into consideration.

The following parameters used for assessing were teacher and peer relations. Detailed observation and recording was made of—

- sighted students' attitude towards blind students and interaction among them.
- teachers' perception of integration of blind students and interaction with them in the classrooms.
- provisions made by the teachers for the inclusion of the blind students in the classroom.

In selecting the parameters a thorough and detailed review of the various Acts of Disability which specified certain standards of staff, equipment and facilities to be provided for the integration and education of the students with disabilities was made. The two Acts that were primarily consulted in this regard were the Scheme of Integrated Education for the Disabled Children, 1992 and Persons with Disabilities (Equal Opportunities, Protection of Rights and Full Participation) Act, 1995. After listing the provisions recommended by the Acts, a comprehensive list of facilities required was made by the researcher in discussion with various school teachers and administrators and members of institutions concerned about the care and rehabilitation of visually impaired individuals. It is however essential to note that according to certain officials not much has been specified in print with regard to facilities to be incorporated in terms of infrastructural facilities for the integration of students with disabilities in the regular schools. According to them such efforts are still in the process.

Pilot Study

The pilot study was conducted on twenty per cent of the actual sample size. Eight blind and sighted students were selected from a single integrated and non-integrated school. Each of the scales was administered to the students individually in order to determine the clarity and usefulness of the tools. On the basis of the responses obtained necessary modifications were incorporated in the scales.

Procedure

Data collection for the measures reported in study involved the target population comprising of blind and sighted adolescent students and class teachers. After fixing an appointment with the respective schools regarding time and place of conducting the final study, the researcher approached one school at a time. The first school approached regarding the integrated setting was the Government Co-education Senior Secondary School, R. K. Puram. Ten blind students were selected from each of the four grades (two sections each). Equivalent number of sighted students was also selected from the same grades and sections.

At the initial stage precautionary measures were taken to conceal the main purpose of researcher's visit to school. For this, the researcher was introduced to students and teachers in one of the sections of grade IX as an observer. The first four days were spent in observing the general classroom activities as well as establishing congenial rapport with the teacher and students. Detailed account of the activities was noted down. After this, interactive sessions were conducted with the blind students. One student was selected at a time for the purpose. At the beginning a brief introductory session was held during which information was obtained about the student's background. Once the rapport was established with the student, the researcher administered questionnaires. One questionnaire was taken up at a time and was read out since it was not typed in Braille. Efforts were made to use simple and clear language. Use of unambiguous terms was avoided as far as possible. No time limit was specified. On the basis of response obtained further questions were asked on each item in the questionnaire to get detailed information. All the responses were noted down as well as recorded by the researcher. Similar procedure was followed while administering the other questionnaires. After all the students from both two sections of grade IX had been interviewed, the similar procedure was used with students of grades X, XI and XII (two sections each).

In case of sighted students also the similar two sections of grade IX were selected. Initially, one questionnaire was distributed among all the students. Specific instructions were provided on them regarding the procedures to be observed while responding to them. Similar procedure was used in administering the other questionnaire. After both the questionnaires were administered, only those students who fulfilled the criteria of required age group and responded to all items were short-listed. From the short-listed candidates, ten students were randomly selected. In-depth interview was then conducted with each of the ten students on an individual basis.

Apart from interviewing students, the researcher also interacted and interviewed the respective class teachers. The teacher rating scale was administered to each teacher for each individual student. The teacher was asked to mark his/her response on the questionnaire itself. On the basis of response obtained, interview was conducted to obtain detailed information about the student. During this process, the researcher also attempted to gather information about the teachers' attitude towards integration of children with special needs in their classrooms.

In addition to interacting with students and teachers at the Government Senior Secondary School, the researcher also prepared a detailed report regarding school infrastructure, teaching aids and appliances, teaching procedures, activities undertaken, nature and level of interaction. This was conducted in reference to the school checklist prepared with the researcher in consultation with concerned authorities. The information was collected based on observation and thorough interaction with the principal, teachers and other staff members of the school.

Similar procedure of students' and teachers' interview as well as observation of school ecology was followed at Upras School, Vasant Marg, Vasant Vihar, New Delhi and Tagore International School, Paschimi Marg, Vasant Vihar, New Delhi.

After the integrated schools, the researcher approached the Blind Relief Association. Similar procedure was followed in selecting students, administering the questionnaires and conducting interview with both students and teachers. However, no detailed observation of school ecology was made as in case of the integrated schools.

The study was carried out in the same procedure with the sighted students from St. Mount Mary's School (non-integrated setting) as in case of sighted students from the integrated schools.

Data Analyses

After the tools had been administered, the data collected was analyzed both quantitatively and qualitatively. For quantitative analysis, the data based on students' responses were coded for statistical application. The response of both blind and sighted students in integrated and non-integrated schools were scored and analyzed for each of the measures in the study. Mean and SD values were computed for each of the four groups of students. Correlational analyses were done the degree of association among self-esteem, adjustment (emotional, social and educational) and academic achievement (also includes students' self-rating of their performance and teachers' rating of students performance) for each group. Analysis of Variance (both 2×2 and 2×2×4) was done to find out the main and interaction effects of each of the variables. Stepwise multiple regression analyses were done to identify different contributing factors of academic achievement.

The data for qualitative analysis was obtained on the basis of the questionnaires administered to both blind and sighted students and the teachers. Detailed semi-structured interviews were also conducted for both the students and teachers based on each of the questionnaires. The recorded interviews were transcribed and the data being descriptive in nature was subjected to content analysis. For case studies, four students were selected from each group. For right to privacy their names were coded. Case studies were then used to make the analysis. Analysis was then done on a comparative basis between three groups of students in order to determine the various factors affecting their self-esteem, adjustment and academic achievement. Ecological analysis of integrated school settings was also conducted.

6

Results

The findings of the study have been organized under the following sections:

Section A: Quantitative analysis of data.

Section B: Qualitative analysis of data. This section has been further sub-divided into—

(I) Comparative analysis of data was done for the following groups:

(a) Blind and sighted students in integrated schools,
(b) Blind and sighted students in non-integrated schools,
(c) Blind students in integrated schools and blind students in non-integrated schools.

(II) Ecological analysis of integrated school settings,

Section C: Overall discussion.

Section A: Quantitative Analysis of Data

The response of both blind and sighted students in integrated and non-integrated schools were scored and analyzed for each of the measures in the study. Mean and SD values were computed for each of the four groups of students and are given in Table 6.1.

Table : 6.1 : Mean and Standard Deviation of blind and sighted students

Students	*Grades*	*Mean*	*S.E*	*ADJUSTMENT*				*AA*	*SSR*	*TR*
	(N)	*(SD)*		*EMO*	*SOC*	*EDU*	*Total*			
Blind	IX	M	66.00	5.00	5.70	6.30	17.00	52.00	27.90	59.10
Integrated	(10)	(SD)	(6.90)	(3.07)	(3.65)	(2.98)	(6.60)	(12.01)	(6.59)	(10.90)
	X	M	66.80	5.80	4.10	5.70	15.60	50.80	27.10	58.70
	(10)	(SD)	(10.51)	(2.70)	(1.91)	(2.16)	(5.99)	(8.34)	(5.51)	(9.83)
	XI	M	70.40	3.70	4.30	6.10	14.10	52.20	31.40	62.30
	(10)	(SD)	(10.36)	(1.77)	(2.36)	(3.00)	(4.75)	(11.94)	(4.95)	(7.44)
	XII	M	66.00	4.40	7.10	5.60	17.10	52.30	32.20	63.00
	(10)	(SD)	(14.51)	(3.47)	(2.42)	(2.68)	(5.88)	(10.04)	(7.18)	(9.78)
Total	(40)	M	67.30	4.73	5.30	5.93	15.95	51.83	29.65	60.78
		(SD)	(10.37)	(3.07)	(2.84)	(2.63)	(10.64)	(10.29)	(6.28)	(9.39)
Blind	IX	M	60.20	2.90	5.60	5.30	13.80	54.40	27.80	55.90
Non-	(10)	(SD)	(17.60)	(1.73)	(3.50)	(1.77)	(5.35)	(9.50)	(4.89)	(12.78)
Integrated	X	M	64.40	4.10	6.10	6.10	16.30	52.50	28.20	55.10
	(10)	(SD)	(11.54)	(2.92)	(2.08)	(2.56)	(5.63)	(10.42)	(4.64)	(8.50)
	XI	M	60.00	4.40	6.20	5.50	16.10	50.50	28.20	61.50
	(10)	(SD)	(15.35)	(2.22)	(2.57)	(2.37)	(4.72)	(9.88)	(3.05)	(9.16)
	XII	M	59.20	3.50	4.60	5.30	13.40	49.40	29.90	67.90
	(10)	(SD)	(20.64)	(1.72)	(1.71)	(3.59)	(5.23)	(12.92)	(4.75)	(13.90)
Total	(40)	M	62.45	4.73	5.63	5.55	14.90	51.70	28.53	60.10
		(SD)	(16.22)	(2.20)	(2.54)	(2.57)	(5.21)	(10.52)	(4.30)	(12.05)
Sighted	IX	M	73.60	2.40	5.80	4.90	13.10	55.40	26.70	53.80
Integrated	(10)	(SD)	(10.86)	(0.97)	(1.75)	(2.19)	(3.51)	(12.09)	(5.03)	(12.73)
	X	M	66.00	3.70	5.60	7.00	16.30	46.70	27.00	53.90
	(10)	(SD)	(22.88)	(2.45)	(1.43)	(1.70)	(2.83)	(9.32)	(2.91)	(6.14)
	XI	M	74.40	2.60	5.10	5.50	14.10	53.70	27.80	57.60
	(10)	(SD)	(12.25)	(1.35)	(3.14)	(1.43)	(4.33)	(10.71)	(2.97)	(9.09)
	XII	M	60.80	3.20	6.90	7.90	18.00	45.50	31.60	68.90
	(10)	(SD)	(18.46)	(2.57)	(3.00)	(2.38)	(5.87)	(5.68)	(4.90)	(13.31)
Total	(40)	M	69.70	2.98	5.85	6.33	15.38	50.33	28.28	58.55
		(SD)	(17.14)	(1.93)	(2.44)	(2.19)	(4.55)	(10.32)	(4.40)	(12.05)
Sighted	IX	M	71.60	2.00	5.20	5.60	12.80	71.80	25.40	55.20
Non-	(10)	(SD)	(13.39)	(1.49)	(1.99)	(3.84)	(5.79)	(14.31)	(6.26)	(11.11)
Integrated	X	M	56.00	6.70	6.40	8.70	21.80	58.50	25.70	55.50
	(10)	(SD)	(13.60)	(3.34)	(1.78)	(3.30)	(6.89)	(14.52)	(2.54)	(5.44)
	XI	M	72.40	1.60	5.80	5.20	12.60	58.50	26.60	58.90
	(10)	(SD)	(14.66)	(2.41)	(1.40)	(3.08)	(4.38)	(11.24)	(4.45)	(7.31)
	XII	M	69.60	2.50	6.00	7.40	16.90	52.00	33.30	67.30
	(10)	(SD)	(16.89)	(1.35)	(2.49)	(2.84)	(6.23)	(9.69)	(6.20)	(11.34)
Total	(40)	M	67.40	3.20	5.85	6.73	16.03	60.20	27.75	59.23
		(SD)	(15.65)	(3.02)	(1.93)	(3.46)	(6.82)	(14.14)	(5.89)	(10.09)

The mean *self-esteem scores* for all the blind and sighted students were 129.75 (SD=26.59) and 137.10 (SD=32.79), respectively. On the basis of type of school setting (integrated and non-integrated), the mean value for all the students were found to be 137.00 (SD=28.51) and 129.85 (SD=31.87), respectively. Grade-wise the mean value for sighted students in integrated schools was found to be higher than blind students for all the corresponding grades except grade XII. For students in non-integrated schools, the mean values were higher for sighted as compared to the blind students in all grades except grade X.

The mean *total adjustment score* for all the blind and sighted students were 30.85 (SD=15.85) and 31.41 (SD=32.79), respectively. In integrated and non-integrated schools, the mean score for all the students were found to be 31.33 (SD=15.19) and 30.93 (SD=12.03), respectively. Grade-wise, the mean scores were found to be higher for sighted students than blind students in integrated schools in grades X and XII. In case of students in non-integrated schools, the mean scores were higher for blind students than the sighted in all the grades except grade X.

For the *emotional adjustment* measure, the mean score for all the blind students 9.46 (SD=5.27) was found to be higher than their sighted counterparts 6.18 (SD=4.95). In respect of integrated and non-integrated schools, the mean score for all the students were found to be 7.71 (SD=5.00) and 7.93 (SD=5.22), respectively. The mean value of blind students in integrated schools was found to be higher than their sighted counterparts for all the corresponding grades. In non-integrated schools, the mean value of blind students was found to be higher than sighted students except in grades IX and X.

The mean value for all the sighted students 11.70 (SD=4.37) was found to be higher than that of blind students 10.93 (SD=5.38) on the *social adjustment* measure. The mean value for all the students in integrated schools and non-integrated schools was found to be 11.15 (SD=5.28) and 11.48 (SD=4.47) respectively. Grade-wise the mean values for sighted students in integrated schools were found to be higher than blind students in all grades except in XII. In non-integrated schools, the mean values for blind students were higher in all grades except in grades IX and X.

For *educational adjustment* measure, the mean value of all sighted students 13.06 (SD=5.65) was found to be higher than blind students 11.48 (SD=5.20). The mean values for students in integrated and non-integrated schools were 12.26 (SD=4.82) and 12.28 (SD=6.03), respectively. The grade-wise mean values were higher for sighted students in integrated schools as compared to their blind counterparts except in grades IX and XII. In non-integrated schools, the mean values were higher for sighted students in all grades as compared to the blind students.

The score on *academic achievement* measure shows that the mean value for all the sighted students 110.53 (SD=24.46) was higher than blind students 103.53 (SD=20.81). In respect of school type, the mean value for all students in non-integrated schools 111.90 (SD=24.66) was found to be higher than those in integrated schools 102.16 (SD=20.61). Grade-wise, the mean values for the sighted students in integrated schools were found to be higher compared to blind students except in grades X and XII. In non-integrated schools, the mean values were higher for the sighted students in all grades.

Students' self-rating of their performance shows a higher mean value for all the blind students 58.18 (SD=10.58) as compared to their sighted counterparts 56.03 (SD=10.29). The students in integrated schools showed a higher mean value 57.93 (SD=10.68) as compared to students in non-integrated schools 56.28 (SD=10.19). Students' self-rating in different grades show a higher mean value for blind students in integrated schools than their sighted counterparts for all the grades. The blind students in non-integrated schools also showed a higher mean value in all grades except in grade XII.

The mean value for *teachers' rating of students performance* was found to be higher for blind students 130.88 (SD=21.44) as compared to sighted students 117.78 (SD=22.14). In integrated and non-integrated schools, the mean value of the students was 119.33 (SD=21.44) and 119.33 (SD=22.14), respectively. Teachers' rating shows a higher mean value for academic performance of blind students in integrated schools than their sighted counterparts in all grades except grade XII. The blind students in non-integrated schools showed a higher mean value in teacher rating score than sighted students except in grade XI.

Intercorrelations between the variables were calculated for each group. The correlation matrices are given in Tables 6.2 to 6.5. Intercorrelation between self-esteem, adjustment (emotional, social and educational) and academic achievement (also includes students' self-rating of their performance and teachers' rating of students performance) for blind students in integrated schools is indicated in Table 6.2.

Table 6.2 : Inter-correlation Matrix for Blind Students in Integrated Schools (N=40)

	SE	*EDU*	*EMO*	*SOC*	*AA*	*SSR*	*TR*
Self-esteem	1.00						
Educational Adjustment	-.26	1.00					
Emotional Adjustment	-.14	.15	1.00				
Social Adjustment	-.18	.28	.11	1.00			
Academic Achievement	.02	-.09	.09	.14	1.00		
Students' self-rating	.50	.01	-.14	.06	.13	1.00	
Teacher rating	-.17	.10	.16	.02	.16	.80(*)	1.00

* p< .01.

A significant correlation was found between students' self-rating of their own performance and teachers' rating of students' performance (r= .80, p< .01). No other correlation was found to be significant.

The intercorrelations between the variables for blind students in non-integrated schools are shown in Table 6.3.

Table 6.3 : Inter-correlation Matrix for Blind Students in Non-Integrated Schools (N=40)

	SE	*EDU*	*EMO*	*SOC*	*AA*	*SSR*	*TR*
Self-esteem	1.00						
Educational Adjustment	-.01	1.00					
Emotional Adjustment	-.11	.40(*)	1.00				
Social Adjustment	-.15	.30	.07	1.00			
Academic Achievement	.63(**)	.15	-.21	-.05	1.00		
Students' self-rating	.21	-.12	-.03	.18	.25	1.00	
Teacher rating	-.19	-.29	-.13	.06	-.27	.56(**)	1.00

* p< .05.
** p< .01.

Significant and positive correlation was found between self-esteem and students' performance in examination (r= .63, p< .01) and students' self-rating of their own performance and teachers' rating of students' performance (r=.56, p< .01). A positive correlation was also found between emotional adjustment and educational adjustment (r= .40, p< .05).

Table 6.4 indicates intercorrelations between the variables for sighted students in integrated schools.

Table 6.4 : Inter-correlation Matrix for Sighted Students in Integrated Schools (N=40)

	SE	*EDU*	*EMO*	*SOC*	*AA*	*SSR*	*TR*
Self-esteem	1.00						
Educational Adjustment	-.04	1.00					
Emotional Adjustment	-.29	.17	1.00				
Social Adjustment	-.36(*)	.07	.35(*)	1.00			
Academic Achievement	.44(**)	-.13	-.10	-.13	1.00		
Students' self-rating	-.20	.25	.06	.01	-.20	1.00	
Teacher rating	-.26	.21	-.01	-.02	-.32(*)	.93(**)	1.00

* p< .05.
** p< .01.

A highly significant and positive correlation was found between students' rating of their own performance and teachers' rating of students' performance (r= .93, p< .01). The intercorrelations also indicate a positive correlation between social adjustment and emotional adjustment (r= .35, p< .05) and self-esteem and academic achievement (r= .44, p< .05). A negative correlation was found between self-esteem and social adjustment (r= -.36, p< .05) and teacher rating and students' performance in examination (r= -.32, p< .05).

Intercorrelations between the variables for sighted students in non-integrated schools are shown in Table 6.5.

A highly significant and positive correlation was also found between students' self-rating of their own performance and teachers' rating of students' performance (r= .95, p< .01). A positive correlation was found between emotional adjustment and educational adjustment (r= .56, p< .01). A negative

Table 6.5 : Inter-correlation Matrix for Sighted Students in Non-Integrated Schools (N=40)

	SE	*EDU*	*EMO*	*SOC*	*AA*	*SSR*	*TR*
Self-esteem	1.00						
Educational Adjustment	-.42(**)	1.00					
Emotional Adjustment	-.33(*)	.56(**)	1.00				
Social Adjustment	-.09	.17	.25	1.00			
Academic Achievement	.24	-.32(*)	-.14	-.02	1.00		
Students' self-rating	.07	.20	-.05	-.10	-.42(**)	1.00	
Teacher rating	.18	.12	-.11	-.20	-.40(*)	.95(**)	1.00

*p < .05.
**p < .01.

correlation was found between self-esteem and educational adjustment (r=-.42, p<.01), self-esteem and emotional adjustment (r=-.33, p<.01), educational adjustment and students' performance in examination (r= -.42, p< .01), students' self-rating and performance in examination (r=-.42, p< .01) and Teachers rating of students performance and students' performance in examination (r= -.40, p< .05).

The scores were analyzed in 2 (Groups) × 2 (School settings) ANOVA for each of the variables and ANOVA Summary are given in Tables 6.6 to 6.11. Table 6.6 gives a 2 (Groups) × 2 (School settings) ANOVA Summary for self-esteem scores.

Table 6.6 : ANOVA Summary for Self-esteem scores (N=160)

Source	*df*	*SS*	*MS*	*F*	*p*
Groups (Blind/Sighted)	1	403.23	403.23	1.76	0.19
School Settings(Int/Non-Int)	1	378.23	378.23	1.65	0.20
Groups × Settings	1	126.03	126.03	0.55	0.46
Error	156	35678.30	228.71		

It is seen from the results that neither the interaction effect (F<1) nor the main effects were found to be significant. The mean scores of all the blind students and sighted students were 129.75 and 137.10 respectively. For students in integrated schools, the mean score was found to be 137.00 and 129.85 for those in non-integrated schools.

A 2 (Groups) × 2 (School settings) ANOVA Summary for Emotional adjustment scores is given in Table 6.7.

Table 6.7 : ANOVA Summary for Emotional Adjustment scores (N=160)

Source	*df*	*SS*	*MS*	*F*	*p*
Groups (Blind/Sighted)	1	51.76	51.76	7.61	0.01**
School Settings(Int/Non-Int)	1	6.01	6.01	0.88	0.35
Groups X Settings	1	15.01	15.01	2.21	0.14
Error	156	1061.33	6.80		

**p < .01.

The main effect of Student group i.e. Blind and Sighted (F=7.61, df=1,156 p> .05) was found to be significant. The mean scores of all the blind students and sighted students were 9.46 and 6.18, respectively (F=7.61, p=.07). The mean score for students in integrated schools was 7.71 and 7.93 for those in non-integrated schools. However, the interaction effect (F<1) was not found to be significant.

Table 6.8 gives 2 (Groups) × 2 (School settings) ANOVA Summary for Social adjustment scores.

Table 6.8 : ANOVA Summary for Social Adjustment scores (N=160)

Source	*df*	*SS*	*MS*	*F*	*p*
Groups (Blind/Sighted)	1	6.01	6.01	0.99	0.32
School Settings(Int/Non-Int)	1	1.06	1.06	0.18	0.68
Groups X Settings	1	1.06	1.06	0.18	0.68
Error	156	943.98	6.05		

The mean scores of all the blind students and sighted students were 10.93 and 11.70 respectively. For students in integrated schools the mean score was found to be 11.15 and 11.48 for those in non-integrated schools. The results reveal that neither the interaction effect (F<1) nor the main effects were found to be significant.

Table 6.9 gives 2 (Groups) × 2 (School settings) ANOVA Summary for Educational adjustment scores. It shows that neither the interaction effect (F<1) nor the main effects were found to be significant.

Table 6.9 : ANOVA Summary for Educational Adjustment scores (N=160)

Source	*df*	*SS*	*MS*	*F*	*p*
Groups (Blind/Sighted)	1	24.81	24.81	3.27	0.07
School Settings(Int/Non-Int)	1	6.25	6.25	0.01	0.98
Groups X Settings	1	6.01	6.01	0.79	0.38
Error	156	1183.43	7.59		

The mean scores of all the blind students and sighted students were 11.48 and 13.06, respectively (F=3.27, p=.07). The mean score for students in integrated schools was 12.26 and 12.28 for those in non-integrated schools. None of the main effects was found to be significant. The Group and School setting interaction were also not significant.

A 2 (Groups) × 2 (School settings) ANOVA Summary for Total adjustment scores is given in Table 6.10.

Table 6.10 : ANOVA Summary for Total Adjustment scores (N=160)

Source	*df*	*SS*	*MS*	*F*	*p*
Groups (Blind/Sighted)	1	3.03	3.03	0.10	0.76
School Settings(Int/Non-Int)	1	1.60	1.60	0.05	0.82
Groups X Settings	1	28.90	28.90	0.91	0.34
Error	156	4967.85	31.85		

The results show that neither the interaction effect nor the main effects were found to be significant (F<1). The mean scores of all the blind students and sighted students were 30.85 and 31.41 respectively. For students in integrated schools, the mean score was found to be 31.33 and 30.93 for those in non-integrated schools.

The main effects of School settings (Integrated and Non-Integrated) was found to be significant (F= 7.27, df=1,156; p>.05) for Academic Achievement as shown in Table 6.11 which gives 2 (Groups) × 2 (School settings) ANOVA Summary for Academic Achievement scores. The interaction of Student Groups with Settings was also found to be significant (F= 7.65, df=1,156; p>.05). The mean score of all the blind students was 103.53 and 110.53 for the sighted (F=3.75, p=.06). This difference was found to be significant. The mean score for students in integrated schools was 102.16 and 111.90 for those in non-integrated schools.

Table 6.11 : ANOVA Summary for Academic Achievement scores (N=160)

Source	*df*	*SS*	*MS*	*F*	*p*
Groups (Blind/Sighted)	1	490.00	490.00	3.75	0.06
School Settings(Int/Non-Int)	1	950.63	950.63	7.27	0.01**
Groups X Settings	1	1000.0	1000.0	7.65	0.01**
Error	156	20401.35	130.78		

**p < .01.

Figure 6.1 shows the nature of interaction between school setting and student groups (blind and sighted) in respect of Academic Achievement scores. The graph shows a higher mean score for students in non-integrated schools 111.90 (SD=24.66) as compared to those in integrated schools 102.16 (SD=20.61).

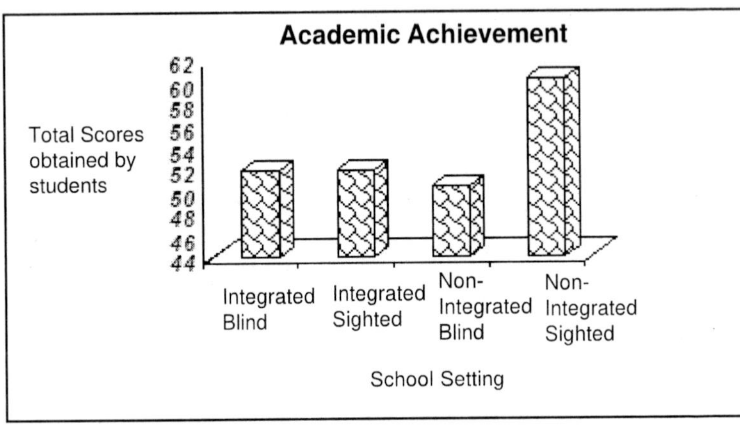

Fig 6.1: Academic Achievement of Blind and Sighted Students in Integrated and Non-Integrated school settings.

The results from 2×2 ANOVA shows that the main effects of Student Group (Blind and Sighted) was found to be significant for Emotional Adjustment and School settings (Integrated and Non-Integrated) for Academic Achievement. The interaction of Student Groups with Settings was also found to be significant for Academic Achievement. However, none of the main effects and interaction effects was significant for Self-esteem, Social, Educational and Total adjustment scores.

The scores were further analyzed in 2 (Groups) × 2 (School settings) × 4 (Grades) ANOVA for each of the variables. The ANOVA Summary tables are given in Tables 6.12 to 6.17.

Table 6.12 gives 2 (Groups) × 2 (School settings) × 4 (grades) ANOVA Summary for Self-esteem scores.

Table 6.12 : 2 (Groups) × 2 (School settings) × 4 (Grades) ANOVA Summary for Self-esteem

Source	*df*	*SS*	*MS*	*F*	*p*
Groups (Blind/Sighted)	1	567.47	567.47	2.245	0.12
School Settings (Int/Non-Int)	1	463.38	463.39	1.99	0.16
Grades	3	565.31	188.44	0.81	0.49
Groups × Settings	1	118.48	118.48	0.51	0.48
Groups × Grades	3	936.16	312.05	1.35	0.26
Settings × Grades	3	395.69	131.90	0.57	0.64
Groups × Settings × Grades	3	665.22	221.74	0.96	0.42
Error	144	3269.89	231.89		

None of the interaction effects or main effects was found to be significant. The mean scores of all the blind students and sighted students were 129.75 and 137.10 respectively. For students in integrated schools, the mean score was found to be 137.00 and 129.85 for those in non-integrated schools.

Self-esteem was also not found to be affected either by the school setting or the grade differences. The mean scores were 271.40 (SD=48.75), 253.20 (SD=58.53), 277.20 (SD=52.62) and 255.60 (SD=70.50) in Grades IX, X, XI and XII respectively.

Table 6.13 gives 2 (Groups) × 2 (School settings) × 4 (grades) ANOVA Summary for Emotional adjustment scores. The result indicates that none of the interaction effects were found to be significant.

Table 6.13 : 2 (Groups) × 2 (School settings) × 4 (Grades) ANOVA Summary for Emotional Adjustment

Source	*df*	*SS*	*MS*	*F*	*p*
Groups (Blind/Sighted)	1	56.56	56.56	9.72	0.02*
School Settings(Int/Non-Int)	1	7.63	7.63	1.31	0.25
Grades	3	105.64	35.21	6.05	0.01**
Groups × Settings	1	10.96	10.96	1.88	0.17
Groups × Grades	3	41.70	13.90	2.39	0.07
Settings × Grades	3	26.62	8.87	1.52	0.21
Groups × Settings × Grades	3	47.04	15.68	2.69	0.48
Error	144	838.42	5.82	5.82	

*p < .05.
**p < .01.

However, the main effect of Student group i.e. Blind and Sighted (F=9.72, df=1,144, p< .05) and Grade (F=6.05, df=3,144, p<.01) was found to be significant. The mean score of all the blind students was 9.46 and 6.18 for the sighted. The mean scores were 12.30 (SD=7.26), 20.30 (SD=11.41), 12.30 (SD=7.75) and 13.60 (SD=9.11) in Grades IX, X, XI and XII respectively.

A 2 (Groups) × 2 (School settings) × 4 (Grades) ANOVA Summary for Social adjustment scores shows that although the main effects were not found to be significant, the interaction of Settings with Grades (F=3.73, df= 3,144; p<.05) was found to be significant. The results are given in Table 6.14.

Table 6.14 : 2 (Groups) × 2 (School settings) × 4 (Grades) ANOVA Summary for Social Adjustment

Source	*df*	*SS*	*MS*	*F*	*p*
Groups (Blind/Sighted)	1	6.01	6.01	1.02	0.31
School Settings(Int/Non-Int)	1	1.06	1.06	0.18	0.67
Grades	3	14.22	4.74	0.81	0.49
Groups × Settings	1	1.06	1.06	0.18	0.67
Groups × Grades	3	6.32	2.11	0.36	0.78
Settings × Grades	3	65.57	21.86	3.73	0.01**
Groups × Settings × Grades	3	13.17	4.39	0.75	0.53
Error	144	844.70	5.87		

**p < .01.

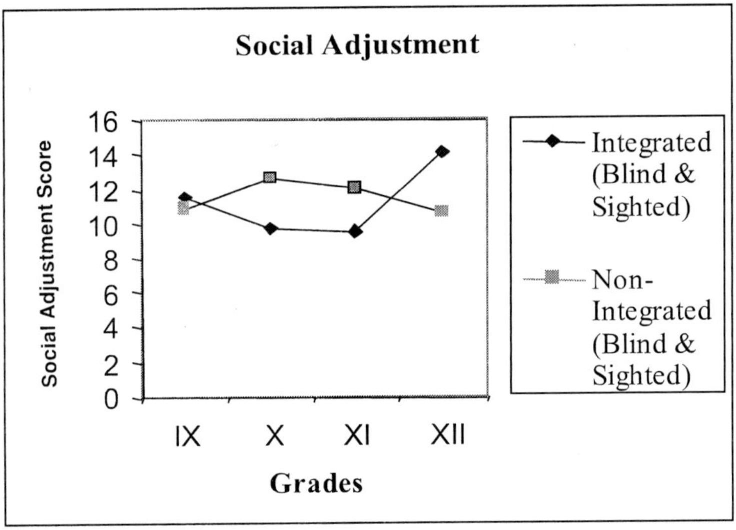

Fig 6.2 : Social adjustment of students in Integrated and Non-Integrated Schools across different grades.

Figure 6.2 shows the nature of interaction between school setting and grades in respect of Social Adjustment Scores. The graph shows a double crossover of the grade-wise scores for integrated and non-integrated schools. In grade IX, integrated school students showed a slightly higher mean 11.50 (SD=5.40) as compared to their non-integrated counterparts 10.80 (SD=5.49). The corresponding scores for the integrated school students were lower in grades X, 9.70 (SD=3.34) and XI, 9.40 (SD=5.50) compared to their counterparts 12.50 (SD=3.86) and 12.00 (SD=3.97), respectively. However in grade XII, the social adjustment score was higher for the integrated 14.00 (SD=5.42) than the non-integrated 10.60 (SD=4.20) school students.

Table 6.15 gives 2 (Groups) × 2 (School settings) × 4 (Grades) ANOVA Summary for educational adjustment scores. The result shows that the interaction effect between student and grades (F=3.08, df=3,144; p<.05) was significant. But the main effects and two-way interaction between Student, Settings and Grades were not found to be significant.

Table 6.15 : 2 (Groups) × 2 (School settings) × 4 (Grades) ANOVA Summary for Educational Adjustment

Source	*df*	*SS*	*MS*	*F*	*p*
Groups (Blind/Sighted)	1	24.81	24.81	3.43	0.07
School Settings(Int/Non-Int)	3	6.25	6.25	0.00	0.98
Grades	3	56.22	18.74	2.60	0.06
Groups × Settings	1	24.81	3.08	0.83	0.36
Groups × Grades	3	6.25	0.69	3.08	0.03*
Settings × Grades	3	56.22	0.27	0.69	0.56
Groups × Settings × Grades	3	5.77	1.92	0.27	0.85
Error	144	1039.90	7.22		

*p < .05.

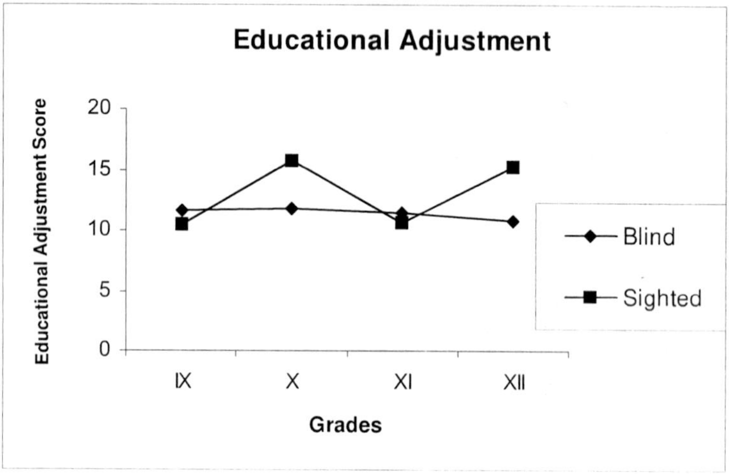

Fig. 6.3 : Educational adjustment of students in Blind and Sighted Students across different grades.

Figure 6.3 shows that the nature of interaction between Groups (blind and sighted) and Grades. The graph for blind students does not show much of a change in educational adjustment scores over the grades except a slight decline in higher grades i.e. grades XI and XII. The mean scores for the blind were 11.60 (SD=4.75), 11.80 (SD=4.72), 11.60 (SD=5.37) and 10.90 (SD=6.27) in Grades IX, X, XI and XII respectively.

A 2 (Groups) × 2 (School settings) × 4 (Grades) ANOVA summary for Total adjustment scores shows that both the interaction effects of Groups and Grades (F=2.70, df=3,144; p< .05) and the main effect of Grade (F=3.76, df=3,144, p<.01) were found to be significant. Grade was found to have a significant effect on total adjustment of students. The mean scores were 56.70 (SD=21.25), 70.00 (SD=21.34), 56.90 (SD=18.18) and 65.40 (SD=23.20) in grades IX, X, XI and XII respectively. The results are given in Table 6.16.

Table 6.16 : 2 (Groups) × 2 (School settings) × 4 (Grades) ANOVA Summary for Total Adjustment

Source	*df*	*SS*	*MS*	*F*	*p*
Groups (Blind/Sighted)	1	3.03	3.03	0.11	0.75
School Settings(Int/Non-Int)	1	1.60	1.60	0.06	0.81
Grades	3	323.53	107.84	3.76	0.01**
Groups × Setting	1	28.90	28.90	1.01	0.32
Groups × Grades	3	232.13	77.38	2.70	0.05*
Settings × Grades	3	183.35	61.12	2.13	0.10
Groups × Settings × Grades	3	97.25	32.42	1.13	0.34
Error	144	4131.60	28.69		

*p < .05.
**p < .01.

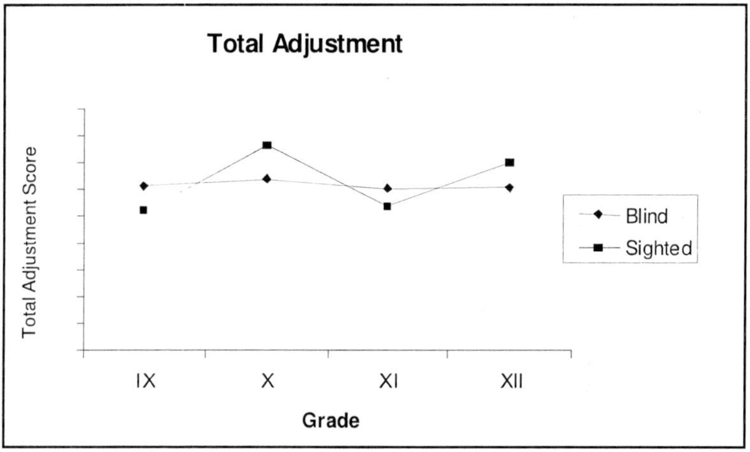

Fig. 6.4: Total Adjustment of students in Blind and Sighted Students across different grades.

Figure 6.4 shows that the nature of interaction between Groups (blind and sighted) and Grades. The graph for blind students does not show significant change in Total adjustment scores over the grades except a slight decline in higher grades i.e. grades XI and XII. The mean scores for the blind were 30.80 (SD=11.95), 31.90 (SD=11.62), 30.20 (SD=9.47) and 30.50 (SD=11.11) in Grades IX, X, XI and XII respectively.

Table 6.17 gives 2 (Groups) × 2 (School setting) × 4 (Grades) ANOVA Summary for Academic Achievement scores. None of the interaction effects were found to be significant. However the main effect of Student group i.e. Blind and Sighted (F=25.54, df=1,144, p< .01) and Grade (F=9.79, df=3,144, p< .01) was found to be significant.

Table 6.17 : 2 (Groups) × 2 (School settings) × 4 (Grades) ANOVA Summary for Academic Achievement

Source	*df*	*SS*	*MS*	*F*	*p*
Groups (Blind/Sighted)	1	3376.41	3376.41	25.54	0.00**
School Settings(Int/Non-Int)	1	18.91	18.91	0.14	0.71
Grades	3	3882.82	1294.27	9.79	0.00**
Groups × Settings	1	18.91	18.91	0.14	0.71
Groups × Grades	3	888.42	296.14	2.24	0.09
Settings × Grades	3	131.32	43.77	0.33	0.80
Groups × Settings × Grades	3	131.32	43.77	0.33	0.80
Error	144	19036.10	132.20		

**p < .01.

The mean values for all the sighted and blind students were 110.53 (SD=24.46) and 103.53 (SD=20.81), respectively. Thus the sighted students had significantly higher academic compared to the blind students. The mean academic achievement scores were 233.60 (SD=47.91), 208.50 (SD=42.60), 214.90 (SD=43.77) and 199.20 (SD=38.33) for grades IX, X, XI, and XII, respectively.

The results from 2×2×4 ANOVA show that the main effects of Student Group (Blind and Sighted) and Grades were found to be significant for Emotional Adjustment and Academic

Achievement, while Grades for Total Adjustment. The interaction of Settings (Integrated and Non-Integrated) and Grades were found to be significant for Social Adjustment while Groups and Grades for Educational Adjustment and Total Adjustment.

Multiple regression analyses were done to identify different contributing factors of academic achievement of students. Multiple Correlation Coefficients (R) were calculated with Self-esteem scores and Total Adjustment scores as the predictors and Academic Achievement criterion variable. Regression was calculated for each group of students (See Appendix FA, B, C & D). For the blind students in integrated schools, R=.089 (R^2 = .008, F= .147, df= 2, 37, p>.05). Thus, the multiple R was not significant. For blind students in non-integrated schools, R= 0.627 (R^2 =.393, F=11.998, df= 2, 37, p<.01). Thus, the multiple R was significant. Self-esteem was found to produce a significant influence on the academic achievement of the students. For the sighted students in integrated schools R=.444 (R^2 = .197, F=4.542, df= 2, 37, p<.05). Thus, the multiple R was significant. Self-esteem as a predictor variable was found to produce a significant influence on the academic achievement of the students. For the sighted students in non-integrated schools R= .301 (R^2 = 090, F= 1.840, df= 2, 37, p>.05). Thus, the multiple R was not significant.

The result of multiple regression shows that self-esteem was found to be one of the significant predictors of academic achievement for blind students in non-integrated schools and sighted students in integrated schools. The other variables were not found produce any statistically significant effect for the same groups. Thus from the results obtained, it can be maintained that several other uncontrollable factors may have had more dominant impact on the academic achievement of the students besides these variables. This will be supported by qualitative analysis of the responses obtained from students.

Overall quantitative analysis of data shows that the blind students, irrespective of the type of school setting did not differ significantly from their sighted counterparts in respect to self-esteem, adjustment and academic achievement. On account of this further attempt was made to undertake a vivid analysis of the qualitative data obtained by means of interviews based on the tools/scales administered.

Section B : Qualitative Analysis of Data

Data for qualitative analysis was obtained on the basis of the questionnaires administered to both blind and sighted students and the teachers. Detailed semi-structured interviews were also conducted for both the students and teachers based on each of the questionnaires. The recorded interviews were transcribed and the data being descriptive in nature was subjected to content analysis. Case studies based on the response of selected students from each group was also used to make the analysis. Analysis was then done on a comparative basis between three groups of students in order to determine the various factors affecting their self-esteem, adjustment and academic achievement. Ecological analysis of integrated school settings were also made on the basis of observations of school and classroom.

(I) Comparative analysis of data

The data based on students' response were subjected to comparative analysis among the following groups of students in order to determine the various factors affecting their self-esteem, adjustment and academic achievement:

(a) Blind and sighted students in integrated schools,
(b) Blind and sighted students in non-integrated schools,
(c) Blind students in integrated schools and blind students in non-integrated schools,

(a) Blind students and sighted students in integrated schools

Perception of the self

Physical Appearance

A sense of physical competence which assumes significance in the area of general mobility, maintaining body functions, enhancing early learning process of social interaction, building of self-esteem and achievement of life goals was emphasized upon by both blind and sighted students. Based on self-evaluation of physical competence, the blind students regarded themselves at par with their sighted counterparts. However at the same time, they laid emphasis on various problems resulting due to lack of sight. According to ten out of forty students, restricted mobility was one of the major problems experienced by them. They accepted that in spite of acquiring training in orientation and mobility it was still difficult for them to access unfamiliar environment. Such circumstances made them depend on others for assistance which in turn lowered their self-confidence and promoted feeling of helplessness.

At the same time, the students also emphasized that though it is the general notion that use of various interventions such as the assistance of animals or instrumental assistance would help to normalize their lives with increased mobility, assist in eliminating social barriers by enhancing how they are socially perceived and would facilitate conversations, but in reality it finds little implementation. According to them, though new and more advanced technological mobility aids are continuously being developed but association of labels and stigma with their usage have negative connotations. In support to this viewpoint, a student of grade ten mentioned that people generally associated the presence of a blind person with a long stick, guide cane or black glasses. According to him, such social and cultural representation of their impairment made them analyze their experiences in light of the existing meanings and practices prevalent in society thus affecting their self-view as well as social functioning.

In addition to these difficulties, the ten students also held that absence of sight made it difficult for them to pursue some of their daily living skills. In this regard two of the students mentioned that they faced a number of difficulties in adjusting to varied life demands during the initial days of their lives but later with increase in age, experience and training they got adjusted to them. In accordance to this, Student A.D. (Sl.No.15)[1] of grade ten while recalling some of the problems experienced by him stated:

> *"I had lost sight at birth. It had been extremely difficult for me to cope with the different life situations because of this. I couldn't play and stayed at home, while others played. I found it difficult to move around and access the environment. Moreover, lack of training in daily living skills made it difficult for me to perform any activity independently. Though my parents and brothers were cooperative, I felt bad at times, it made me feel so helpless".*

Besides the difficulties associated with movement, loss of sight was also found to make the students apprehensive of their future. While expressing some of the problems in their lives, six out of the ten students stated that they were at a crucial stage in life when certain important decisions had to be taken regarding their lives. According to them, though at present they could take care of themselves with assistance from their family members but they felt apprehensive of their future. Deciding on career options and leading a completely independent life, in particular caused anxiety and stress in them. This was evident from the students' response. For instance Student D.S. (Sl.No.6) of grade ten said:

> *"I want to live an independent life like others. I want to become a teacher, but I'm not sure how. I wish I*

1. The serial number of the respective student in the sample is indicated in parentheses.

could see then things would have more clearly, but today everything is so confusing. Every time I think of an option the next moment various thoughts come, I feel I can't then new thoughts come again".

Similarly Student A.G. (Sl.No.39) of grade twelve said:

"Other things are good in life, but if I was sighted I could become a cricketer. There is no career for the blind in sports".

Hence based on the responses of ten students mentioned above it was seen that effects of impairment of vision was found to extend from both perceptual and non-perceptual domains of development. The unexpressed feeling of loss of sight was frequently associated with helplessness, inferiority, mobility related stress and anxiety, depression, loss of self-efficacy and poor performance by these students. Since the desired outcome of life is preparation for independent living and to become a contributing member of the society, physical constraints in case of these students was found to be associated with developmental delays in motor skills. Restricted mobility was found to effect the development of identity by giving rise to feelings of helplessness and dependence. Besides this, constant presence of adults or other support services due to restricted mobility made these individuals more dependent and maintain negative or low self-esteem.

However, it is important to note that despite emphasizing various difficulties resulting due to their physical limitations, the blind students maintained a positive view regarding themselves. When asked if they wanted to incorporate certain changes in themselves, the remaining thirty students did not make much reference to physical changes. The students were satisfied by the way they appeared. It was observed that apart from their own self-view, others' opinions played a significant role in formation of their self-image. In view of this, Student S.V. (Sl.No.2) of grade nine said:

> *"I cannot see myself through my own eyes but I assume I am good looking. Some of my friends at school and of course my parents also say so. They find me as smart as others."*

The blind students did not perceive any difference in physical appearance as compared to their sighted counterparts. Hence, they showed no inclination towards incorporating changes. However on the contrary, they wanted certain changes in their personality such as develop more patience, reduce anger, be more approachable etc. According to them, such changes contributed immensely towards their self-development and also better social acceptance. Student S.D. (Sl.No.18) of grade ten said,

> *'I try to find out if I am wrong, then try to correct it. I need to be more patient towards others".*

Similarly laying emphasis on the need to bring changes in their behaviour, Student A.S. (Sl.No.31) of grade twelve said:

> *"I give up in performing an activity easily; I need to develop more persistence and concentration. In addition to this my reserved nature makes it difficult for people to approach me. I also want to talk to others, but feel awkward in doing so. I want to develop a more friendly nature".*

Hence it was seen from students' responses that although physical ability constitutes a basis for individuals to develop unique identities, blind students did not hold any low opinion of themselves. They did not attach much significance to their physical appearance, but rather wanted to incorporate changes in their behaviour for better acceptance by others. On the whole, they rated their lives positively and considered themselves to be at par with the sighted counterparts. They preferred to be addressed to as 'differently abled' rather than 'disabled'.

Unlike blind students, the sighted students made greater reference to their physical self. Since the students were at the adolescent stage their body image was found have an important influence on their self-esteem and adjustment mechanism. Twenty-six out of forty students did not regard themselves as good looking as others and desired to be 'someone else'. For instance, Student M.M. (Sl.No.13) of grade ten said:

> *'Like every person of my age I also want to look good. I have been fat and short since my childhood. My friends always made fun of me and called me 'shorty'. I wish I can reduce and also have a better height".*

Similarly, Student R.B. (Sl.No.28) of class eleven stated:

> *"I want to become a pilot. This requires not only a good personality but also healthy physique. I have always been lean and weak. I wish I can acquire these qualities soon".*

Two other students of grade nine and ten also expressed their desire for an increase in their height so that they could look good as others and also take up professions of their preference (both want to become police officers). Thus it is seen that physical ability played an important role in the formation and maintenance of self-evaluation and social image of sighted individuals.

Self-identity

Besides contributing towards formation of self and social image, physical competence also had significant influence on the development of various characteristics such as feeling of independence, adaptability, etc. Adaptability which includes the ability to satisfactorily adjust to new and diverse situations and activities emerged as noteworthy characteristic among both blind and sighted students. When asked about their adaptability to new things, situations and people, twenty-nine out of forty blind students regarded themselves to be at par with their sighted counterparts. According to them despite physical limitations, they were confident that with concentration and desire to learn more they can take up and perform well in various activities. The students acknowledged that the training in orientation and mobility provided by their institutions contributed towards instilling such confidence in them.

The blind students had similar opinion regarding their adaptability to people or life related situations. However in adjusting to people, their confidence was found to vary in situations especially where important decisions had to be made. This according to them was primarily due to fear making their dear ones feel embarrassed. Under such circumstances even if they undertook certain decisions on their own, they were always ready to incorporate changes in consultation with others.

The sighted students were also found to maintain positive self-identity. They regarded themselves to be confident and independent. However, ten out of forty students accepted that they required more time to get used to anything new. In spite of this, they believed that provided with more time and focussed effort some of the activities can be executed properly. The students preferred performing things on their own and taking responsibility for all decisions. They found their decisions to be correct on most occasions but regarding certain major issues in life such as career, relationships, etc. they found it suitable to consult their parents and siblings. They also required more time in dealing and adjusting with people.

Concern about life conditions

Both blind and sighted students expressed numerous concerns regarding their life and studies. Despite regarding themselves at par with the sighted, blind students mentioned of being apprehensive about their academic performance, independent mobility, ability to interact with others and their future. When asked if "Things usually don't bother", twenty-six blind students expressed their concern regarding their academic performance, free mobility, ability to interact with others and future. At the same time despite the apprehensions and difficulties, they showed good academic performance (as evident from their school marks). They did not believe in giving up on doing things and were determined to continuously proceed ahead despite difficulties.

The sighted students were found to be more relaxed in their approach towards life. They were confident of facing the numerous problems and preferred challenges and competition in life. Such an attitude made them less bothered about trivial matters. Despite referring to several problems such as apprehension regarding their future, performance at school, interaction with people, etc., they were confident that with persistence and dedication they will overcome them and attain higher goals in life.

Social Identity

Social acceptability and popularity was found to play a major part in the formation and maintenance of personality for both blind and sighted students. When asked "Most people are better liked than me", twenty-eight out of forty blind students held that they were equally liked by others as their sighted counterparts. According to them, their good behaviour made people prefer their company. They were popular among people of their same age group as well as those younger than them. In describing his social life, Student A.J. (Sl.No.4) of grade nine said:

> *"Even when I was absent for a single day only, everyone was asking about me to my class teacher. Everyone was so worried. They are really concerned about my welfare. This makes me feel good and well accepted".*

However, the remaining twelve students held that although they did not perceive of any difference between themselves and their sighted counterparts, they were often made to feel conscious of their physical inability by other people through various activities and behaviour manifestations. On being subjected to comparison with the sighted children they felt stigmatized and segregated. Emphasizing on the negative impact of comparison, sixteen-year old Student N.G. (Sl.No.25) stated:

> *"Sometimes I really feel bad when people around me, compare me with others. It hurts more when based on such comparisons I am not included in the group since they feel I can't be good like them".*

Besides subjection to comparisons, the sympathetic feelings that are often associated by people with their loss of vision also caused anxiety among the students. According to them, when such emotional manifestations related to their physical capabilities it accelerated feelings of helplessness in them. It also made them feel that their company was less preferred to that of others. Recalling his own experiences, Student B.J. (Sl.No.37) of grade twelve said:

> *"I don't know why people consider us 'different'. They either avoid our company or sympathise with us. I feel this more when I am travelling or am in an unknown place or am there in a social party. People come ahead trying to help me insistently because they feel I can't do so on my own. Even on social occasions people tend to avoid speaking to me in the normal manner, I think they feel uneasy in speaking to me using certain specific terms such as 'see', 'can you do' etc. These things make me feel 'different', which I don't like".*

Social support plays a dominant role in affecting the social image of an individual. In case of blind students it was found to have diverse effects. On the one hand, the students mentioned of better acceptance by 'others' in the mainstream society whereby their social popularity positively boosted their self-confidence. On the other hand, they laid stress on the detrimental impact of social comparisons that adversely affected their mental make-up. For them social acceptability based on capabilities were more significant rather than their acceptance into the social structure due to "sympathetic" attitudes.

In comparison to blind students, the sighted also showed more positive social identity. According to them, positive attitude towards life and friendly nature made people prefer their company. They preferred interacting with people of different age groups and were also popular. Their associates accepted their suggestions and advices. According to the students, popularity contributed towards enhancing their social image. However at the same time, it also gave rise to intense sense of competition among individuals of the same age group to attain greater popularity. This often resulted in severing good relations. It also pressurized them to make constant efforts for maintaining proper social behaviour to be accepted by all. All these cumulatively had severe implications on their psychological make-up wherein they felt insecure regarding their acceptance or rejection by others.

Perception of Family Relations: Parents, siblings and relatives

Home is the social institution where an individual acquires a sense of belongingness. It was found to play an important role in the establishment and maintenance of self-esteem and adjustment for both blind and sighted students. Both the groups positively responded to questions like 'My parents usually consider my feelings', 'My parents respect too much of me', 'My parents understand me'. According to them, parents considered their feelings, provided motivation to become independent and study properly. They also provided valuable guidance and assistance and gave due weightage to their viewpoints.

Of the forty blind students, thirty-eight of them mentioned

of receiving adequate attention from their parents and preferred staying at home. Responding to questions such as "I get easily upset at home" or "There are many times when I would like to leave home", the students expressed great desire to be at home forever and continue to do things that would make their parents proud. Responding regarding his parents, Student H.A. (Sl.No. 37) of grade twelve said:

> *"My parents are the best in the world. They understand and love me. They are the best people I know. They never consider me different, but rather encourage me to go ahead in life. I would never think about leaving them, I want to do good things for them".*

Even when the students were asked if they felt that their parents were pushing them to do things, they mentioned of being provided sufficient space to decide and do things independently. Though in certain instances parents pressurized them but the students accepted that it was for their benefit only. Student N.T. (Sl.No.17), a fifteen-year old student stated:

> *"I know at time my parents tell me to study hard and participate. This makes me surely feel pressurized but then I also know that my parents love me a lot; they are always worried about my welfare. So they push me hard in various activities so that I can move forward".*

In addition to their parents, the blind students regarded their siblings as constant source of support and motivation. They engaged in diverse activities such as study, play games, help academically, etc. Their siblings did not differentiate them from "others". Elaborating the relation with his siblings, Student M.T. (Sl.No.33) of grade twelve said:

> *"My brother and sister are extremely good. Though I am the youngest in the family they treat me like their*

friend. They never differentiate me. They have always been of great support to me especially at times when I felt depressed. They encouraged me to do things on my own and move ahead in life. Besides helping me in my studies and daily work they also take me out to places and encourage me to interact with people. We really share a great relationship and hope it would always remain".

Apart from the parents and siblings, "significant others" (relatives) also affected the lives of blind students. However, regarding the 'others', the students laid more emphasis on the negative impact. According to the students, though their parents did not subject them to any differentiation or comparison their relatives often made unnecessary comparisons. This caused depression and lowered their self-confidence.

Thus home or family for the blind students was supportive and permissive which had positive impact on their psychological make-up. According to them, life at home was a pleasurable experience and they preferred staying there. They mentioned of having great fun with their parents and siblings like going out, talking, playing, etc. However, the students maintained negative opinion regarding the "significant others", specifically their relatives.

Of the forty sighted students who were interviewed, thirty-two of them held that they preferred their homes and mentioned of receiving good treatment. They regarded their parents to be understanding and cooperative. They respected their individuality and encouraged them to engage in independent work. In this regard seventeen year old Student H.R. (Sl.No.31) said:

"My parents are the 'best' parents in the world, who not only love me and respect my feelings. We share great moments discussing personal issues, this helps me a lot. Sometimes, I really feel relaxed having shared my thoughts and feelings with them. Although the

shower affection on me they also encourage me to engage in independent work and experimentation so that I can grow up as a responsible person. I love my parents and being at home, I can never think of staying away from them".

However, the remaining eight students provided varied response regarding the influence of home or family. Four of the students mentioned feeling deprived of adequate attention and time since they had working parents. Expressing his sadness, Student U.S. (Sl.No.29) said:

"I know my parents are concerned about me and my welfare but they never have adequate time. They are always busy with their own work. There are times I want to discuss things with them, but fail to do so. Then I feel very depressed. I wish my parents can give more time to me so that things can be better".

Similarly, fifteen-year old, Student R.M. (Sl.No.21) stated:

"I don't like being at home, there's no one to interact with. My parents are always out for work, I feel bored and low. That's why I prefer being at school, at least I have a few friends to discuss my problems with".

In addition to inadequate parental attention and support, high parental expectations emerged as another factor affecting students desire to avoid the home environment. According to them, the inability to attain the expected standards caused great anxiety and helplessness. In reference to the various difficulties faced by him, Student J.K. (Sl. No.20) of grade ten said:

"Since my childhood I always had to shoulder great responsibilities. My parents have very high dreams for me, but I find it so difficult to keep up with them. They expect me to maintain an extremely good academic as well as social profile, which I cannot; I want to live a

regular life. They want me to take up Science but I don't like it, I prefer Commerce, it's interesting. I also like going out to certain places with them. I get tired, but they fail to understand it. All these make me angry as well as depressed".

Hence for the sighted students, the home or family was found to have a mixed impact. While the permissiveness of parents instilled confidence in them to face the challenges in life; inadequate parental attention and support and high parental expectations made them feel neglected and negatively affected their opinion regarding the importance of home. This had significant impact on their self-view and adjustment mechanisms. Alienation and lack of effective communication (especially in case of those having working parents) were found to be some of the other factors affecting the adjustment of sighted individuals.

Perception of School

Besides family, school was also found to play an important role in affecting the development and maintenance of self-esteem and adjustment of both blind and sighted students. Both groups maintained positive approach towards school and its related activities. The blind students, in particular regarded the school as a 'miniature home' and maintained positive approach towards their integration into regular schools. According to them, placement in heterogeneous setting enabled them to develop new skills of communication, social dealings, adjustment and concern for others. They accepted that despite certain initial adjustment problems, they soon got accustomed to the varying demands of the school environment. Referring to this, Student S.R. (Sl.No.30) of grade twelve said:

"Initially on entering school I did have some minor problems in adjusting. My classmates were not very forthcoming to me, they avoided my company. I felt

neglected. However, soon they became sensitive to my 'different' needs. Today I enjoy the ambience at school and find all my peers, teachers and other school authorities highly cooperative. Since then they have never made me feel different from others."

The blind students mentioned of being regular at school. They did not find the curriculum to be a load and took active interest and participated in both curricular and co-curricular activities. However, they were moderately satisfied with their present level of academic performance, especially in grades 10 and 12. Commenting on the nature of their performance, the students felt that though they regularly attended classes, paid attention to the lessons taught, participated in classroom discussions, their performance was not in accordance to their own expectations. With regard to this, they emphasized the need for more focussed attention and efforts.

Referring to some of the constraints limiting their performance, the blind students mentioned that though no less capable than their sighted counterparts, their lack of vision was a major constraint in pursuing certain activities such as drawing, mathematics particularly geometry, science practical, computers and geography. The difficulty was more evident in case of geography where they had to deal with abstract concepts such as 'types of clouds', 'leeward and windward side', course of river, etc. They also faced similar problems in learning mathematics and history. Though they appreciated the assistance offered by teachers and peers in clarifying their doubts with the use of aids, yet they failed to understand these concepts which their sighted counterparts acquired through 'observation'. It was due to this limitation that they were excluded from science practical and had to depend on theoretical explanations only.

Referring to their difficulties in other subjects they mentioned that although special computer programmes are being developed for them yet they fail to access certain important programmes designed especially for the "sighted".

In addition to these, the students also mentioned of other associated problems such as unavailability of adequate text. Regarding this they held that though efforts were made by their residential institution (National Association for the Blind) to equip them with the necessary materials the schools failed to adequately address this issue. Moreover, they also faced problems in learning certain topics due to limited use of models. The instructions being primarily theoretical in nature made them dependent on class lectures and their sighted classmates to note or read them out for them. This inevitably affected their clarity of concepts and level of performance. To reduce this difficulty they depended on special teachers to clarify their doubts in the special classes held at the Institute (NAB) after the school hours. They held that these factors cumulatively limited their performance.

The blind students also laid stress on their hesitation in communication and need for more time to complete given tasks. According to them, limitations in their range and variety of experiences made them hesitate from communicating confidently with others. Moreover, it also affected their participation in outside classroom activities especially in sports, etc. However, the students were found to actively participate and excel in activities like debates, chess, elocution, etc.

Relations with Teachers and Peers

Within the school environment, the blind students shared close rapport with both their teachers and peers. Elaborating on these relationships, the students appreciated the efforts made by their teachers in providing adequate attention and guidance to them despite their busy schedules and large class size. On most occasions, the teachers encouraged them to engage in independent work. The peers were also of great assistance to them. They helped them in taking down class notes, accessing the school campus, discussing academic and personal difficulties etc. According to the students, some of their friends even took time after class hours to explain concepts to them if they had any problems.

Like their blind counterparts, the sighted students also actively participated in both curricular and co-curricular activities at school. They regarded the school as a platform that enabled them to acquire new knowledge and experiences as well as give expressions to their manifold talents. They appreciated the assistance and cooperation received from their friends and teachers. Their teachers were cooperative and understanding, paid adequate attention to their difficulties and always encouraged them to actively participate in various activities. According to the students, the teachers contributed immensely towards their academic as well as personal welfare. In this regard, seventeen-year old, Student S.R. (Sl.No.26) said:

> *"I have always been shy by nature. I generally preferred being on my own and kept to myself and my studies. This made people stay away from me and it also affected my performance very badly. Soon my teachers encouraged me to interact with others. At times they even forced me to participate in classroom discussions and give up additional assignments. These brought about remarkable changes in me. Today I owe whatever I am to my parents and my teachers".*

Thus, social competence was found to be a powerful predictor among several factors affecting academic achievement of students. Peer acceptance enabled the students to display prosocial and responsible forms of behaviour at school and also affected their achievement. In case of both blind and sighted students, peer support was primarily in the form of students providing mutual assistance by clarifying and interpreting their teacher's instructions, sharing various resources such as notes and books, etc.

Academic Achievement

However on self-assessment, the students were not adequately satisfied with their own academic progress especially in grades

10 and 12. According to them, increasing curricular pressure, parental expectations, lack of adequate guidance limited their ability to perform as per their expectation. They also laid great emphasis on the negative effects of high parental expectations and lack of required guidance. Referring to parental pressures, they held that though parents pressurized them to engage in certain activities for their own welfare, it also prevented them from performing according to their own capacities. Under such circumstances, they often failed to produce the expected results that caused emotional turmoil and lowered their self-confidence etc. The students also laid stress on lack of adequate attention and academic guidance from their parents. This was mostly evident in cases where both the parents were employed. Moreover, the students held that though they wanted to participate in co-curricular activities such as debates, elocution, science contests, etc., academic pressures restricted their participation.

(b) Blind students and sighted students in non-integrated schools

Perception of the self

Physical Appearance

Adolescence marks a period of transition which encompasses within it not only cognitive, physical, personality and social changes but a phase wherein individuals strive to seek for identity formation and value clarification. Among the various factors, physical ability was found to be a crucial requisite for facilitating conceptualization of information and of paramount importance in the area of general mobility, enhancing the whole early learning process of social interaction, maintenance of self-esteem and adjustment and achievement of life goals. Both blind and sighted students laid emphasis on their physical self. However for the blind students, physical self was found to be closely related to their sense of independence. The students were found to be confident and regarded themselves as capable as their sighted counterparts. They also expressed the desire to undertake independent responsibilities despite their physical limitations. According to them, in spite of requiring more time than others to get used to anything new, they could perform well if clear instructions were provided. However, while emphasizing on the need for adequately performing social skills, the students made reference to their physical limitations and the associated difficulties.

According to the students, though the training in orientation and mobility and vocational skills provided at school prepared them to learn new things and move about more freely and independently but it was more confined to known environment. Whenever they had to travel to new places, absence of sight imposed severe constrictions in their exploration and interaction with the environment. This resulted in delays in movement, motor skills and physical competence, concept formation, learning of social conventions and also made them dependent on others. The students further mentioned that since limitations in mobility necessitated the constant presence of adults or other support services, it in turn made them become more dependent and develop feelings of helplessness.

Besides causing delay in mobility, lack of sight also made the students apprehensive about their future. In this regard, fourteen-year old Student F.G. (Sl.No.7) stated:

> *"I have had no sight since my birth. Things were so difficult for me then, I took time to learn things. My parents have always been by my side. However, when I think my parents will go away I'm not sure what will I do, how will I do work, whether I'll be happy or not. I don't know my future".*

Similarly, Student M.B. (Sl.No.18) of grade ten said:

> *"I do not know what my future is; I wish I could see*

then I would have become a doctor. Today even though I try my level best to do well in work but I fail to do adequately, if I could see then I would have done far better. Things would have been better. My parents are also worried about me. This further increases my tensions".

Hence according to the students, their physical limitation exposed them to various difficulties ranging from imposing restrictions to their accessibility, developing feeling of helplessness to becoming apprehensive of their future. All these cumulatively affected their psychological make-up.

Besides significance of sight, the blind students also emphasized that behaviour plays significant role in determining the identity of an individual. In view of this, they expressed their deep desire to incorporate certain changes in behaviour for better acceptance by others. They laid great emphasis on behaviour characteristics such as politeness in speech, helpfulness, friendly nature, attentiveness, patience, etc.

The sighted students as compared to their blind counterparts maintained a more positive attitude towards life. They regarded themselves to be confident and independent. They expressed their desire to undertake all sorts of challenges in life and did not like relying on others. Rather, they preferred engaging in independent work and experimenting on things. At the same time, they accepted that regarding certain academic and career issues they took more time and preferred consulting others, especially their parents. They also showed great confidence in getting adjusted to new situations and acquiring competence in performing new activities.

It is important to note that despite showing better confidence as compared to their blind counterparts, the sighted laid more importance on their physical appearance. Sixteen year old, Student R.D. (Sl.No.22) said:

"I am not as good looking as others. My height makes me feel so small next to my other classmates. I want my height to increase and even my face. Then more people will pay attention to me".

Being at the adolescence stage when others perception played significant role in formation of self-view and social image, the sighted students laid more importance on their physical competence. They were found to make conscious attempts towards adjusting to the varied biological changes. Inability to make these adjustments made the students show symptoms of depression and behaviour problems such as withdrawn, impulsive, etc.

Social Identity

Besides accepting and feeling comfortable with their body image, adolescents also engage in evaluating themselves along with several other dimensions such as, academics, athletics, appearance, social relations and moral conduct. In view of this, appropriate assistance and support from family or parents, peers and teachers were found to play a dominant role in the formation of self-view and adjustment. Social network (family, peer group) was found to make an important impact on self-esteem, adjustment and academic achievement of both groups of students. The blind students showed good social adjustment. Thirty out of forty students had access to a wider social circle and were popular among them. However, nature of their social group was limited only to the homogeneous setting. According to them such a placement enabled them to relate well with the problems of other children having similar needs, facilitated better interaction and also strengthened their bondage. They also preferred interacting with people mostly of their own age group due to ease in relating. They were found to engage in wide variety of activities such as playing, talking, going to places, etc. When enquired if others enjoyed their company, they specified that despite being considered "different" by others their company was preferred. According to them, ability to interact with people, humorous nature and good behaviour greatly contributed towards their popularity. Student Z.A. (Sl.No.16) of grade ten at the Blind Relief Association mentioned in this regard:

> *"I am cheerful, friendly, humorous and outgoing in nature. My ability to adjust with different people and environment makes me more acceptable by others, my parents, friends and teachers. There is nothing wrong in me and so people like me. My friends like me since I speak and behave well, it's important".*

The sighted students also maintained positive social identity of themselves. They preferred interacting with large social groups comprising of people from various age groups. According to them, exposure to a greater number of people helped them in acquiring new social skills as well as learn to deal with relationships. Popularity for them played a major role since it determined their social importance. However, while emphasizing on the need for greater social acceptance, they also mentioned of certain problems faced by them in their social life. The students accepted that though popularity was important it was also acted as a constraint in their social adaptability. According to them, though every individual aspires to create a place of their own and be accepted by all, this can also result in emotional turmoil if overemphasized on. Sometimes, they felt highly pressurized to conform to group norms in order to feel accepted by others. Failure on their part to conform to the expected standards subjected them to fear of rejection and lowered their self-confidence. On certain other occasions such incidences were traumatizing because they faced rejection despite being good as others. According to the students, such circumstances also cumulatively contributed towards breeding unhealthy competition among friends, caused stress, etc.

Perception of Family Relations: Parents, siblings and relatives

Besides the peers and the wider social circle, the family was found to have an effective impact on self-esteem and adjustment of both blind and sighted students. Both the groups of students considered their family members to be cooperative and understanding. The students were found to share positive relationship with their parents. According to them, their parents paid adequate attention and support which made their stay at home pleasurable. However, the responses of blind students were found to be more positive as compared to their sighted counterparts. The blind students emphasized that their parents understood them well and treated them just like any other children of their age group. They shared great moments going out to places, discussing problems, etc. Sharing the experiences of his family life, sixteen-year old, Student N.J. (Sl.No.23) stated:

> *"My parents are the best parents in the world. They are so understanding. I discuss all my problems with them and so do they involve me in all the decisions and activities of the family. They have never for a moment considered me to be 'incapable' or 'different'. They have always been by my side through good and bad times. They are always concerned about my welfare. I love being with my family".*

Elaborating on the nature of relationship with their family members, the blind students emphasized that their parents always paid attention to their numerous problems—both personal and otherwise. They always respected their feelings and gave due weightage to their viewpoints and actions. Besides being provided with attention and affection the students also mentioned of being subjected to positive criticism by their parents. According to them, they realized that this was obvious since like parents of sighted children, their parents also had high expectations from them. They accepted that on certain occasions parental pressures and positive criticism motivated them for better performance. None of the students mentioned of feeling pressurized but instead felt encouraged to work hard and attain higher goals.

Besides parents, the students mentioned of sharing close, 'intimate' and positive relationship with their siblings. For most of them their siblings were a "play partner". Twenty eight of the forty students mentioned that during vacations they preferred being at home, playing and studying with their siblings. According to them their siblings helped them in doing their homework, explained certain subjects, went out for picnics and even at times had friendly fights. They were never made to feel "different" from others by their siblings in any manner. Student T.D. (Sl.No.13) of grade ten held:

> *"Never have I been made to feel that I'm different by my parents and sister. Though they can see but I can't, they always encouraged me to move ahead in life. They help me in my studies, but at the same time stress that I try on my own. They even defend me when others compare or tease me. Like all other families we brothers also have fights but soon make over. It's lovely being with them. I never feel the lack of friends".*

However, the remaining twelve students maintained negative attitude regarding their siblings. According to them, they felt neglected when their siblings avoided their company and failed to acknowledge their importance in public. Student M.P. (Sl.No.33) of grade eleven stated:

> *"I feel bad when my brother is there at home, I don't want to be with him. He doesn't care for me. Even when his friends make fun of me, he doesn't say anything. He also avoids interacting with me, he leaves me home alone".*

Thus for the blind students avoidance and neglect from their siblings affected their psychological make-up. In addition to this, the students also maintained negative opinion about their relatives. They specified that their relatives subjected them to comparison with their cousins or other people of their age regarding their competency and performance in academic as well as other activities. This hurt their sentiments as they did not consider themselves to be different from others in any manner. Such circumstances made the students prefer school to home.

Adolescence is generally referred to as a period of "stress and storm" and demands careful and affectionate understanding and treatment, parental care and support for fostering healthy adjustment. This was widely evident in case of the blind students in non-integrated school settings. Both students and parents were found to maintain 'close' and 'intimate' relationship. The subjects were found to be well adjusted on the dimensions of family relationship, emotional stability and adjustment to reality. Positive interaction with family members, substantial ability to maintain and restructure relationships emerging from such attitudes and acceptance of blindness were found to have significant positive influence on the psychosocial development of the blind adolescents. However at the same time, strained relationships with siblings and negative attitude of relatives made the students prefer the school environment more to home.

Like blind students, the sighted also referred to their parents as being understanding and cooperative in nature. According to them, their parents motivated them to take initiative towards facing the diverse challenges of life. Both the students and parents shared cordial relationships. According to the students, they spend a lot of time going out to places, playing and discussing various issues. They were comfortable in discussing both personal as well as other academic related topics. Elaborating on the significance of parents, five out of forty students mentioned that in spite of their parents working they were provided adequate time and attention. This was essential because the realization of being a valued part of the social network not only helps to foster self-esteem and self-assurance but also feelings of security and control over oneself and the environment while failure in attaining acceptance resulted in stress, anxiety and a feeling of helplessness.

It is essential to note besides emphasizing on the positive impact of parental treatment, ten students also highlighted some of the associated problems. According to them, though they did not experience any negligence, but high parental expectations often made them feel pressurized. On certain occasions they were subjected to too much of strict discipline which in turn adversely affected their ability to form positive approach towards their own self as well as undertake responsibilities. Failure to conform to parental standards and live up to their expectations further lowered their self-confidence.

The sighted students were also found to maintain a mixed attitude towards their siblings. While thirty-six out of forty students regarded their siblings as cooperative, the remaining four referred to them as "opponents". Those maintaining positive relationship held that they often played, studied, and spent considerable time with their siblings. Though the students who referred to their siblings as "opponents" did not have any personal problems with their siblings but at the same time specified that they felt 'hurt', 'rejected', 'embarrassed', etc. on occasions when they were compared with their siblings by others. This adversely affected the relationship between them.

Perception of School

Though both groups of students maintained positive approach towards school and its related activities, it was more evident in case of the blind. The blind students expressed great admiration for their school with special reference to the type of school setting. According to them, the homogeneous setting made it easier for them to relate well with others having similar problems and need. The students assisted each other in games, studies, etc. and also spend a great deal of time discussing problems with each other. They were regular to school and actively participated in various activities. Moreover, they also stressed that such a setting also prevented them from facing the stress of undue competition with the sighted students in integrated schools.

The sighted students also regarded the school as a miniature society which enabled them to interact with a large number of people. They were regular to school and its various activities.

Relations with Teachers and Peers

Referring to other school related issues, the blind students laid emphasis on the role of teachers. They regarded their teachers to be supportive. According to them, their teachers took good personal care and never made them feel inferior or different in anyway. Despite their heavy workload the teachers provided them with individualized attention and devised new teaching techniques to cater to their diverse needs. They even spent adequate time after the school hours to help clarify doubts.

The sighted were also found to share cordial relations with both their teachers and peers. They found their teachers to be cooperative and understanding. They offered assistance to the students both academically as well as personally. This played a very important role according to the students. According to them, there were certain important issues in their lives that they couldn't discuss with their parents but they needed urgent attention.

Therefore among the numerous social factors, supportive school environment along with students' perception of goals, academic efficacy, use of effective learning strategies and homogeneous ability grouping had wide implications on the adjustment and academic performance of blind students. Perception of a sense of belongingness or connectedness with one's school was found to be positively related to their academic, psychological and behavioural outcomes. The peer group affiliation played a significant role in the lives of the students. At an age when most of the students were undergoing similar personal and professional situations, they found it easy to relate to each other. This facilitated both personal growth as well as increased social interaction.

Academic Achievement

It is important to note that based on self-assessment, despite being satisfied with their placement in homogeneous setting, the blind students were moderately satisfied with their own academic performance especially in grades 10, 11 and 12. According to them, their performance was not at par with the expected standards due to several factors ranging from studies being too theoretical in nature, shortage of adequate material facilities such as Braille books and equipments, "too vast syllabus", lack of concentration, adequate guidance, etc. In relation to these problems, Student P.K. (Sl.No.29) of grade eleven stated:

> *"There is the urgent need for the educational authorities to reconsider the content of the curriculum and reduce the unnecessary issues from them. It needs to be made more focussed and practical or career oriented. It is so difficult to concentrate on the vast and 'too theoretical' syllabi. In addition to this there is also lack of adequate text and teaching aids. This is seriously affecting our performance. We can't afford to show bad performance, this phase is crucial for our future".*

Therefore, despite receiving attention from school authorities, the blind students were unable to keep up with the pace of work and academic challenges. The vast syllabi, "too theoretical" curriculum, shortage of adequate material facilities such as Braille books and equipments, lack of adequate guidance along with the pressures of preparing for the board examinations that played a crucial role in determining their future made the students feel insecure about their ability to perform better. In view of this, the students held that there is the urgency for the concerned authorities to focus attention and address all these issues since they had negative affect on their achievement.

On the other hand, the sighted students particularly in grades 10 and 12 were not satisfied with their present level of achievement. According to them, sudden increase in syllabi along with the pressures of preparing for board examinations made them feel insecure since their future career plans were dependent on their performance. In addition to this, theoretical nature of work, old methods of teaching adopted by the teachers coupled with vast syllabi and high parental expectations and pressure, etc. were all found to cumulatively lower their performance. They were dissatisfied with some of the teaching strategies adopted by their teachers which were "uninteresting", "too boring", etc. On the contrary, they mentioned that the teachers should adopt strategies that would be interesting with adequate scope for practical application, more simplified and creative. Besides the teaching methods, the students also held that greater number of students in the classroom and heavy workload prevented teachers from providing adequate attention to them. Five of the forty students also laid considerable emphasis on parental pressures for having negative impact on their performance.

Thus academic achievement was found to be associated with social functioning at both individual level and social level. The associations at the individual level were found to evolve from intrapersonal processes such as individual social-cognitive competence or specific family socialization experiences. Associations at the group level also indicated the significance of the group and affected the performance of students.

(c) Blind students in integrated and non-integrated schools

Perception of the self

Physical Appearance

Physical competence which forms an integral part of an individual's personality contributes immensely towards the development and maintenance of a separate identity. However, on the other hand, restrictions in movement may reduce the opportunities for interaction as well as stimulation for cognitive growth and personal development. In view of this, formation of positive self-view largely depends on the extent to which one perceives his or her physical competence. Irrespective of type of school setting, the blind students made reference to their physical self. Students in both settings were aware of their physical limitations. According to them, lack of sight culminated into certain associated problems such as restricted mobility, apprehension about their future, limited social interaction, low classroom participation, etc. While enquiring into the numerous problems that they experienced in their life, the influence that additional physical effort has upon the alteration of feelings emerged as one of the dominant difficulties. According to the students, though they experienced limitations in opportunities to control and manipulate their environment, their self-confidence wavered more on occasions when they had to abandon their own methods of manipulating the visual environment conveniently and substitute it by socially approved procedure of the sighted. They further mentioned that although training in orientation and mobility and vocational skills that was provided in schools prepared them to learn new things and move about independently, they experienced problems in unfamiliar environments. Under such circumstances, they had to depend on others which lowered their confidence.

On the other hand, despite emphasizing on physical limitations, the blind students irrespective of school setting maintained positive view regarding their physical appearance. When asked if they wanted to incorporate certain changes in themselves, the students did not make much reference to physical changes. They were satisfied by the way they appeared. This was primarily because the students regarded themselves to be similar to their counterparts in physical appearance and hence did not feel the need to incorporate changes. However, on the other hand they wanted certain changes in personality such as develop more patience, reduce their anger, be more approachable, etc. It is important to note that apart from their own self-view, the students also laid emphasis on significance of others' opinions in formation of their self-image.

Self-identity

Physical self, for both groups of blind students was found to be closely related to their sense of independence, adaptability, etc. Regarding their adaptability to new situations and activities, the blind students were found to be confident and expressed the desire to learn more and perform well in various activities. They accepted that though due to their visual limitation they required "more" time for certain activities but if specific and clear explanations and instructions can be provided then it facilitates better functioning.

Restricted mobility was also found to affect the development of identity of blind students because it is through different interplay situations with others that an individual develops a self-image/identity. In this relation social support, self-esteem and emotional support from family and friends, perceived discrimination and disability conditions were found to play important roles in students' adjustment to their disability condition. When asked "Most people are better liked than me", twenty-eight out of forty students from integrated and thirty from non-integrated schools held that they were equally liked by others. According to them, people preferred them because of their good nature and not their physical capabilities.

Social Identity

However, a major difference was observed among the students regarding the nature of their membership to social groups. While the students in integrated school setting preferred membership in the heterogeneous circle, those in non-integrated schools were confined to homogeneous groups. The integrated students held that a heterogeneous setting enabled them to develop new skills of communication, social dealings, adjustment and concern for others. Hence, analysis of students self-report showed that they were less withdrawn, more attentive, had wider social contacts and interaction. They also preferred interacting with people of different age groups. On the other hand, the non-integrated students held that they preferred being in small groups and with people who had similar needs. This helped them to relate more, facilitated better interaction and also strengthened their bondage. They also preferred interacting with people mostly of their own age group due to ease in relating. Despite differences in the nature of their group membership, both groups of blind students were found to engage in wide variety of activities such as playing, talking, going to places, etc. According to them, their ability to interact with people, humorous nature and good behaviour made them popular among others.

Perception of Family Relations: Parents, siblings and relatives

Students in both integrated and non-integrated schools were found to maintain positive relationship with their parents. They mentioned of receiving adequate attention and support from their parents. According to them, since their parents understood and respected their feelings and viewpoints, they felt at ease in discussing their problems and secrets with them. Another factor that positively affected the confidence of students was the impartial or 'undifferentiated' treatment they received from their parents. According to them, their parents did not discriminate between them and their sighted siblings and accepted them just as they were. Moreover, since they gave due importance to their viewpoints and decisions, they preferred staying at home in the company of their parents and siblings. Such permissive parental treatment and high parental involvement positively contributed towards making the blind students socially responsible, independent and more competent than their peers.

The students in integrated schools also mentioned of sharing close, 'intimate' and positive relationship with their siblings. They regarded them to be understanding, helpful and "fun loving". According to them, though they had occasional fights among themselves like any other siblings, they were also cooperative to each other. Their siblings interacted and assisted them in homework, explained certain subjects, discussed their personal problems, etc. They never made them feel being "different" from others. Rather they always encouraged them to engage in more independent and productive work. In this regard, Student L.V. (Sl.No.24) of grade 11 said:

> *"I love interacting with my brother and sister. They never have been made to feel me that I'm different. Instead of helping me they sometimes pressurize me to do things on my own, they want me to do well. They do feel bad when others make fun of my blindness at times".*

On the other hand, students in non-integrated schools were found to be restrained in their preference for home primarily due to their siblings. According to them, they did not share the same cordial relationship with their siblings and other members as with their parents. Such feelings were more evident when other members of the family compared them with their sighted siblings. Such comparisons and impartial treatment made them feel bad and also hampered the relationship with their siblings. It also made them feel like leaving home. In certain cases students who had fewer friends and depended more on their siblings for interaction, felt depressed and neglected at home if their siblings did not understand and quarrelled with them. Relating some of the experience with his siblings, Student N.G. (Sl.No. 14) stated:

> *"I get upset when my brothers beat me up. They do*

not regard me to be of any use. I want to do things on my own but whenever I make mistake they behave rudely. They never encourage me. I don't have very many friends to share my pain also".

According to two students, inability to participate in various activities at par with their sighted siblings at home made them avoid their company. Such instances lowered the self-confidence of the blind students and affected their level of social interaction. They tended to become more reserved, solitary, insecure, withdrawn and impulsive.

Besides their siblings, the blind students from non-integrated schools also emphasized of being subjected to comparison and neglect by their relatives. According to them, continuous comparison with their sighted siblings or other children of their own age group made the home environment less preferable, lowered their self-confidence and also strained relationships. Such circumstances made them prefer school more to home.

Perception of School

School climate was also found to play a dominant role in influencing the psychological adjustment of blind students. Students from both integrated and non-integrated settings maintained positive approach towards school. However, as compared to students in non-integrated schools, blind students in integrated schools showed greater confidence in their ability to participate in classroom activities and communicate. According to the students in non-integrated schools, their lack of confidence in deciding whether they will be able to speak correctly or not often prevented them from engaging in productive interaction and also adversely affected their academic performance. Besides this, frequent occurrence of mistakes, repeated failures and inability to keep up with the pace of work or to follow instructions properly made them scared of undertaking initiatives.

Relations with Teachers and Peers

Within the school environment, peers and teachers were found to have significant influence on the personality development and academic achievement of both groups of students. Peers, in particular were found to play an increasingly important role in the lives of the adolescents by helping them develop a sense of belongingness, cooperation, binding to the group, self-esteem and identification. However, certain differences were evident among both groups of blind students regarding the nature of peer-group affiliations. The students in non-integrated schools mentioned of having greater peer assistance as compared to those in integrated schools. According to them, placement in a homogeneous group promoted better understanding and awareness of the problems and needs of each other thereby fostering better and more intimate relationships. Although the students in integrated schools mentioned of sharing good and cordial relationships with their sighted peers they still felt the difference as in certain cases their peers failed to understand them primarily because of being less acquainted with their needs.

The blind students in both types of schools were also found to maintain cordial relationship with their teachers. They widely appreciated their teachers for understanding and catering to their diverse needs. However regarding this aspect, the students in the integrated schools held that although their teachers were cooperative they failed to give adequate individual attention to them largely due to their heavy workload, large class size, etc.

Academic Achievement

Irrespective of type of school setting, the blind students were moderately satisfied with their present level of achievement especially in grades 10 and 12. According to them besides sudden increase in syllabi along with the pressures of preparing for board examinations, numerous other factors such as inability in pursuing certain activities such as drawing, mathematics particularly geometry, science practical, computers and geography, understanding abstract concepts etc. contributed towards limiting their level of performance. Moreover, they also faced problems in learning certain topics due to unavailability of adequate text and limited use of models. The instructions being primarily theoretical in nature made them dependent on class lectures. In case of students in the integrated schools, such method of instruction made them depend on their sighted classmates to note or read them out for instructions for them and on special teachers to clarify their doubts in the special classes held at the National Association for the Blind (NAB) after school hours.

Overall analyses of self-esteem, adjustment and academic achievement of blind and sighted students in integrated and non-integrated schools brought out certain similarities and differences to the forefront. Physical competence was found to play a dominant role in influencing mobility, maintenance of self-esteem, building of social interaction and achievement of students. Both the blind and the sighted students made reference to their physical self. It is important to note in this regard that despite referring to various associated problems resulting due to lack of vision such as inability to move about independently in unknown areas, ability to play, do drawing, etc. the blind students irrespective of school setting maintained positive self-esteem. They did not regard themselves to be different from their sighted counterparts in any dimension. On the basis of student' response, it was seen that physical incompetence need not always result in feelings of helplessness and dependence. On instances social attitude and representation of a 'disabled' condition may also play a significant role in affecting the formation of self-image. This was emphasized by the blind students in integrated schools who held that such circumstances made them analyze their experiences in light of the existing meanings and practices prevalent in society and affected their functioning. However, despite innumerable constraints the blind students in both school settings were found to maintain positive self-view and did not refer to the need to incorporate any change in their physical appearance. On the other hand, they laid more stress on changes in their behaviour for better social interaction and acceptance.

As compared to blind students, the sighted laid more emphasis on their physical self. They stressed on the need to incorporate certain changes for better adjustment and acceptance. According to them, physical competence played an important role in influencing formation and maintenance of self-evaluation and social image.

Besides the physical self, social network (family, peer group) was also found to make an important impact on self-esteem, adjustment and academic achievement of all groups of students. Both blind and sighted students regarded their family members to be cooperative and understanding. They shared good rapport with both their parents and siblings. However, the blind students in non-integrated schools and sighted students in both school settings expressed their dissatisfaction regarding the approach of their relatives towards them. According to them, unnecessary and impartial comparisons made them feel depressed and neglected. It was found to make the individuals more withdrawn and affected their social interaction.

The school was considered by students in all the schools as a 'miniature home'. They were positively influenced by the ambience at school. They actively participated in various curricular and co-curricular activities. However, the range of the participation of co-curricular activities was limited due to several factors such as increased workload, pressure of board examinations, etc. In case of blind students, their participation was more confined to activities like debates, elocutions, etc. Absence of sight restricted their scope of participation in other "physically" related activities. Unlike the blind, the sighted students were found to excel in both activities.

All the four groups of students were found to be moderately satisfied with their own academic performance. While the blind students in the integrated schools felt that they needed to put in more focussed efforts in order to keep pace with their sighted counterparts, those students in non-integrated schools emphasized on the need for more individual efforts as well institutional arrangements. The sighted students also expressed that better performance would result with more focussed efforts and proper guidance.

(II) Ecological Analysis of Integrated School Settings

Ecological analysis of school and classroom environment was made on the basis of observation of school and classroom. Three schools integrating students with visual impairments were selected for the study undertaken— Government Co-education Senior Secondary School, R. K. Puram, Sector V, New Delhi; Upras School, Vasant Marg, Vasant Vihar, New Delhi and Tagore International School, Vasant Vihar, New Delhi.

School 1: Government Co-education Senior Secondary School

Government Co-education Senior Secondary School located at R. K. Puram, Sector V, New Delhi is a co-educational school accommodating students from grades 1 to 12. One of the noteworthy characteristics of the school is that it integrates students with disabilities. The school was located away from the main road and hence was found to be safe in terms of traffic hazards. There was adequate space in front of the school for the vehicles to park and drop the children to school. The school had two entrances facilitating ease in movement.

The main building of the school was located at a distance from the main entrance. The Principal's office was located on the left of the corridor while the Staff room was on the right hand as one enters the main building. The playground was located behind the main school building. It was found to be spacious and free from any physical hazards. The main school building was three storey building and spacious. It had a wide staircase on the side while classrooms, laboratories, toilets were located on the other side of the staircase. Inside the school building, the children were observed to move around quite comfortably, particularly those with visual impairment. However, there were no ramps constructed for the visually impaired students to facilitate their movement. The students were found to be aware of the location of the different places in the school such as the school office, Principal's office, staff room, classrooms, library, sick room, toilets, canteen, exits and entrances.

The classrooms were spacious with linear arrangement of tables and chairs in rows and columns each having double seating arrangements. There was adequate space for the children to move in and out. The classroom also had adequate arrangements for lighting and ventilation. There was a common entrance and exit in each classroom. The other furnishings in the classroom included a seating arrangement for the teacher in the front and centre of the class and a blackboard. There were no additional arrangements in the form of storage facilities for the students to store their books and other essentials.

Instructional strategies and adaptations

There was no facility for the school to provide for the Braille writers, magnification devices etc. to the visually challenged students. The Braille writers etc. were all furnished to the students by the National Association for the Blind (NAB) which they carried to the class regularly. Sometimes, they noted down the instructions or notes provided in the class using them while on other occasions they only listened.

Recorded cassettes containing instructions or lessons taught in the class (based on the advance notice given by the respective teachers) were prepared and distributed by the NAB amongst the students. There was no use of models in the process of instruction.

The teachers were found to provide instructions at the outset of the class on the topics to be discussed in clear and simple language. The teacher took up each topic and divided them into sub-topics and discussed them in bullets/point method. Sometimes, they wrote the bullet points on the blackboard as well as read them aloud for the convenience of the students. They encouraged the students, particularly the visually challenged students to answer and contribute actively in covering the topics. Sometimes, the teacher facilitated a topic taught by furnishing examples from the daily life situations.

Interpersonal relations: teachers and peers

The teachers reported that initially they had difficulty in dealing with the inclusion of the students having disabilities in their classroom since they were not aware of their needs and were not sure of their ability to deal with them. However with the support of the special educators from NAB they are now confident in interacting with such children. Though their daily work schedule and added responsibilities put a lot of work pressure on them at times they are trying their level best to cater to the needs of such children with the help of the limited facilities provided to them.

The teachers and the students were found to maintain a positive rapport. The teachers encouraged the visually challenged students to participate in actively classroom discussions and activities. They also encouraged the students to participate in extra-curricular activities such as planting trees in the school compound, debates, etc. They however reported that the students with disabilities were not allowed to engage much in outdoor games considering their safety factor.

The sighted counterparts were found to maintain a cordial relation with the visually challenged students. They assisted them in copying the class notes, read out sections of the book as and when required, accompanied them during the recess hours, played games, discussed studies, etc.

School 2: Upras School

Upras School located at Vasant Marg, Vasant Vihar, New Delhi is a co-educational school from grades 1 to 12. It integrates students with disabilities. The location of the school was found to be free of any potential safety hazards. It was located away from the main road. There was sufficient parking space between the main school building and the school gate which enabled the school buses to drop the students at a safer zone. The main school building was separated from the entrance gate by a corridor. The Principal's office, staff room, science laboratories and a few classrooms were located on the ground floor. A staircase is situated on the one side of the building but there were no ramps for the visually impaired students. A spacious playground was located behind the main school building with facilities available for various outdoor games such as basketball, cricket, etc. The visually impaired students were found to be aware of the location of the various places in the school compound and were at ease in their mobility.

The classrooms were spacious with facilities for adequate ventilation and lighting. There were combined seating arrangements for two people at a time. The classroom was furnished with a seating arrangement for the teacher, a blackboard but had no other additional arrangements. The visually challenged students were seated in the front row.

Instructional strategies and adaptations

At the outset of the class the teacher told the students of the topic to be discussed. After stating the broad outline she started to lay emphasis on the specifics. The teacher chiefly used the lecture method but simultaneously noted down whatever was said on the blackboard for the convenience of the other students in the class. The teacher used clear and simple language in imparting the instructions which was frequently repeated. She actively involved all the children (sighted as well the visually challenged) in the classroom discussion. The discussion was marked by interchange of views, questioning and answering. The teacher especially motivated the visually challenged children to ask and answer questions so as to clear their doubts. In order to clear any doubts the teacher sought examples from the daily life situations.

The population under observation actively participated in the classroom activities and discussions. However, the children were not found to note down the class notes using Braille. When the researcher inquired it was informed that they have already been provided with recorded cassettes on the topics to be discussed in advance. During the classroom session it was observed that despite a large class the teacher made attempt to distribute as much as equal time as possible among the children though she was unable to provide individual attention.

The teachers mentioned that for subjects such as geography and history where map work had to be done the task was modified for the visually challenged who instead had to name the place and its location (continent, etc.). The teachers also mentioned that they participated in lab work. On most occasions, they attended the lab classes, listened to the instructions given, noted them using Braille or at times their peers helped them to note down. For practical examinations *vivavoce* was held for them in place of conducting experiments in person. There was however limited use of models due to limited facilities available in the school.

The teachers reported that participation of the visually challenged students in both curricular and co-curricular activities were satisfactory. However, their participation was less in case of outdoor games.

Interpersonal relations: teachers and peers

Cordial relations were found to exist between the teachers and the students. The students freely approached the teachers to clear their doubts. The students mentioned that the teachers were understanding and helped them in doing work. The teachers mentioned that though initially they had some problems in dealing with the students having disabilities they are now at ease. Whenever they have any problems they do consult the special educators and counsellors from NAB.

Healthy relations were found between the visually challenged students and their classmates. The peers assisted them in lab work, in taking notes, read out instructions, sit, talk and play with them. They reported that their classmates never made them feel different from others.

School 3: Tagore International School

Tagore International School located at Paschimi Marg, Vasant Vihar, New Delhi is a co-educational school from grades 1 to 12. The school has differently abled children studying along with the other students. On observation the location of the school was found to be free of any potential safety hazards. It was located away from the main road. There was a parking space in front of the school that reduced the difficulties associated with parking and free movement of the school children. A wide corridor separated the two storied main building from the entrance gate. The Principal's office, school office and the staff room were located down the corridor. The staircase was located in middle of the building but there were no ramps for the visually impaired students. The playground was located behind the main school building and was spacious. On closely observing it was found that the visually impaired students were found to be aware of the location of the various places within the school compound.

The classrooms were found to be spacious. The arrangement of the classrooms was noticeable as the tables and chairs were arranged in semi-circular pattern with four children in each row. The visually challenged children sat amidst the other children and were assisted with a volunteer (one of his classmates). The classroom was found to be adequately equipped in terms of lighting and ventilation, seating arrangement for the teacher in the front and a blackboard. However, there were no additional arrangements in the form of storage facilities for the students to store their books and other essentials.

Instructional strategies and adaptations

The method adopted in teaching the students was essentially lecture based at the outset. The class teacher introduced a topic in simple and clear language. This was generally followed by repeated examples from daily life situations to facilitate the understanding of the students. Care was taken to introduce one concept at a time and the teacher proceeded from concrete to abstract and easy to difficult concepts. They made a constant attempt to actively involve the children (sighted as well as the visually challenged) in the classroom discussion. The discussion was marked by interchange of views, questioning and answering. In case of the subject class attended i.e. Geography the teacher made comprehensive use of hand symbols to teach the children the concept of mountain, the two sides (Leeward and Windward), the concept of slope, etc. The Geography teacher mentioned in case of map work the task was modified for the visually challenged who were asked to name the place and its location (continent, etc.) rather than mark.

The visually challenged students were also participated in laboratory work. They generally listened to the instructions given while their peers performed them. They were evaluated by way of *vivavoce*.

Besides academics the visually challenged students were found to actively participate in co-curricular activities which were more evident in indoor rather than outdoor games.

Interpersonal relations: teachers and peers

Cordial relations were found to exist between the teachers and the students. Both the teachers and students were found to work in close cooperation with each other. The teachers despite the various difficulties such as large class size and workload paid adequate individual attention to the students particularly the visually challenged. At the initial stages, the teachers reported of the innumerable difficulties they underwent in dealing with the inclusion of the students having disabilities in their classroom. These were primarily due to their unawareness of the needs of such children but with the support of the special educators from NAB they later became confident in interacting with such children.

The sighted peers were also found to maintain positive and healthy relationship with the visually challenged students. They were found to be sensitive to their needs and make conscious attempts to assist them such as taking notes, interact with them, encourage to do independent work, etc.

Analysis of ecology of school and classroom environment

Though emphasis is continually being laid on integrating students with disabilities into the regular schools the population/number of students enrolled in each of the schools surveyed was miniscule. Several reasons emerged on inquiring about the enrolment rates with some of the concerned authorities in the institutions aiming to integrate the students into the mainstream schools. Some of the authorities mentioned that the central problem lay in the attitude of the parents of the children. Till date some of the parents opined that their children would be best taken care of in special schools with special assistance. They felt that apart from the benefits of special aids and teachers the issue of being placed with other students having similar needs would be an added advantage and have a positive impact on the psychological make-up of their children. Moreover, the notion that their children may be subjected to unnecessary criticism, abuse, unavailability of adequate and essential facilities accounted for some of the apprehensions that seem to restrain the parents from admitting their children to regular schools.

Though a number of policies have envisaged the need to adopt adequate measures for creating a barrier-free environment and prescribed guidelines and space standards much is left to be attained. While observing the schools selected for the study based on the School Observation Checklist prepared in consultation with some concerned authorities as in the light of the standards prescribed by the Integrated Education for the Disabled Act (IEDC) and Persons With Disabilities Act (PWD) 1995 certain issues emerged to the forefront.

The PWD Act detailed out the architectural and instructional barriers and specified the need for each institute to identify the type of infrastructure to be/modified for enabling the Government to provide financial assistance for such upgradation/modification. It laid down detailed guidelines for creating barrier-free environment specifying the modifications required regarding corridors, stairways, entrances, lighting, classroom arrangements, etc. thereby increasing the level of accessibility. On observing the schools, it was evident that more concrete and large scale efforts need to be made in this direction. Most of the schools did not possess many of the prescribed infrastructural standards. There was lack of ramps, modifications in terms of entrance, class arrangements. One of the major hurdles encountered by the visually challenged students was in accessing the stairways and corridors. None of the schools investigated were found to have the facility of ramps which is one of the most essential requirements for schools integrating students with disabilities. All the schools had broad stairways with maximum number of risers and inadequate hand rails. This is in contrast to the guidelines specified in the PWD Act — schools would have stairs of 135 cm width in minimum, the maximum number of risers shall be limited to 12 and hand rails shall be provided on both sides. Moreover, the classrooms being located on both sides of the corridor made it difficult for the children to access them comfortably although some of the students were aware of their location and could access them with assistance from their fellow students. In addition to the classrooms the location of the toilets, laboratories, cafeteria, etc. were also at a distance and required the students to travel across floors. All these factors restricted the mobility of the students with disabilities and made them dependent on others.

As far as the classrooms were concerned they did not have separate entrances and exits. The seating arrangements also did not facilitate adequate mobility. The tables and chairs were closely arranged and there was no adequate space to facilitate easy movement. Moreover in case of most of the classrooms, the lighting was not adequate and there was no arrangement for students to store their books, school bags and other personal items.

Regarding the aids and equipments to be owned by the schools, the IEDC prescribed certain guidelines—Equipments and materials to include Braille slate and stylus, Abacus, Taylor Frame, mobility canes, Braille sheets, thermoform machines, embossed recreational materials, Cassette and talking books, etc.

In all the three schools most of the materials were not available. The students reported that they acquired the aids such as Braille writer, slate and stylus, Magnification device, Cassette tape recorder/player, etc. on their own from the training institute i.e. National Institute for the Blind (NAB). Moreover, the libraries also did not have reading materials for the visually impaired students. This caused the students to depend on their sighted counterparts to read out to them or in certain cases the students reported that they did not access the library.

Though it is emphasized that use of models was to facilitate imparting of instruction this facility was not there in the case of the schools. The teaching was observed to be purely theoretical in nature and lecture based. Commenting on this issue the concerned authorities, parents as well as the teachers held that the theoretical nature of the curriculum and work pressure prevents the students from continuing in the integrated schools. Under such circumstances they often preferred the alternative schooling i.e. National Institute of Open Schooling that offered courses that have an advantage of specially adapted to the needs of every child thereby giving them the opportunity to progress at his/her own pace or join the Community Based Rehabilitation Programmes.

In view of these it is maintained that despite the attempts towards integration the efforts fail to meet the requirements of the "basics" of curricular aspects of such children such as facilities for reading, writing, field trips, standards of attendance, participation, etc. This is supported by the fact that recently in an attempt by the Government to evaluate the curricular issues in CBSE schools several difficulties emerged related to the provision of barrier-free environment, adequate and appropriate study materials such as rarity in the availability of Braille books, necessary support services as well as adequate transport services.

On final analysis of the observation of the ecology of schools and classrooms made concerning the integration of students with disabilities certain inadequacies emerged. Several reasons can be attributed accounting for them. One of the reasons behind the inadequacies in making provisions for the disabled is due to the fact that in most cases the policy-makers, planners and administrators are not adequately aware of the needs of the disabled population. As a result of this, the nature and modalities of the provisions tend to be merely adoptive forms of the various programmes from developed countries that may not be suitably adaptable to the requirements of the nation implementating it.

Among the other factors that can be accounted for the restrictions on the legislative measures undertaken for the empowerment of people with disabilities is the limitations in the enforcement of the provisions specified has been the lack of detail of the follow-up procedures for their implementation which has been primarily left to the Court of Law. This dilutes the entire process whereby it becomes difficult for those people with disabilities who have limited resources and legal knowledge to take initiative on their personal front in the legal process.

Moreover, diverse issues of the people with disabilities continue to be addressed to in a marginal way in plans and policies. The notion that education and management of disabled children relies on voluntary organizations further affects the initiatives on the part of the Government. This account for the policies towards the disabled is equivocal and full of ambiguities. Moreover, the functioning of the NGOs is also limited to the micro level due to lack of continuous funding and good infrastructural support. In addition to these the changing Governmental policies further limits the functioning of the various agencies.

Section C: Overall Discussion

Though the type of school placement/setting was not found to produce any significant difference in self-esteem, adjustment and academic achievement of blind and sighted students in the integrated schools, blind and sighted students in the non-integrated schools as well as blind students in integrated and non-integrated schools, analysis of qualitative data based on the response of students obtained through interviews helped to obtain a holistic picture of the sources and processes involved in the development and maintenance of their self-esteem, adjustment and academic achievement.

Both blind and sighted students, irrespective of the type of school placement were found to base their self-evaluation and adjustment mechanisms on two major factors—their physical self and significant others, particularly parents and siblings. Regarding the physical self, it is important to note that blind students in both school settings made occasional reference to loss of vision despite regarding themselves as capable as others (sighted). According to them, loss of sight at times prevented them from leading a normal life by placing certain undue restrictions on their mobility, achievement of goals and social interaction. Besides this they realized their physical limitation only when people around them made any reference to it such as undue comparisons, overconcern or overprotectiveness, usage of stigmatized terms, etc. It was on such occasions that they felt the desire to see. However in general, they expressed the desire to incorporate certain changes in themselves but they were more inclined towards behavioural modifications such as develop more patience, concern for others, less anger, etc. Hence, it is evident from their response that although physical ability constitutes a basis for an individual to develop an unique and separate identity, blind students in spite of their limitation did not hold any low opinion of themselves, rated their lives positively and considered themselves to be at par with their sighted counterparts. The students preferred to refer to themselves as 'differently abled' rather than 'disabled'.

As compared to the blind students, the sighted students in both integrated and non-integrated schools laid considerable emphasis upon the physical aspect. They were found to be more concerned about their looks (fair complexion, fatness, etc.). Though some students expressed their desire to incorporate behavioural changes in themselves, majority of laid more emphasis on their looks such as become "taller", "fairer", "less fat", better physique etc. For them better physical appearance greatly affected how others perceived and accepted them.

The role of significant others, particularly parents and teachers was largely emphasized by both groups — blind as well as sighted students, thereby indicating that self-esteem and adjustment is not a mere function of perception of self but also social identification. Social acceptance and popularity emerged as important aspects whereby members of each of the groups attached great importance to the role of 'significant others' in their lives. Though social acceptance and popularity attained was found to be one of the essential prerequisites for the psychological well-being of all individuals certain intra as well as inter-group differences were reflected. In case of blind students in the integrated schools, the social circle was found to be wider than the students in non-integrated schools and at par with their sighted counterparts. Placement in heterogeneous setting was found to provide students with greater opportunities to develop new skills of communication, social dealings, adjustment and concern for others. Though the students made occasional reference to some of the problems they encountered at the initial stages but at present they are well adjusted to their environment. They enjoyed the company of both their 'differently abled' as well as sighted peers. However, the blind students in non-integrated schools regarded their homogeneous placement as the ideal social environment for themselves. In their viewpoint such an environment ensured better interaction and adjustment.

Social circle and popularity emerged as central features for the sighted students. They were a part of a wider social circle and considered themselves to be easily adaptable and accepted by people. Besides this they held that their good communicative skills further facilitated their inclusion in various groups. While emphasizing on the significance of popularity in their social life they also made occasional reference to the pressures that it inflicted on them such as maintenance of certain specific behaviour norms, lifestyle, etc.

Regarding the significance of family, both blind students as well as sighted students reported of receiving good treatment from their family members. For the blind students in integrated schools their home environment was supportive, caring both in terms of parents and siblings as well as other members.

They held all the family members maintained a considerate view of them, made no attempts to make them feel inferior or different in anyway. Their responses revealed that the parents of blind children were concerned, permissive and protective about their welfare.

The blind students in non-integrated schools also mentioned of receiving good parental treatment but reported of negative attitude on the part of other members of the family. They recalled of instances of being subjected to comparison and neglect and in such situations expressed their preference for school to home. However on overall analysis, the family was found to have an influential impact wherein the students regarded their parents to be cooperative and understanding.

Regarding family experiences the sighted students in both type of school settings revealed a mixed picture. On the one hand, some students reported of receiving adequate parental love, consideration and assistance from their parents, siblings and other members of the family. They however did not mention of their parents being overprotective, but rather directive as well permissive in their approach encouraging them to be self-dependent. On the other hand, other students felt that their family, i.e. both parents and siblings restrained their independence and negatively affected their behaviour and adjustment pattern.

However, overall qualitative analysis of the influence of family showed that it was found to produce differential impact on the developmental process of both blind and sighted students. In case of the blind students, their parents were found to be more permissive and overconcerned about their safety. On the other hand, though the sighted students also preferred their home but for them it was an institution where they were showered with love as well as were subjected to criticism. They did not report of over parental attention or indulgence.

All groups of students from both settings were found to maintain positive approach towards school and its related activities. They referred it as their "second home", an institution which provided them with a wider arena for interaction, a yardstick to evaluate themselves, both in terms of social and academic competence and also incorporate necessary changes in themselves for their own betterment. The blind students in non-integrated schools, in particular laid more emphasis on the school environment and the approach of the teachers towards them. According to them, the homogeneous setting made it easier for them to relate well with others having similar problems and need. Besides this, they also regarded their teachers to be supportive and understanding. They provided more individualized attention and encouraged them towards independent thinking and initiatives.

The blind students in integrated schools also stressed that their placement with sighted students provided an opportunity for them to develop greater communication and academic skills. This in turn provided them a parameter to evaluate themselves and their performances. They reported of having received undifferentiated attention from both the teachers as well as their sighted classmates. This raised their level of self-confidence, encouraged them to take more independent initiatives and also affected their performance. However, at the same time the students also mentioned that despite being cooperative their teachers at times failed to provide individualized attention due to their workload.

It is essential to point out that although the blind students reported of 'feeling accepted' in the integrated schools both academically as well as socially, analyses of the ecology of the schools showed certain limitations. Shortcomings in infrastructural requirements, teaching strategies, equipments, biased attitude of teachers, parents, etc. were seen to play significant role in slowing down the process of integrating the students with disabilities into mainstream school environment. This was also seen on the performance level of the students (as evident from qualitative data). However, despite these limitations since the blind students in integrated schools were mostly from a comparatively higher socio-economic class and had access to education in schools with better facilities it had a positive affect on their performance.

Regarding the blind students in non-integrated schools, good educational facilities, individualized attention and congenial school climate facilitated better performance. On the other hand, the sighted students in both school settings laid emphasis on several factors like theoretical nature of work, old methods of teaching adopted by the teachers coupled with vast syllabi and high parental expectations and pressure, etc. which cumulatively lowered their performance.

The sighted students in both integrated and non-integrated schools regarded school as a miniature society where they found the opportunity to interact with a large number of people and improve their performance through active participation in school activities. However, while analyzing their overall academic achievement the students laid emphasis on several factors like theoretical nature of work, old methods of teaching adopted by the teachers coupled with vast syllabi and high parental expectations and pressure, etc. which cumulatively lowered their performance.

Another significant effect that was evident closely related to the school dimension was the influence of the grade on the self-esteem, adjustment and academic achievement of blind and sighted students in integrated and non-integrated schools. The students irrespective of the type of school placement were found to show better adjustment patterns in grades 9 and 11. They felt more relaxed and better socially and emotionally accepted during these grades. They showed good control over their social, emotional as well as academic life. The role of the family, teachers and peers was found to play a more dominant role in the process of their development. The students demonstrated better control over their emotions and social behaviour. Those in grades 10 and 12 were generally found to be more burdened by the academic and social pressures. Parental expectations and career aspirations posed certain difficulties for the individuals.

7

Discussion and Conclusion

Analyses of research on visual impairment, particularly the blind emphasize that they were expected to have low self-esteem and adjustment. However, findings of the present study show that they were as well adjusted as their sighted counterparts and also had a comparable self-esteem. This was consistent with several research findings that emphasize that visually impaired people are not at a high risk of developing low self-esteem than their sighted counterparts (Williams, 1971; Brewer, 1979; Sinha, 1982; Kaur, Singh & Jain, 1984; Kapoor & Sen, 1984; Obiakor, 1986; Obiakor & Stile, 1990; Dodds, et al., 1994; Beaty, 1994). On the contrary, those individuals showed better control of their lives, positively accepted their state of disability and a sense of responsibility to affect changes in their lives.

Though research evidences emphasize that the type of school setting largely affects psychological well-being of blind children, no difference in self-esteem and adjustment among blind students in both integrated and non-integrated school setting shows that integration of students did not make significant impact. This is in agreement with the findings of Schindele (1975), Kielly (1994) and Gronmo and Augestad (2000). According to them, differences in educational settings did not have significant impact on the self-esteem, social behaviour and participation of blind individuals. Schindele (1975) and Kielly (1994) while comparing the social adjustment and self-esteem of visually impaired children in different educational settings, where some of them were from residential schools and some from resource programmes in regular schools found no difference in their social adjustment and self-esteem. Gronmo and Augestad (2000) also concluded that type of school provisions were not crucial in indicating differences in physical competence, physical and social self-concept and global self-worth of blind individuals.

However, the affect of ongoing social relationships in recurring social settings on the psychological well-being of blind children as found in the present study appears to be in agreement with the findings of Goldstein and Cisar (1992), Pellegrini (1984), Burgess and Fordyce (1989), Ladd and Price (1993). Attitude and interaction with the peers and teachers was found to play significant role.

Physical self, emerged as one among the factors playing a dominant role in shaping the self-esteem and adjustment pattern of both blind and sighted students in integrated and non-integrated school settings. Adolescence being a myriad of changes both physically and psychologically, a high level of physical ability reinforces positive evaluation of physical self and global self-evaluation. In accordance with the biological changes that occur during this age phase, the extent to which individuals accept and feel comfortable with their body image affects their self-perception and self-esteem (Allgood-Merten, Lewinson & Hop, 1999; Williams & Currie, 2000). The findings of the present study also lend support to the above argument. Both blind and sighted students were conscious of their physical appearance. However, it is essential to note that although the blind students laid emphasis on their physical appearance and expressed desire to incorporate certain changes, they did not associate loss of vision with any negative connotation. Despite occasional reference to loss of vision, they regarded themselves to be as capable as their sighted counterparts and referred to themselves as 'differently abled' rather than 'disabled'. This contradicted the general notion that unexpressed feeling of loss of sight is frequently associated with helplessness, inferiority, mobility related stress and anxiety, depression, loss of self-efficacy, and poor performance.

Besides the significance of physical ability, family also played an important role in affecting the developmental process of both blind and sighted students. The students regarded their home environment to be supportive. The blind students in particular, reported of receiving good treatment from their family members and found their parents to be concerned, permissive and protective about their welfare. This was in agreement with the findings of Wright (1983), Dote-Kwan (1995), Behl, Akers, Boyce and Taylor (1996), according to whom parents with visually impaired children tend to be more overprotective than the parents of sighted children.

However in case of sighted students, family was found to cast diverse influence. On the one hand, it provided positive stimulation to the students thus their ensuring healthy adjustment and self-approach. This was found to be in conjunction with researches which show that permissive parental attitude had positive impact upon children's self-esteem (Anderson & Hughes, 1990; Tennent & Berthelson, 1997; Kernis, Brown & Brady, 2000). On the other hand, parental overcontrol and less emotional support from parents promoted undesirable adjustment problems among students and was found to be associated with lower self-concept. This related to a number of studies which show that adolescents with inadequate family support and excessive parental control suffer from poorer mental health, low self-concept, retarded social development and attenuated overall well-being (Yoshikawa, 1994; Barber & Olsen, 1997; Conger, Conger & Scaramella, 1997; Wenz-Gross, Siperstein & Untch, 1997).

Both blind and sighted students emphasized on the role of "significant others" besides their families. Generally, the students reported being subjected to comparison and neglect (Simmons, Rosenberg & Rosenberg, 1973; Rosenblum, 2000).

Findings of the study relates to the theoretical framework of Mead (1934) who contended that development of knowledge concerning self was entirely dependent upon one's experience with others. Such experiences provide information about one's expectations from the self. The context of blind students' self-esteem being affected by judgement of others, relates it to the principle of Social Comparison theory (Festinger, 1954) and the Social Identity theory (Tajfel, 1981, 1982; Turner, 1987). In accordance with the Social Comparison theory, wherein individuals gather positive, neutral or negative self-ratings by comparing themselves with others, the result of the study shows that blind students indulged in social comparisons (parallel, downward and upward) for maintaining their optimal functioning and subjective well-being. According to them, such comparisons enabled them to develop new skills of communication, social dealings, adjustment and concern for others. It also encouraged them to improve their level of achievement. According to Turner (1958), one's stability in self-definition was accompanied by the need for maintaining or enhancing self-evaluations. When one had low self-esteem or if one's evaluation of self was not socially approved, one experienced anxiety and felt highly agitated to do something about such failures (Gecas, 1986). Under such circumstances stigmatized people might use mechanism of selective downward comparison i.e. compare oneself with someone who is worse off contrast effect, which is perceived as less threatening for enhancement and maintenance of their self-esteem.

The advocates of Social Identity theory (Tajfel, 1982; Tajfel & Turner, 1979, 1985) maintained that there would be higher cognitive preference for intra-personal similarities and interpersonal differences which help to enhance psychological distinctiveness of individuals. Identifying more with in-group members and selective comparison can be gratifying especially for stigmatized persons (Gecas, 1986). This was evident in the present study, wherein blind students in both integrated and non-integrated school settings maintained comparable self-esteem and adjustment as their sighted counterparts. Certain observations were made regarding this. Similarity of socio-economic background and standard of schooling enabled the students to relate with the needs and requirements of their counterparts. This in turn helped to strengthen the intra-personal similarities among the students. Strong in-group identification was prevalent among the blind students, but more in case of those in non-integrated schools. According to students in non-integrated schools, their placement in homogeneous setting helped them to relate well with each others, needs and problems as well avoid undesired comparison with the sighted prevalent in integrated schools.

In comparison to the non-integrated school counterparts, blind students in integrated schools also identified with their in-group members but at the same time maintained that comparison with their sighted counterparts contributed towards the maintenance of their positive self-view. Thus, greater identification with in-group members, parallel comparisons and fewer experiences of problems in social interaction emerged as chief reasons for maintenance of positive self-esteem and adjustment of blind students. These factors also enabled them in distancing themselves from the out groups (Tajfel, 1982) and maintaining higher self-esteem. Extensive identification with their in-group demonstrated their group solidarity, helped them to combat their perceived insecurities (Brewer, 1979) and foster positive self-esteem (Gupta, 1989).

In addition to above theories, findings of the study also relates to the theoretical framework of Bandura's Self-efficacy theory. In case of blind students irrespective of school setting, their self-identity developed through a combination of sources such as previous performance, experience of observing others perform tasks and the affective reaction that accompanied apprehensions about their own capabilities. The students engaged in several tasks and activities, interpreted results of the actions which determined the base for further actions. On most occasions their outcomes were successful which raised their self-efficacy, self-esteem and adjustment. Moreover, the extent of similarity or divergence of attributes of the "significant other" and their own capabilities affected their self-beliefs. The blind students laid emphasis on the significance of observing and performing in accordance with the views of the "significant others". It produced strong influence on their adjustment.

It was evident from the study that both the groups of blind

and sighted students in integrated and non-integrated schools expressed liking for their school environment and satisfaction with their academic achievement. Blind students, in both school settings showed evidence of good academic achievement. Jangira (1987), Haider (1990) and Beaty (1994) also reported similar findings. Jangira (1987) reported that visually impaired students were neither isolated nor were they below average in their achievement. Haider (1990) and Beaty (1994) further mentioned that sometimes the visually impaired students showed better academic performance than the non-impaired students. Based on the students' rating of their own performances as well as the teachers' ratings no significant difference was evident in the performance of blind and sighted students in both school settings.

The Self-determination theory (Deci et al., 1991) emphasize that students become actively engaged in educational activities to the extent that classroom endeavours affirm their competencies and prove themselves to be interesting and relevant to the students' lives was applicable in the present study. Supportive environment had wide implications on the academic performance of students. Both groups of blind students regarded their school environment to be stimulating and conducive to their needs. This had a significant influence on their performance level. Similar to blind students, the sighted students also appreciated their school environment but reported of greater academic stress resulting due to high parental pressures. Dornbusch et al. (1987) and Steinberg, Elmen and Mounts (1989) in their findings have emphasized that authoritative parenting was positively correlated with adolescent school performance but negatively correlated with authoritarian and permissive parenting. Therefore, adolescents who described their parents as behaving more democratically, more warmly and more encouraging showed better academic performance.

According to Coopersmith (1967), self-esteem had two main sources i.e. a sense of self-worth acquired through being loved and accepted during childhood, and the other being a sense of competence acquired during through adulthood. Veroff and Veroff (1980) and Rubel (1983) also noted the positive role of cognitive abilities in subsequent self-esteem evaluations and making social comparisons. In other words, when academic area is perceived to be important, positive self-evaluations results in more positive global self-evaluations and negative academic self-evaluation to negative global self-devaluation, (Alasker, 1989). Self-esteem, satisfactory adjustment and academic competence of blind students were depended upon positive reinforcement and feedback from their teachers. Johnson, Vincent and Ross (1997) proposed that self-esteem was built upon many positive experiences of success and positive reinforcement from others.

The findings of the present study is in agreement with the earlier research findings of Goldstein and Cisar (1992) and Pellegrini (1984) that positive experiences in interpersonal relationships with peers and teachers help to strengthen the self-esteem, adjustment and academic achievement of both blind and sighted students. There were evidences of positive interaction with the peers and teachers. The socio-metric status of blind children in integrated classes was not found to be lower compared to their sighted classmates as argued in the findings of Havill (1972). The students reported of receiving undifferentiated attention from their sighted classmates. This raised their level of self-confidence, encouraged them to take more independent initiatives and positively affected their performance. The findings also showed no evidence of negative attitude or differential treatment as found by Murphy (1960), Diamond (1979), Bulloile and Rigg (1980), Pastor and Jimenez (1994) and Glaubman and Lifshitz (2001). Teachers were found to maintain positive and healthy relations with the students and provide constant assistance.

However it is important to note that besides numerous benefits derived from integrated school settings, the students also made reference to certain associated problems such as lack of adequate study materials such as Braille books, inadequate individualized attention, etc. This in turn highlights the various important issues that need to be addressed in order to ensure complete integration of the disabled not only into educational programmes but also the mainstream society.

Conclusion

The present study attempted at a comparative analysis of blind and sighted adolescents with respect to their self-esteem and adjustment (social, emotional and educational adjustment) in two types of school settings (integrated and non-integrated). It also explored relation of the psycho-social variables with academic achievement for all the four groups of students. Besides these, ecological analysis of school and classroom environment was carried out in order to investigate and interpret the effect of type of school placement on self-esteem and adjustment (social, emotional and academic adjustment) and academic achievement of blind students.

Four groups of students—blind students in integrated schools, blind students in non-integrated schools, sighted students in integrated schools and sighted students in non-integrated schools—each comprising of 40 male students within the age group of 14-17 years and grade levels of IX-XII each were selected for the study. In case of blind students only totally and congenitally blind adolescents were selected. Those having any additional impairment were not included in the sample.

Data were collected using questionnaire technique, observational methods and school record sheets. A questionnaire was used to collect background information of the students. Students' self-esteem was measured using the translated and adapted version of Coopersmith Self-esteem Inventory—Adult Form. The Adjustment Inventory for the School students by A. K. P. Sinha and R. P. Singh (Hindi) was used for assessing Emotional, Social and Educational adjustment of students. The academic achievement of students was assessed by using the percentage of marks obtained by them in their last school examination. Besides this, self-rating scales of students' own performance and teachers' ratings of students' performance were administered. An in-depth study of the ecology of classrooms was done at the larger institutional level in the context of the schools and also in terms of interpersonal relations prevalent in the classrooms. Classroom observations and interviews were employed in order to observe the attitude and interaction of blind and sighted students and teachers in integrated schools.

The response of both blind and sighted students in integrated and non-integrated schools were scored and analyzed for each of the measures in the study. Mean and SD values were computed for each of the four groups of students. Correlations were found out to assess the degree of association among self-esteem, adjustment (emotional, social and educational) and academic achievement, students' self-rating of their performance and teachers' rating of students performance) for each group. 2 (Group) × 2 (School setting) × 4 (Grades) ANOVA were used to find out the main and interaction effects of each of the variables. Stepwise multiple regression analyses were done to identify different contributing factors of academic achievement.

The data obtained on the basis of questionnaires administered to blind and sighted students and the teachers was used for qualitative analysis. Detailed semi-structured interviews were also conducted for both the students and teachers. The recorded interviews were transcribed and subjected to content analysis. Case studies based on the response of selected students from each group were also used for further analysis. Ecological analysis of integrated school settings was also conducted.

The findings of the study in relation to the proposed hypotheses are as follows

- There will be significant difference between blind and sighted students (integrated and non-integrated) in respect of self-esteem, adjustment and academic achievement.

The above hypothesis was found to be rejected in the study. Findings show that blind and sighted students (integrated and non-integrated) did not differ in respect of their self-esteem, adjustment and academic achievement. All the four groups of students were found to be confident, capable of shouldering responsibilities, adaptable and determined. Among the several factors, parents and teachers were found to play a dominant role in shaping the behaviour of students. This shows that self-esteem and adjustment are not a mere function of perception of self but also of social identification. However, differences in response were found among both blind and sighted students regarding the role of their parents. While the blind students laid more emphasis on more positive parental approach that affected their self-image, adjustment and academic achievement, the sighted students focussed on certain constraints resulting due to parental overcontrol and adversely affected their behaviour and performance.

Regarding academic achievement also, both blind and sighted students were found to be competent, hardworking and interested in school related activities. The role of peers and teachers was emphasized by all students. Besides this since the blind students in integrated schools were mostly from a comparatively higher socio-economic class it may have had an effect on their psychological development. The students had access to education in schools with better facilities which positively affected their performance. Regarding the blind students in non-integrated schools, good educational facilities, individualized attention and congenial school climate facilitated better performance. On the other hand, the sighted students in both school settings laid emphasis on several factors like theoretical nature of work, old methods of teaching adopted by the teachers coupled with vast syllabi and high parental expectations and pressure, etc. which cumulatively lowered their performance.

- Integrated and Non-integrated school settings will have significant effect on self-esteem, adjustment and academic achievement of blind students.

The above hypothesis was found to be rejected in the study. The findings showed no statistically significant difference in self-esteem and adjustment of blind students in non-integrated schools as compared to those in integrated schools. Both groups of students were found to possess positive self-esteem and better adjustment. However, based on analysis of qualitative response of students certain differences were evident which were not found to be statistically significant. Ecological analysis of integrated schools, ascertained the argument that the type of school setting failed to produce any significant difference among blind students. The findings contradicted the arguments that integration of blind students into mainstream schools ensures greater gains in self-esteem, adjustment and degree of independence. The results show that although the process of integration was implemented in most schools, its impact was confined to mere physical placement of students than their complete integration into the mainstream educational structure.

Moreover, architectural and instructional barriers such as lack of barrier free environment, adequate and appropriate study materials such as non-availability of Braille books, necessary support services, adequate transport services, lack of continuous funding, restrictions on the legislative measures undertaken for the empowerment of people with disabilities, lack of follow-up procedures for their implementation, etc. emerged as some of the loopholes in implementation of educational programmes. Based on these, it can be concluded that all these factors cumulatively contributed towards diluting the process of integration which aims at integrating people with disabilities into the mainstream society.

On the contrary, blind students in non-integrated schools held that the homogeneous grouping made it possible for them to relate to and make more realistic comparisons between their own achievements and those of their peers. Moreover, they also emphasized that more individualized attention, educational resources and guidance of specially trained teachers facilitated good academic performance.

The attitude of other family members (relatives) was found to have adverse affect on the self-esteem, adjustment and academic achievement of both groups of students. Though both groups maintained positive view of their parents for being sensitive to their diverse needs, respecting them and providing assistance, love and affection, they maintained a negative opinion of their relatives. The blind students from non-integrated schools, in particular emphasized of being subjected to comparison and neglect by their relatives. According to them, continuous comparison with their sighted siblings made the home environment less preferable, lowered their self-confidence and also strained relationships. Such circumstances made them prefer school more to home.

- The difference between blind and sighted students in self-esteem, adjustment and academic achievement will be less in integrated schools than blind and sighted students in non-integrated schools.

The above hypothesis was found to be rejected in the study. The findings showed no statistically significant difference in self-esteem, adjustment and academic achievement of blind and sighted students in integrated schools as compared to the students in non-integrated schools. All the students showed positive self-esteem and adjustment. However, the interaction effects of student groups and settings was significant on academic achievement. The results showed a higher mean score for students in non-integrated schools as compared to those in integrated schools. However, none of the main effects and interaction effects was significant for Self-esteem, Social, Educational and Total adjustment scores. This questions the relevance of the effect of school setting on the psycho-social development of blind students. The findings failed to lend adequate support to the arguments of research evidences which maintained that the process of integrating blind students into mainstream schools facilitated greater social interaction, peer and teacher support, better facilities of learning, etc.

Analysis of students' response and ecological analysis of integrated schools show that the two different school settings were not found to produce any significant and diverse effect on the psycho-social well-being of both groups of blind students. The sighted students in both integrated and non-integrated schools demonstrated similar self-esteem, adjustment pattern and academic achievement.

The interaction effects of school setting and grades on social adjustment were significant. The findings show that integrated school students showed better social adjustment in grades IX and XII as compared to their non-integrated counterparts. However, it was lower in grades X and XI. The students were more attentive, less withdrawn and had positive social interaction in grades IX and XII. However, the ever changing and widening social relationships and expectations in the higher grades had adverse affect on social competence of students from both settings.

Besides the school setting, family was found to produce significant influence on both groups of blind and sighted students. The home environment of blind students was found to be more protective than that of the sighted. The parents were found to be overconcerned about their children's safety and well-being and provided additional attention to them. Though the sighted students also preferred their home but they did not report of parental overattention or indulgence. Hence, it can be assumed that the care and attention that was provided to the blind students by their parents positively affected their psychological make-up as against the undifferentiated attention provided to both groups of sighted students.

- Disability condition (blindness and sighted), school settings, self-esteem and adjustment will be significant predictors of academic achievement.

The above hypothesis was found to be rejected. However, only self-esteem was found to be one of the significant predictors of academic achievement in case of blind students in non-integrated schools and sighted students in integrated schools. According to the blind students, additional resources and homogeneous placement boosted their self-confidence and skills. The other variables were not found to produce any statistically significant effect for the same groups.

Other findings of the study

- Significant positive correlation was found to exist between teachers' rating of students' performance and students' self-rating of their own performance. The teachers were satisfied with academic as well as non-academic performance of both blind and sighted students in integrated and non-integrated school settings. This shows that teachers maintained positive attitude towards the integration of blind students in regular classrooms. They were sensitive to the needs and problems of blind individuals which in turn affected their behaviour pattern, teaching methods, etc. while dealing with exceptional children. All these cumulatively affected the self-esteem, adjustment and academic achievement of students.

Thus, comparative analysis of blind and sighted adolescents with respect to self-esteem and adjustment (social, emotional and educational adjustment) and academic achievement showed no significant difference. Ecological analysis of school and classroom environment also showed that the type of school setting (integrated and non-integrated) did not have any significant effect on their self-esteem and adjustment and academic achievement. However, analysis of qualitative data revealed that irrespective of the school setting, home or family had a major role in affecting the behaviour and development of both blind and sighted students.

Limitations of the study

- The study was carried out under a variety of methodological constraints like limited time, availability of only a few integrated and non-integrated schools and required number of sample size. These restricted the scope to look into the socio-psychological factors, their causes and effects in greater depth.
- The study was limited to only a few socio-psychological variables (self-esteem and adjustment).
- Due to unavailability of the required number of students within specified age and grade levels from a single school, sample for the integrated setting had to be selected from three different institutions. Though attempts were made to select the students from similar socio-economic background so as to maintain uniformity and reduce the effect of class difference as far as possible, yet precautionary measures needs to be taken in generalizing the results.
- The results of this study are sample specific. Since the sample selected was small, cautious measures needs to be taken in making generalizations.

Despite the limitations, the present study attempted to provide a base for further studies in the area of integration and segregation of blind individuals and its effect on their self-esteem, adjustment and academic achievement.

Implications of the study

- Knowledge about the impact of type of school settings on self-esteem and adjustment of blind individuals can provide insight into the changes that needs to be incorporated in the various educational policies and programmes, such as mainstreaming and training. Further studies can be made in this area to facilitate in-depth understanding of their problems and complexities.
- Study of self-esteem and adjustment can prove helpful in installing guidance and counselling programmes for blind individuals. Since enhancement of self-concept and adjustment of handicapped children constitutes an important goal in education, hence each case must be properly monitored to determine their benefit.
- Knowledge about differences in self-esteem and adjustment patterns and their impact on academic achievement of blind students in integrated and non-integrated schools can be helpful to educators, administrators, curriculum planners to understand the educational needs of these children and direct efforts towards their effective implementation.
- Knowledge of blind individuals reflects the critical need to educate parents regarding psycho-social well-being of their children. This is because parents were found to be a powerful force in monitoring the progress of children. One such programme could be to provide total communication training to the parents. They should be encouraged to keep regular contact with teachers in order to ensure their child's psychological and academic progress.
- Knowledge of psycho-social development of blind can make sighted siblings and other members of the society conscious and sensitive to their needs and problems

and help to ensure their healthy development.

- As teachers require special training to cater to the needs of blind children, knowledge of their psycho-social development can be used to organize their training programmes accordingly. Teachers should be trained as teacher counsellors. Appropriate teacher training programmes should be organized and existing programmes such as those provided by National Council for Teacher Training, Rehabilitation Council of India, etc. should be reviewed and strengthened.

Suggestions for further Research

- Longitudinal study with larger sample size can be undertaken to look into the interactions between school setting and its impact on self-esteem, adjustment and academic achievement of blind students.
- Comparative studies can be undertaken to find out differences in self-esteem, adjustment and academic achievement between blind and individuals having other forms of handicap.
- Comparative studies can be undertaken to find out differences in self-esteem, adjustment and academic achievement among individuals with various categories of visually impairment, i.e. blind, partially sighted and low vision and also among congenitally and adventitiously blind individuals.

Appendix-A

Background Information

1. Name:
2. Age:
3. Sex:
4. Class:
5. Address:
   a. Type of residence
      Own/Rental:
   b. Number of Rooms:
   c. Does the child have personal room of his/her own:
6. Type of family:
   a. Extended/nuclear:
   b. Number of members in the family:
   c. Whether grandparents live with them:
7. Name of the school:
8. Address of the school:
9. Type of school:
   a. Single sex/Co-education:
   b. Regular/Residential:
10. Parents education (highest level/degree obtained):
    Mother:
    Father:
11. Parents' occupation:
    Mother:
    Father:
12. Monthly income:
    Mother:
    Father:
13. Total Family income:

14. Number of siblings:
    a. Education:
    b. Occupation, if any:
    c. Position of the child among the siblings:
15. Does any other member of the family have any type of impairment/disability:
    Father:
    Mother:
    Brother:
    Sister:
16. Any pre-school training received prior to admission in the present school:

Appendix-BIA

Coopersmith Self-esteem Inventory - Adult Form

1. आमतौर से परिस्थितियाँ मुझे परेशान नहीं करती हैं।
2. लोगों के सामने बात करने में मुझे कठिनाई होती है।
3. मुझमें ऐसी कई बातें हैं जिन्हें मौका मिलने पर मैं बदलना चाहुँगा।
4. मैं ज्यादा कठिनाई के बिना ही अपने मन को बना सकता हूँ।
5. लोगों को मेरा साथ बहुत अच्छा लगता है।
6. घर पर छोटी सी बात में मैं जल्दी ही अस्त–व्यस्त/परेशान हो जाता हूँ।
7. नई चीजों से आदी होने में मुझे काफी समय लगता है।
8. हम उम्र के लड़के/लड़कियों में बहुत लोकप्रिय/प्रसिद्ध हूँ।
9. अक्सर मेरे परिवार के लोग मेरी भावनाओं का ध्यान रखते हैं।
10. मैं कुछ करने या पाने के प्रयत्न से आसानी से रुक जाता/हार मान जाता हूँ।
11. मुझसे मेरे परिवार के लोगों को काफी अपेक्षाएँ हैं।
12. मेरे अपने स्वअस्तित्व को दिखा पाने में कई कठिनाईयाँ हैं।
13. मेरे जीवन में सब कुछ खिंचपिच हैं।
14. लोग अक्सर मेरे विचारों को मान लेते हैं।
15. मैं अपने बारे में नीचा सोचता हूँ।
16. मेरे मन में कई बार घर छोड़ देने की इच्छा होती हैं।
17. मैं अक्सर अपने काम से परेशान रहता हूँ।
18. मैं औरों के जैसा अच्छा देखने में नहीं हूँ।
19. अगर मुझे कुछ बोलना होता है, तो मैं अक्सर बोल देता हूँ।
20. मेरे परिवार के लोग मुझे समझते हैं।
21. अधिकतर दूसरे लोग मुझ से ज्यादा पसन्द किए जाते हैं।

22. मुझे अक्सर लगता है कि मेरे परिवार के लोग मुझ पर दबाव डालते हैं।
23. मैं अपने काम में जल्द ही हतोत्साहित हो जाता हूँ।
24. काश मैं कोई और होता!
25. मैं निर्भरशील नहीं हूँ।

Appendix-BIB

Interview Schedule-Coopersmith Scale

1a. किस तरह की परिस्थितियों में तुम अक्सर परेशान हो जाते हो-
   (i) घर में
   (ii) स्कूल में
   (iii) रोज की जिन्दगी में
   (iv) अन्य

1b. उन परिस्थितियों से निकलने के लिए तुम क्या करते हो-
   (i) अपने आप उनका समाधान निकालने की कोशिश करते हो।
   (ii) दूसरों की मदद लेते हो।

2a. किन लोगों के समाने बात करने में तुम्हें कठिनाई होती है-
   (i) अनजाने लोग
   (ii) घर वाले
   (iii) दोस्त
   (iv) अध्यापक

2b. क्या तुम्हें कभी ऐसी मुश्किल का सामना करना पड़ा है-

2c. तुम्हें किस प्रकार की परेशानी होती है-
   (i) निंदा किये जाने पर या दोष निकाले जाने पर
   (ii) भाषा की समस्या के कारण जैसे आवश्यक शब्दों की कमी, भाषा पर अच्छी पकड़ न होना, अपनी भावनाओं को व्यक्त करने की कुशलता की कमी के कारण इत्यादि।
   (iii) ज्यादा या अपरिचित लोग होने के कारण
   (iv) जानकारी की कमी के कारण

3a. तुम अपने आप में किस तरह का बदलाव या परिवर्तन लाना चाहोगें-

(i) शारीरिक गुणों में

(ii) स्वाभाविक गुणों में

(iii) शैक्षिक गुणों में

(iv) अन्य

3b. इन बदलावों को लाने के लिए तुम क्या कर सकते हो या करना चाहोगे?

4. किन परिस्थितियों में तुम्हें अपने मन को बनाने में कठिनाई होती है-

(i) पारिवारिक विषयों पर

(ii) व्यक्तिगत विषयों पर (जैसे दोस्तों के साथ रिश्ता, अपने स्वभाव इत्यादि)

(iii) शैक्षिक विषयों पर

(iv) अन्य

5a. किस तरह के लोग तुम्हारा साथ पसन्द करते हैं- परिचित लोग जैसे परिवार वाले, दोस्त, या अपरिचित लोग।

5b. तुममें कौन से गुण है जिनके लिए लोग तुम्हारा साथ पसन्द या नापसन्द करते हैं।

6a. तुम्हें घर की चीजें या परिस्थितियाँ अच्छी या बुरी लगती है जैसे भाई, बहन में अन्तर या प्यार, माता-पिता के ध्यान में कमी या समानान्तर प्यार।

6b. अपने रिश्तेदारों के साथ तुम्हारा रिश्ता कैसा है?

7. किस तरह के नए काम या चीजों में तुम्हें कम या काफी समय लगता है?

(i) नया पढ़ाया गया पाठ

(ii) नये लोगों के साथ

(iii) दूसरों की राय/बातों को मानना

(iv) नई जगह जाने में

(v) नई खेल।

8. तुम्हारे कितने दोस्त हैं? क्या तुम्हारा कोई प्रिय मित्र है?

(i) अगर हाँ, तब तुम लोग साथ में क्या-क्या करते हो, जैसे- खेलना, घूमने जाना, पढ़ना इत्यादि।

(ii) अग नहीं तो, तुम्हें दोस्त बनाने में किस तरह की परेशानी होती है?

9a. अगर तुम्हें कोई परेशानी होती है तो क्या वह समझ जाते हैं या उन्हें बताना पड़ता है।

9b. तुम उनके साथ किस तरह की बातचीत करते हो?

(i) व्यक्तिगत

(ii) शैक्षिक

(iii) अन्य

10a. तुम्हें किस तरह की परेशानियों में ऐसा महसूस होता है–

10b. तुम्हें क्यों लगता है कि तुम उस कार्य को अच्छी तरह कर या नहीं कर पाओगें, कभी तुम्हें ऐसी समस्या का सामना करना पड़ता है?

10c. तुम्हें ना कर पाने की भावना से निकलने के लिए क्या करना चाहिए?

11a. तुम बड़े होने पर क्या बनना चाहते हो?

11b. तुम्हारी माता–पिता की तुमसे किस तरह की अपेक्षाएं हैं?

11c. क्या तुम्हारी और उनकी अपेक्षाओं में कोई अन्तर है, अगर हाँ तो इनकी वजह से तुम्हें किन समस्याओं का सामना करना पड़ता है?

12a. अगर कठिनाई होती है तो किस प्रकार की?

12b. क्या तुम्हें लगता है कि तुम इन कठिनाइयों का समाधान निकाल पाओगे?

12c. अगर कठिनाई नहीं होती है, तो तुम्हारे व्यक्तित्व में कौन सी बात है जिससे तुम्हें प्रकट करने में समस्या नहीं होती है?

13a. तुम्हें अपने जीवन के किन विषयों में सब खिचपिच लगता है?

13b. इनकी वजह से तुम्हें किस तरह की समस्याएँ होती हैं?

13c. क्या तुम्हें आशा है कि यह सब जल्द ठीक हो जाएंगे?

14a. क्या तुम्हारे साथ कोई घटना हुई है जहाँ लोगों ने तुम्हारे विचारों को माना या नहीं माना है?

14b. तुम्हारे विचारों के माने या न माने जाने पर तुम्हें कैसा महसूस होता है और उनके लिए कोई वजह।

14c. क्या तुम्हें भी दूसरों के विचारों का ख्याल होता है?
15a. तुम्हें अपने आप में क्या सबसे अच्छा या बुरा लगता है?
15b. तुम अपने आप के बारे में क्या सोचते हो?
16a. तुम घर पर अक्सर क्या-क्या करते हो?
16b. घर की कौन-कौन सी बातें तुम्हें पसन्द या नापसन्द हैं?
16c. तुम घर में रहना या न रहना क्यों चाहते हो?
16d. अगर तुम घर छोड़ना चाहते हो तो कहाँ रहना पसन्द करोगे?
17a. तुम्हें किस तरह के काम या परिस्थितियों में परेशान होते हो?
17b. उन मुश्किलों के समाधान में तुम क्या करना चाहोंगे?
18a. अपने और दूसरों के बारे में तुम्हें कौन सी बातें अच्छी या बुरी लगती हैं?
18b. तुम अच्छे दिखने के लिए क्या करना पसन्द करोगे?
19a. क्या तुम्हें हर परिस्थिति में बोलना आसान लगता है?
19b. क्या कभी ऐसा हुआ है जहाँ तुम बोलने में नाकामयाब रहे। किस तरह की मुश्किल हुई थी। तुमने क्या किया था?
20a. क्या तुम अपनी सारी बातें अपने घर के लोगों को बताते हो।
20b. अपने परिवार के सदस्यों का आपकी परिस्थितियों की तरफ कैसा व्यवहार है।
21a. तुम्हें कभी ऐसा एहसास हुआ है- अगर हाँ-
उनमें कौन सी बाते हैं जो उन्हें तुमसे ज्यादा प्रसिद्ध बनाती हैं?
21b. क्या तुम उन गुणों को अपनाना चाहते हो?
22. तुम्हें किस तरह के दबाव महसूस होते हैं?
(i) सामाजिक अपेक्षाएं
(ii) भविष्य की अपेक्षाएं
(iii) शैक्षिक/स्कूल के कार्यो में अच्छी प्रदर्शनी
(iv) अन्य
23a. किस प्रकार के काम/हालत में तुम्हें ऐसा लगता है-
23b. तुम उस हालत में निकलने के लिए क्या कोशिश करते हो?

24. तुम कौन होना पसन्द करोगे और क्यों?

25a. तुम्हारे साथ कभी ऐसी कोई घटना घटी है जिसमें ऐसा महसूस हुआ हो।

25b. क्या तुम्हें कभी घर/स्कूल में कोई काम की जिम्मेदारी दी गई है? तुमने उनको कैसे निभाया?

Appendix-CIA

Adjustment Inventory for School Students- A.K.P. Sinha and R.P. Singh

1. क्या तुमको स्कूल में हमेशा किसी भी बात पर डर लगा रहता है?
2. क्या तुम अपने सहपाठियों से मिलने से भागते हो?
3. पढ़ी हुई चीज को क्या तुम जल्दी भूल जाते हो?
4. किसी सहपाठी से कुछ अनुचित बात अनजाने में बोली जाती है तो क्या तुम तुरन्त क्रुद्ध हो जाते हो?
5. क्या तुम लजालू स्वभाव के हो?
6. क्या तुमको परीक्षा से डर लगता है?
7. किसी शिक्षक द्वारा किसी गलती के लिए डांटे जाने पर तुम चिंतित रहते हो?
8. क्या तुम क्लास में किसी चीज को नहीं समझने पर शिक्षक से उठकर प्रश्न करने में हिचकिचाते हो?
9. क्या क्लास की पढ़ाई को समझने में तुम्हें कठिनाई होती है?
10. क्या तुम्हारे उन सहपाठियों को जिन्हें शिक्षक अधिक मानते हैं, ईर्ष्या करते हो?
11. क्या तुम शिक्षकों के बीच बेखटके जाते हो?
12. क्या क्लास की पढ़ाई को तुम ठीक से नोट नहीं कर लेते हो?
13. क्या तुम यह देखकर कि तुम्हारे बहुत से सहपाठी तुमसे अच्छे हैं, द्वेष करने लगते हो?
14. क्या स्कूल में तुम्हें कभी–कभी ऐसा लगता है कि तुम्हारा कोई मित्र नहीं है?

15. क्या क्लास में पढ़ाई के समय तुम प्राय: ऊँघते हो?
16. कुछ विद्यार्थियों को आपस में बात करते देखकर क्या तुम्हें लगता है कि शायद तुम्हारी निन्दा कर रहे हों?
17. क्या तुम आसानी से दोस्ती कर लेते हो?
18. क्या तुम इस स्कूल के शिक्षकों की पढ़ाई से संतुष्ट नहीं हो?
19. क्या तुम स्कूल के किसी भी कार्यक्रम में आगे नहीं आने पर दूसरों पर अपना क्रोध प्रकट करने लगते हो?
20. जब कुछ लड़के इकट्ठे होकर बात करते हैं तो क्या तुम भी बेखटके उसमें शामिल हो जाते हो?
21. क्या तुम ऐसा समझते हो कि स्कूल के शिक्षक तुम्हारी कठिनाई पर ध्यान नहीं देते हैं?
22. क्या तुम स्कूल में प्राय: उदास और खिन्न रहते हो?
23. क्या तुम सहपाठियों से मिलकर एक साथ काम करना चाहते हो?
24. क्या तुम अपनी पढ़ाई की प्रगति से संतुष्ट हो?
25. क्या तुमको ऐसा लगता है कि शिक्षक तुम्हारी अवहेलना करते हैं?
26. क्या तुम क्लास में शिक्षक का ध्यान अपनी ओर आकर्षित करने की चेष्टा करते हो?
27. क्या पढ़ाना तुम्हारे लिए भार मालूम पड़ता है?
28. क्या जब विद्यार्थी शिक्षक से तुम्हारी साधारण शिकायत की बात करता है तो तुम आवेश में आकर उसको हानि पहुँचाने के लिए प्रयत्न करना चाहते हो?
29. क्या तुम प्राय: एकान्त में रहना पसन्द करते हो?
30. क्या तुम्हारे शिक्षक पठन सम्बन्धी तुम्हारी कठिनाई को दूर करने के लिए हमेश तत्पर रहते हैं?
31. क्या तुम अपने स्कूल से प्राय: असन्तुष्ट रहते हो?
32. क्या तुम अपने स्कूल के विद्यार्थियों से मेल–जोल बढ़ाते रहते हो?
33. क्या तुम्हारे स्कूल के शिक्षक तुम्हारी प्रशंसा करते हैं?
34. क्या तुम गलती करने पर भी सीना जोरी करने पर तुल जाते हो?

35. क्या तुम क्लास में आगे की सीट पर बैठना पसन्द नहीं करते हो?
36. क्या परीक्षा में प्रायः तुम कम अंक पाते हो?
37. क्या जब शिक्षक तुमसे कोई प्रश्न पूछते हैं तो तुम्हारे मन में उनके प्रति द्वेष का भाव उत्पन्न हो जाता है?
38. क्या तुम्हारा अपने सहपाठियों से मेलजोल रहता है?
39. क्या तुम चाहते हो कि स्कूल में अधिक छुट्टियाँ रहें?
40. क्या तुम अपने सहपाठी द्वारा किये गये कुछ हंसी-मजाक की बात पर भी तुरन्त तमतमा जाते हो?
41. क्या स्कूल की गोष्ठियों में तुम खुलकर भाग लेते हो?
42. क्या तुम छुट्टी से पहले ही कभी-कभी स्कूल से चले जाते हो?
43. क्या तुम अपने सहपाठी से प्रायः झगड़ लेते हो?
44. क्या तुम स्कूल के खेल-कूद में भाग लेते हो?
45. क्या तुम्हारे कुछ शिक्षक तुम्हें प्रायः पढ़ाई के लिए डाँटते रहते हैं?
46. क्या तुमको प्रायः स्कूल में दूसरों के प्रति शक बना रहता है?
47. क्या तुम अपने से ऊँचे क्लास के छात्रों से बातचीत करने में लजाते हो?
48. क्या तुम अपने शिक्षक को आदर की दृष्टि से देखते हो?
49. जिस साथी से तुम्हारी पटती नहीं है उसके द्वारा कही गयी सभी अच्छी बात पर भी क्या तुम उद्दण्डता दिखाते हो?
50. क्या इस स्कूल में तुम्हारे कुछ घनिष्ठ मित्र हैं?
51. क्या क्लास में तुम्हारा ध्यान पढ़ाई की ओर लगा रहता है?
52. क्या परीक्षा में कम अंक पाने पर तुममें शिक्षक के प्रति द्वेष भाव उत्पन्न हो जाता है?
53. क्या तुम अपने सहपाठियों की हर प्रकार से सहायता करने में तत्पर रहते हो?
54. क्या तुम स्कूल के पुस्तकालय से किताब तथा पत्र-पत्रिकाएँ लेकर पढ़ते हो?
55. क्या तुम अपने से ऊपर क्लास के छात्रों से मिलने से प्रायः डरते हो?

56. क्या तुम स्कूल के अन्य कुछ विद्यार्थियों को चिढ़ाकर मजा लेते हो?
57. क्या तुम वाद-विवाद में भाग लेते हो?
58. क्या अपने से नीचे क्लास के छात्रों से मिलने में तुम्हें ग्लानि होती है?
59. क्या तुम अपनी नोट बुक या पुस्तक अपने सहपाठियों के माँगने पर सहर्ष देते हो?
60. क्या तुम्हें शिक्षा सम्बन्धी बातों में दिलचस्पी है?

Appendix-C1B

SCORING KEY FOR ADJUSTMENT INVENTORY FOR THE SCHOOL STUDENTS—
A. K. P. SINHA AND R. P. SINGH

Scoring Key for Emotional Adjustment

Items	*Responses indicative of Lack of Adjustment*
1	Y
4	Y
7	Y
10	Y
13	Y
16	Y
19	Y
22	Y
25	Y
28	Y
31	Y
34	Y
37	Y
40	Y
43	Y
46	Y
49	Y
52	Y
55	Y
58	Y

Scoring Key for Social Adjustment

Items	*Responses indicative of Lack of Adjustment*
2	Y
5	Y
8	Y
11	Y
14	Y
17	Y
20	N
23	N
26	N

29	Y
32	N
35	Y
38	N
41	N
44	N
47	Y
50	N
53	N
56	N
59	N

Scoring Key for Educational Adjustment

Items	*Responses indicative of Lack of Adjustment*
3	Y
6	Y
9	Y
12	N
15	Y
18	N
21	Y
24	Y
27	Y
30	N
33	N
36	Y
39	Y
42	Y
45	Y
48	N
51	N
54	N
57	N
60	N

Appendix-D1

MARKS OBTAINED BY STUDENTS IN LAST EXAMINATION IN DIFFERENT SCHOOL SETTINGS

Percentage of marks obtained by the Blind Students in Integrated Schools

Sl. No. of Students	*Marks*
1	50
2	65
3	40
4	40
5	68
6	50
7	55
8	42
9	40
10	70
11	48
12	50
13	72
14	45
15	48
16	44
17	53
18	47
19	45
20	56
21	42
22	54
23	40
24	75
25	42
26	47
27	45
28	55
29	52
30	70
31	69
32	49
33	52
34	39
35	46
36	57
37	68
38	41
39	52
40	50

Percentage of Marks obtained by the Blind Students in Non-Integrated Schools

Sl. No. of Students	Marks
1	50
2	70
3	62
4	50
5	45
6	42
7	65
8	62
9	48
10	50
11	39
12	68
13	58
14	46
15	48
16	70
17	56
18	42
19	51
20	47
21	51
22	44
23	70
24	65
25	43
26	47
27	50
28	44
29	52
30	39
31	71
32	32
33	36
34	45
35	41
36	69
37	55
38	43
39	52
40	50

Percentage of Marks obtained by the Sighted Students in Integrated Schools

Sl. No. of Students	*Marks*
1	65
2	55
3	42
4	52
5	48
6	52
7	39
8	80
9	56
10	65
11	42
12	51
13	39
14	45
15	69
16	43
17	52
18	35
19	46
20	45
21	52
22	47
23	68
24	52
25	57
26	55
27	43
28	75
29	42
30	46
31	44
32	48
33	40
34	53
35	44
36	49
37	47
38	42
39	53
40	35

Percentage of Marks obtained by the Sighted Students in Non-Integrated Schools

Sl. No. of Students	*Marks*
1	82
2	56
3	67
4	88
5	48
6	73
7	59
8	82
9	91
10	72
11	40
12	54
13	50
14	69
15	75
16	87
17	48
18	46
19	59
20	57
21	68
22	41
23	58
24	70
25	52
26	55
27	55
28	44
29	68
30	74
31	43
32	54
33	39
34	50
35	46
36	49
37	62
38	72
39	48
40	57

Appendix-D2A

STUDENT RATING SCALE

Instructions

Given below is a rating scale. There are items each of which is accompanied by certain columns containing numbers to be marked. Each of these numbers denote certain categories such as :

1-Very Good, 2-Good, 3-Average, 4-Poor and 5-Very Poor.

In case of yourself kindly read the items carefully and rate yourself accordingly by marking a Tick (   ) in the respective boxes. The information furnished would be kept confidential.

Student's Name:
Class:

	1	2	3	4	5
Overall individual academic performance					
Academic performance of the student in relation to other students in the class					
Participation in—					
(a) Classroom activities and discussions					
(b) Co-curricular activities					
Ability to complete work properly and in given time					
Ability to work independently					
Ability to follow instructions in the class					
Ability to solve any problem related to various subjects					
The quality of work done					
Self-confidence.					
Interaction with other students in different situations					
Interaction with other teachers/staff					
Behaviour in the classroom					

Thank You for your kind Cooperation.

Appendix-D2B

INTERVIEW SCHEDULE FOR STUDENTS

1. Are you regular in school? What are some of the things that make you like or dislike your school?
2. Do you regularly participate in activities of school? Do you prefer curricular or co-curricular activities?
3. Are you active in classroom participation? What are the kinds of activities that stimulate the most?
4. Which are the subjects that you enjoy the most or the least? Can you mention some of the problems that you have faced recently?
5. Have you ever faced any problem in following classroom instructions? Mention.
6. Do you face any difficulties in completing work on time? Have you experienced any such situation? What would your reaction be in such cases?
7. Do you prefer engaging in individual or group work? Can you mention of any one such activity that you have recently engaged in?
8. Do you think participation in co-curricular activities is important? Do you engage in such activities at school?
9. Are you satisfied with your present level of academic as well as non-academic achievement?–
   If yes, do you still intend to incorporate any change in your manner of performance?
   If no, what are the factors that limit your performance? What are the measures you intend to undertake to bring about improvements?
10. Do you love interacting with your peers? Can you mention of some activities you all engage in? Have you ever faced any peer related problems during your stay at school?
11. Can you mention some of the qualities in yourself that makes others prefer your company?

Appendix-D3A

TEACHER RATING SCALE

Instructions

Given below is a rating scale. There are items each of which is accompanied by certain columns containing numbers to be marked. Each of these numbers denote certain categories such as :

1-Very Good, 2-Good, 3-Average, 4-Poor and 5-Very Poor.

In case of each student kindly read the items carefully and rate the student accordingly by marking a Tick ( ) in the respective boxes. The information furnished would be kept confidential.

Student's Name:
Class:

	1	2	3	4	5
1. Regularity of attendance in the class					
2. Overall individual academic performance					
3. Academic performance of the student in relation to other students in the class					
4. Participation in—					
(a) Classroom activities and discussions					
(b) Co-curricular activities					
5. Ability to concentrate on work					
6. Ability to complete work properly and in given time					
7. Ability to work independently					
8. Ability to ask questions					
9. Ability to answer questions					
10. Ability to follow instructions in the class					
11. Ability to solve any problem related to various subjects					

	1	2	3	4	5
12. The quality of work done					
13. Social Skills					
14. Self-care					
15. Self-Expression					
16. Self-confidence					
17. Behaviour in the classroom					
18. Time management					
19. Recreation					
20. Career development					
21. Work with others					
22. Interaction with other students in different situations					
23. Interaction with other teachers/staff					
24. Attitude of other students towards individual					
25. Attitude of other teachers towards the student					
26. Emotional responses to different situations appropriate for his age					

Thank You for your kind Cooperation.

Appendix-D3B

INTERVIEW SCHEDULE FOR TEACHERS

1. Is the student regular at school and for classes?
2. How is the student's approach towards school? Does he enjoy his stay there? What are the things he likes and dislikes there?
3. What is the student's nature of participation in—
   a. classroom activities and discussions
   b. co-curricular activities
   c. any other
4. Is the student able to complete the assigned tasks on time?
5. What is the nature of the work of the student: methodological, systematic, haphazard, structured, etc.?
6. What are the common difficulties faced by him in performing his work in the classroom?
7. a. Are there any specific areas or subjects in which the student requires special assistance?
   b. What measures do you undertake to help them in such situations?
   c. What are the problems you face in this process?
8. What sort of rapport exists between the student concerned and others in both classroom and outside classroom situations?
9. a. What is the general attitude of the other students towards the inclusion of the students with special needs in the classroom?
   b. Do they engage in activities with them? If yes, then the nature of the activities they involve in? If no, then the reasons.
   c. Do they face any problem due to their inclusion in the regular classroom?
   d. What efforts they make to adjust with them?

Appendix-E

SCHOOL OBSERVATION CHECKLIST

Checklist for School Climate/Organization (Institutional Level)

Outdoor Orientation and Mobility:

- Basic traffic safety
- Location of zone in relation to building entrance
- Procedure for getting on and off vehicle
- Configuration of the playground
    a. location of the boundaries of the playground in relation to the classroom, buildings, streets, etc.
    b. location and nature of playground equipment
    c. safety rules of using playground equipments

Indoor Orientation and Mobility:

A. In the school building the student knows location of

- Main/School office
- Principal's office
- Staff room
- Library
- Clinic/sick room
- Toilets
- Classrooms
- Canteen/Cafeteria
- Exits and entrances
- Potential hazards

B. In the classroom the student knows location of

- Exit and entrance (areas often used are readily accessible)

- Configuration of desks, chairs
- Storage areas for books, school bags and other personal items
- Location of adapted computers and printers

Checklist for Instructional Strategies and Adaptations

A. Classroom supplies and equipments

- Braille writer, slate and stylus
- Magnification device
- Cassette tape recorder/player
- Raised-line or bold line paper, templates and/or writing guides
- Physical education equipment with auditory signals
- Use of models

B. Safety considerations

- Evaluate environment for potential hazards (e.g. playground structures, stairs, ramps, etc.)
- Ensure students know routines for fire drills and other emergency procedures
- Exits and entrances

C. Instructional strategies

- Reads notes aloud while writing them on board
- Provide audio tapes of reading materials
- Provide opportunities for hands-on-learning
- Specifies the instructional procedure for each lesson clearly
- Emphasizes on individualized instruction

D. Additional Curriculum Areas

- Listening skills
- Daily living skills
- Orientation and mobility

- Social skills
- Braille literacy

E. Other information

- Learn how and when students use guide, long cane etc. for travel
- Learn about magnification devices, braillers and other equipments available to and used by the students
- Familiarity with individualized education programme goals and objectives and related services
- Collaboration with other specialists working with the students (e.g. special/itinerant educator, physical trainer, counsellor, etc.)

Checklist for Interpersonal relations

Teacher

- Approves/supports inclusion/integration of students with special needs in the regular classroom
- Aware of the needs of the students with special needs
- Gives individual attention
- Personal interaction with the students
- Easily approachable
- Discusses problems, if any
- Monitors students behaviour from time to time
- Encourages and reinforces self-expression and participation of the students
- Provides assistance and structures learners' responses

Peer

- Supports the integration of students with special needs in the regular classroom
- Aware of the needs of the students with special needs

- Personal interaction with the students with special needs
  a. Sits with them
  b. Works with them
  c. Includes them in group activities
  d. Offers assistance when required
- Problems faced by the peers, if any.

Appendix-FA

REGRESSION RESULT FOR BLIND STUDENTS IN INTEGRATED SCHOOLS

Table 4.18 : Regression Summary for Self-esteem and Total Adjustment as predictor variables

R	R^2	*Adjusted* R^2	*Std. Error of the Estimate*
.089	.008	-.046	10.5232

ANOVA

	Sum of Squares	*df*	*Mean Square*	*F*	*Sig*
Regression	32.475	2	16.238	.147	.864
Residual	4097.300	37	110.738		
Total	4129.775	39			

Co-efficient Summary for Self-esteem and Total Adjustment as predictor variables

	Unstandardized Co-efficients		*Standardized Coefficients*	*t*	*Sig*
	β	*Std. Error*	β		
Constant	46.571	13.455		3.461	.001
SE	3.93	.165	.041	.238	.813
TTL ADJUST	.163	.306	.091	.534	.597

Appendix-FB

REGRESSION RESULT FOR BLIND STUDENTS IN NON-INTEGRATED SCHOOLS

Table 4.19 : Regression Summary for Self-esteem and Total Adjustment as predictor variables

R	R^2	*Adjusted* R^2	*Std. Error of the Estimate*
.627	.393	.361	8.4123

ANOVA

	Sum of Squares	*df*	*Mean Square*	*F*	*Sig*
Regression	1698.055	2	849.028	11.998	.000**
Residual	2618.345	37	70.766		
Total	4316.400	39			

**p<.01.

Co-efficient Summary for Self-esteem and Total Adjustment as predictor variables

	Unstandardized Co-efficients		*Standardized Coefficients*	*t*	*Sig*
	β	*Std. Error*	β		
Constant	24.925	7.016		3.552	.001
SE	.409	.084	.631	4.889	.000
TTL ADJUST	8.163	.260	.040	.313	.756

Appendix-FC

REGRESSION RESULT FOR SIGHTED STUDENTS IN INTEGRATED SCHOOLS

Table 4.20 : Regression Summary for Self-esteem and Total Adjustment as predictor variables

R	R^2	*Adjusted* R^2	*Std. Error of the Estimate*
.444	.197	.154	9.4973

ANOVA

	Sum of Squares	*df*	*Mean Square*	*F*	*Sig*
Regression	819.420	2	409.710	4.542	.017*
Residual	3337.355	37	90.199		
Total	4156.775	39			

* p<.05.

Coefficient Summary for Self-esteem and Total Adjustment as predictor variables

	Unstandardized Co-efficients		*Standardized Co-efficients*	*t*	*Sig*
	β	*Std. Error*	β		
Constant	32.348	9.709		3.332	.002
SE	.266	.093	.441	2.847	.007
TTL	-1.884	.352	-.008	-.054	.958

Appendix-FD

REGRESSION RESULT FOR SIGHTED STUDENTS IN NON-INTEGRATED SCHOOLS

Table 4.21 : Regression Summary for Self-esteem and Total Adjustment as predictor variables

R	*R^2*	*Adjusted R^2*	*Std. Error of the Estimate*
.301	.090	.041	13.8455

ANOVA

	Sum of Squares	*df*	*Mean Square*	*F*	*Sig*
Regression	705.566	2	352.783	1.840	.173
Residual	7092.834	37	191.698		
Total	7798.400	39			

Co-efficient Summary for Self-esteem and Total Adjustment as predictor variables

	Unstandardized Co-efficients		*Standardized Co-efficients*	*t*	*Sig*
	β	*Std. Error*	*β*		
Constant	57.797	14.244		4.058	.000
SE	.136	.157	.151	.866	.392
TTL	-.422	.360	-.203	-1.171	.249

Appendix-G

CASE STUDIES

(a) Blind students from integrated schools

Case study 1

Student V.M. (Sl.No.5)[1] of grade nine at Upras School comes from a middle class family. Treading down the memory lane, he recalled of having lost his sight at birth. The eldest of two children and having working parents made V.M. conscious of additional responsibilities of life at a very young age. Unfolding his life story he mentioned that with the growing years he has undergone several changes on his personal front from being an individual who was greatly sceptic about his life to a confident young adolescent. Referring to his childhood days he mentioned that initially adjusting to lack of sight was a difficult and traumatizing phase for him. His life was inactive and dull without any access to the external world around. V.M. mentioned that during that phase he did not have many friends or much dreams for his future. He was more dependent on other members of the family to assist him on all his daily chores. Moreover, at an age when he required continuous parental assistance he suffered a setback. Since both his parents were employed they were unable to provide adequate attention to him. Today, however, V.M. appreciates despite his parents' inability to provide time they always cared a lot and showered him with love and affection. They were always by his side encouraging him to do things on his own. He also greatly appreciated the role played by his younger sister in his life. He mentioned that although younger than him she has been his "best friend". They still share great moments together playing games, sharing

1. The serial number of the respective student in the sample is indicated in parentheses.

"secrets". She often helps to read out text material to him which he notes down in Braille.

Later on concern regarding V.M'.s future caused his parents to admit him to a special school. He was in the special school for the "differently abled" for two years after which he was shifted to a regular/integrated school (his present school). V.M. regards his entrance to the present school as beginning of a new phase in his life which ushered in him a new direction, hope and confidence. It is here that he came into contact with lots of other children, both having similar problems as his as well as non-disabled peers which eventually increased his level of confidence. On being enquired if he wanted to incorporate any change in his present life he expressed his only desire is to get rid of his anger and be good in his behaviour towards others.

Referring to his life at the school, V.M. cited innumerable incidences to show his preference for school. Today his love for school is such that he now prefers being at the school even during the school vacations. In reference to this he mentioned that initially when he had entered the school there were certain adjustment problems faced both by him as well as his sighted peers. This he feels was primarily due to their lack of awareness about dealing with individuals with "special needs". Gradually, the relationships became very cordial and helpful in nature. At present he enjoys the ambience at school and finds all his peers, teachers and other school authorities highly cooperative. He did not mention of any incidence where he had being made to feel different from others. For him his friends (sighted) were all forthcoming. They all not only share a great relationship in academic activities but they also spend a considerable time playing together, going out to picnics, etc. They also help him in taking down class notes and some of them even take time after their class hours to explain concepts to him if in case he has any problems.

V.M. appreciated his teachers who were very cooperative and understanding. They paid adequate attention to his needs and problems despite their busy work schedules. They always encouraged him engage in independent work and study. He shyly mentioned that at times they scolded him if he did any wrong with the hope that he would strive harder and perform a lot better.

Today a proud student of grade nine, V.M. is filled with confidence and acknowledges at each step that he was able to reach this stage due to the great support he received from others. Now he strongly believes that there is nothing wrong in him and like any other youth is ready to undertake the problems and challenges of life and overcome them.

Case study 2

Student A.D. (Sl.No.15) studies in grade ten at the Tagore International School. He had no sight since his birth. Recalling his childhood days, A.D. mentioned that during the initial stage of his life it was extremely difficult to cope with his blindness. He expressed deep grievance recalling the several occasions when he missed his childhood plays and had to sit back home while others played. During that period he mentioned that his parents have been understanding and supportive. They paid a lot of attention to him as well as encouraged him do things on his own. He recalled instances when his parents sat for hours pushing him to do certain things like study better, do his daily activities on his own, etc. so that he can become independent.

However, A.D'.s depressions soon caused his parents to initially admit him to a regular/integrated school with the assumption that contact with other children would make him feel better, boost his confidence thus making him feel good. Entrance to the school was a new experience for him. Initially, due to his reserved nature A.D. faced some difficulties in adjusting to his new environment. This also prevented the teachers and his sighted peers from approaching to offer assistance to him. This phase further increased A.D'.s depression and apprehensions. He mostly kept to himself and his academic activities. He also found certain difficulties in coping up with the course and the method of classroom instruction. Despite these problems, his hard work attracted a large number of people towards him and he came to be accepted by his peers (sighted) who had earlier neglected him. Interactive sessions with people soon made A.D. start liking school and the various things associated with it. Today he regards his classmates to be considerate, friendly and good to him. Soon his teachers also started regarding him to be capable of doing a lot of activities and entrusted to him a lot of responsibilities. Today he feels quite contended with whatever he is doing and has managed to achieve. He really admires his school so much that he leaves for school at the earliest possible time and even thinks of not returning home sometimes. When enquired if faced with any problems at school, he mentioned lack of adequate individualized attention and pressures of the syllabi. A.D. also mentioned that he loves reading a lot of general knowledge and fictional books. In this regard he held that although there are recorded books on various subjects in their school library there are not many for fictions. Therefore, for this, he depends on his sighted classmates to read them out to him. It is important to note that despite referring to his difficulties he is confident that since he has always been eager to learn new things he would soon be able to overcome these difficulties. Besides academics, he also likes participating in co-curricular activities such as, chess, recitation, etc.

Today after ten years in his school A.D. appears as a confident young person who is all prepared to face the diverse problems in life with the strong determination to overcome them through hard work and necessary support from others. He regards himself to be as capable as others and holds that at the end that being blind today does not matter him as much as to progress and move ahead in life. He firmly believes in the concept that 'life is to lead and not a hope to be given up'.

Case study 3

Student P.M. (Sl.No.23) of grade eleven at the Government Senior Secondary School is the eldest of four siblings. He had lost his vision at birth. For him life has been quite a long journey of varied experiences which have had significant effect on his personality. He coyly recalled the days when he was sceptic about his life, did not have much to dream and aspire for his future. It was during this difficult phase that his family especially his mother provided him great encouragement. She motivated him to take initiative in doing various activities, go out and make new acquaintances and develop confidence within himself. He laughs and recalls the moments when he even got severely scolded by her for his lack of enthusiasm despite constant encouragement. The desire to acquire a more secured future for P.M. made his parents to get him admitted to a special school for the visually handicapped. He was in the school for a brief period of 2 years during which his life took a new turn. Exposure to the world of independence taught him to do things on his own which in turn made him a little more confident. Being in contact and interacting with lots of other children having similar problems installed some hope in him. He recalled of innumerable incidences of sharing close relationship with his peers. They engaged in playing and studying together. However amidst all these he missed the company of his parents and his little sister. He made special reference to his little sister who fought but also loved him a lot. They had shared great moments playing and listening to music.

Soon after grade four he was transferred to an integrated school. Though the sudden shift in environment was initially difficult for him to adjust he mentioned that today he feels most comfortable in such an environment. With continuous assistance from parents, friends and teachers he started taking interest in various activities and managed to farewell in them. This provided a tremendous boost to his confidence. Today he is quite satisfied with his performance both at school as well as at home.

P.M. described himself as a friendly and confident individual who just like any other person of his age group is capable of doing everything. Today he is quite a social person who enjoys the company of limited but really dependable people. He has some great friends with whom he engages in playing and studying. Even within the classroom his sighted peers were found to have a positive view of him and enjoy his company. They assisted him in both his educational endeavours as well as included him in their various social activities.

Regarding his academic performance he attempts not to depend on others as far as possible. With dedication and hardwork he has reached a stage when he feels confident enough to help the other weaker students in his class. However, he gave a depressed look at the mention of doing mathematics and geography wherein he feels his lack of vision prevents him pursuing these subjects. The teachers also widely appreciated his performance and behaviour. Regarding his future aim in life, P.M. mentioned that though his parents aspire for him to become a teacher he is still engaged in exploring the various career options.

Case study 4

Student S.R. (Sl.No. 30) of grade twelve is the youngest of three children and belongs to an upper middle class family. Life for him has been a mixed experience of pain and affection. Having had lost his mother to whom he was greatly attached to at an early age greatly affected his mental make up. In addition to this since lack of vision limited his range of experiences, he gradually started developing a feeling of helplessness. According to him, his family has been of immense support during that phase. He shyly confessed that although his elder brother and sister made innumerable attempts to boost his confidence they mostly met with failure. Despite continuous encouragement from his family members he continued being a reserved child. He had little or no friends and generally avoided the company of people. He engaged in self-play and was hesitant to undertake any activities. Elaborating on his relationship with his father and siblings, he mentioned that they shared an extremely close relationship with each other. They often discussed their personal as well as other problems. They gave due respect to his feelings and showered him with affection. They also subjected him to certain disciplinary measures in order to avoid any form of unnecessary overprotective shelter. He however sadly mentioned that his father failed to provide adequate attention to his needs and problems due to his work pressures.

Soon unable to adequately cater to S.R'.s 'different' and 'diverse' needs his family admitted him to an integrated school where he continues till date. The initial few years at school was a sad experience for him. Away from his family he mostly kept to himself. Even with the classrooms he restrained from participating in activities. He did not find his sighted peers to be very forthcoming and they avoided his company. Moreover, he also found it difficult to cope up with the academic pressures. Gradually with constant pressure from his teachers he started interacting with a few children and was able to make friends. The support from teachers also helped him to adjust to the new academic requirements and his performance showed marked improvement. It was during this phase that his soft nature and good academic performance made him feel accepted by his classmates. This sense of belongingness fostered a new confidence in S.R. for whom the school soon became his favourite place besides home.

Today S.R. thoroughly enjoys the school environment and everything associated with it. Being serious in his educational endeavour has been a dominant factor that has contributed to his consistently outstanding performance. Today he is proud of his performance (he is among the top five students) and expressed his intentions to improve further.

Having undergone the diverse experiences and changes in life S.R. now believes that only work and no play makes a person dull. Today his cheerful and friendly as well as his capacity to participate in co-curricular activities in the school makes him popular among his colleagues. His social circle is quite large comprising of people both his age as well as those younger. S.R. regards himself to be a simple person and considers that everything in his life is better and he does not bother himself much regarding trivial issues. He believes in seeking perfection and has strong faith that his hard work and dedication would definitely help to attain success in life. With this in objective, he expressed his desire to become more focussed and approachable in nature so that he is liked by all and can perform his best in life.

(b) Blind students from non-integrated schools

Case study 1

Student T.P. (Sl.No.4) of grade nine at the Blind Relief Association had been blind since birth. He belongs to a middle class family and is the youngest of two siblings. Just like any other young person he expressed dissatisfaction while recalling some of his early experiences in life. During his early days he found it extremely difficult to cope with his blindness, and felt bad when he missed his childhood plays and had to sit back home while others played. He mentioned that though his parents have been highly supportive during that phase but lack of adequate knowledge to deal with a child with special needs they also faced numerous difficulties. Soon, they were informed about special schools dealing with such children and he was admitted to such institution in class one.

Entrance to the school was a new experience for him. At the initial stage it was difficult for him to adjust to the new environment. He had to undertake more independent responsibilities and decisions which he was not accustomed to. Moreover, life away from his family caused a lot of depression in him. He also faced some hesitation in making friends. However, with the passage of time his hard work and simplicity attracted a large number of people towards him and he came to be well accepted by his peers and teachers. Today most of them are considerate, friendly and good to him. He mentioned that soon his teachers also started regarding him to be capable of doing a lot of activities and entrusted to him a lot of responsibilities.

School for T.P. is second home where he is able to express himself and showcase his talents. He regards himself to be no less as compared to others in any manner. He actively participates in the daily school activities and has also managed to be awarded in a number of them. He mentioned that he has always been eager to learn new things and makes serious efforts to learn new activities and concepts as early as possible. However, the greatest challenge for him to overcome is his fear for Mathematics and History. He is however confident that with the continuous supervision of his teachers and his consistent efforts he would soon be able to overcome this shortcoming.

Revealing about his personality and life, T.P. mentioned a few problems in his life. He held that although he does not generally repent his lack of vision he occasionally realizes the importance of it in his daily life situations. This occurs when he has to travel in unknown places and has to depend on others. Moreover, even if he travels alone using his cane he is greatly pained by the sympathetic attitude expressed by the sighted for him. He feels bad when people consider him helpless and offer him assistance with that attitude. In addition to this, with his growing years and the need to establish a career, T.P. feels apprehensive of certain issues. He also wants to become a contributing member of the family. However, when further enquired on what he intends to do, T.P. mentioned that although there seems to be a lot of problems in his present life and would also be there in the future he has hope that he will overcome them with his determination, hard work and necessary support from others. He aspires for a bright future as a teacher and wants to make his parents proud and serve the country by spreading knowledge.

Case study 2

Student D.T. (Sl.No.12) is a student at the Blind Relief Association in grade ten. He has been in the institution since grade one. Being the eldest of two children (other being sighted) from a middle class background tremendous responsibilities and expectations had been placed on the shoulders of the fifteen year old.

According to D.T., he always had a simple but a well protected childhood under the careful supervision of his parents. Later with his growing years, apprehensions about his future caused his parents to admit him to a specialized school for the blind at the age of six years where he continues his education till date. D.T. shyly related some of the traumas and doubts that flashed across his mind at the mention of being admitted to a school away from his family who had been a pillar of support for him in times thick and thin. He mentioned of numerous difficulties he faced in the process of to get used to his hostel and school life at the initial stage. One of the major problems that he faced was in getting used to the ecology of the school. It was a new environment for him and he lacked training in orientation and mobility. Hence, he found it extremely difficult to access the different places. Moreover, the hostel life was also a new experience for him. Due to his reserved nature D.T. found it difficult to relate to people. For a long time, he was without any company. Later he became accustomed to the lifestyle at school. Later when he realized that there were other children in the school who faced similar difficulties it became easier for him to open up and interact with them. He soon developed a liking towards the school and started enjoying the company of his friends and teachers who were very cooperative and understanding. With their support he soon developed skills such as independent mobility, self-performing all his daily chores, adjusting to the school curriculum, etc.

According to D.T., the family has been of tremendous support in bringing about positive developments in his life.

They Till date his parents continue to be a constant source of encouragement for him, assisting him in various activities and motivating him to proceed ahead in life. At the same time, he mentioned that amidst constant encouragement they also exposed him to strict discipline so that he did not develop a sense of overdependency. He recalled instances of being scolded by his father for being unable to do certain work. Mentioning about his social life outside his family he held that though he has good friends but they are limited in numbers. He generally prefers being on his own or with his family.

Mentioning about his academic life, D.T. considers himself to be a good student. He takes great interest in the classroom activities and participates in discussions and projects. He loves studying Science and Mathematics. Regarding some of the academic difficulties he experiences he made reference to the course structure which was at times difficult for him to adjust. Initially, this made him dependent on others for assistance. This in turn caused an internal rift within himself since he thought he was not as capable as others. However, his teachers and classmates encouraged him to do work on his own despite making mistakes. This made him more responsible as he learnt to learn from mistakes and attempt to master new skills to avoid any further mistakes. Today he feels proud with his good academic result which causes a smile to flash across his parents face. However, he showed limited participation in co-curricular activities. According to him, this was partly due to his lack of interest and academic pressure.

With reference to his future dreams, D.T. mentioned that though at times he wished that he could see the world through his own eyes as his other friends, yet he doesn't repent much since he is able to do as much as others. Today he dreams big and a tint of glow appears on his face as he discloses that he aspires to be a police officer one day and remove the crime from his city. Though he has not much idea as to how his dream would reach its fulfilment but he still holds on to the hope that it would materialize one day.

Case study 3

Student S.J. (Sl.No.28) studying in grade eleven at the Blind Relief Association is the youngest of three children and belongs to an upper middle class family. From the very outset he appreciated of being born in an extremely supportive family. He proudly recalled that as a child all his needs were met with great affection. His parents loved him and respected his feelings. However, along with love and affection he was also subjected to a certain disciplinary measures. From the initial stage of his life he was not subjected to any form of unnecessary overprotective shelter. He recalled with great pride certain instances when he was even scolded for having committed mistakes, "They love and respect me, but they don't pamper me. They always taught me to be independent and have confidence and faith in myself". Although S.J. maintained low profile did not refer to any comparison by his parents with other individuals of his age group, he felt bad on being subjected to it by his other relatives. Their comparison made him feel 'different' but his parents encouraged him to overcome such thoughts.

On reaching his school going age, S.J. was admitted to the institution he is at present which opened a wide new world of experience before him. School has always been his favourite place besides home. He thoroughly enjoyed the school environment and everything associated with it. He has always been sincere towards schoolwork since the beginning and also actively participated in other co-curricular activities. He takes great interest in activities such as elocution, debates, etc. and participates whenever such programmes take place. He widely appreciated the encouragement and assistance that he received from his teachers and other school authorities which motivated him towards undertaking new initiatives. He held that his teachers paid adequate attention not only to him but also other students having similar needs. They always encouraged him to engage in independent endeavours and attempt to participate in all activities. Today he feels proud of his performance (he ranks second in his class) and expressed his intentions to improve further.

On the social front, S.J. considers himself to be cheerful, friendly, humorous and outgoing. His social circle is quite large and he is quite popular among the other kids of his age. He shares an extremely close rapport with his friends. They spend a lot of time playing games, sharing personal information, going out for movies together. According to him, the ability to adjust with different people and environment made him more acceptable by others— parents, friends and teachers.

S.J. aims to become a writer when he grows up. He feels that he needs to address some of the social issues and bring about some changes in the society. He also wishes to voice the challenges and problems of people with disabilities, so that they can progress in life. He feels that his own experience would help in expressing their needs in a more concrete manner. He hopes that his parents would continue lending their support to him in this endeavour also.

Case study 4

Student D.M. (Sl.No.30) is a student of grade twelve at the Blind Relief Association. He has been a student of this institution since grade one. He is the eldest of two children (other being sighted) and hails from a middle class background. D.M. has been blind since his birth and related several difficulties that he had to undergo and still have due to his lack of sight. Referring to his early days he mentioned that one of the major problems that he faced was his inability to move around freely and independently. At an age when all children of his age group engaged in games he recalled of gloomy times when he sat in his room. He felt angry of his helpless situation which increased all the more with his growing years. The concept of depending on others to do his work made him feel "useless".

D.M'.s parents whom he considers to be the 'best' parents in the world soon became concerned about his future and tried out various ways and means to help him. He mentioned that his parents really understood him and still continues to do so standing by him through thick and thin. However, he maintained a negative view of relatives who at times subjected him to unnecessary comparisons based on his physical "inability'. He however feels relaxed that his parents were sensitive to his needs and provided him support during those occasions.

With the attainment of school going age it became difficult in deciding on the type of educational setting for D.M. However, he was finally admitted to a special school for the visually challenged where he continues his education till date. Student H mentioned that initially he underwent a trauma at the mention of school and became apprehensive of his future. However, after a few visits he got adjusted to the newly acquired setting. He soon developed a liking towards the school, enjoying the company of his friends and teachers whom he claimed to be cooperative and understanding. Despite getting used to the school environment even today at times D.M. feels that although he participates in activities and performs his school work, he is not being able to invest his best and often feels frustrated. Relying on others for small chores even today makes him feel unhappy. Regarding his career D.M. seems to be at crossroads. He mentioned that he wishes to become a teacher but sometimes doubts if he can ever become one.

For D.M. his family members are a constant source of encouragement. They assisted him in various activities, but this help also at times made him feel overdependent. He mentioned that his parents loved him but also emphasized upon maintenance of discipline. He recalled instances when due to his repeated failures he had to get scolding from his father. Such instances of inability to do things properly made him feel bad. However, he soon realised that those immensely contributed towards his well-being.

According to him, his social life was confined to his parents and a few close friends. He generally did not enjoy the company of a lot of people and preferred staying alone. He feels that since he is not as outgoing as others it in turn limits others, preference of his company.

(c) Sighted students from integrated schools

Case study 1

Student A. R. (Sl.No.3) is a student of grade nine at the Government Co-education Senior Secondary School. Despite being the youngest of two siblings from a middle class background, he has strong faith in hard work and traditional and cultural norms. He owes this quality to his parents who from a tender age instilled good values and appreciation of culture in him. They had always been a pillar of strength for him especially his mother with whom he always shared his feelings and problems. He feels proud that she understands him well and involves his active participation in the diverse family issues. This has contributed towards making him feel confident in taking responsibilities and accomplishing them. He pointed out that his parents regarded him to be a bright child and even admitted him to school at an early age. He holds that he had always been a dedicated student and maintained a good academic record. His hard work and sincerity was even appreciated by his teachers and parents. A. R. however accepted that it would not have been possible for him to attain all these without the assistance of his parents and teachers. He strongly believes that the good habits and discipline instilled in him by all of them finds reflection in his work.

At school, the teachers continuously encouraged A. R. to actively participate in academic as well as co-curricular activities. Science and Computers are his favourite subjects and he makes conscious efforts to participate in all competitions concerning them such as Science Hunt, quizzes, etc. Referring to co-curricular activities he confessed that although he attempted several times to take active part in sports and other related activities he failed to meet with much success. He feels more comfortable being with the academics. He held that today being in grade nine he thoroughly realises the importance of the need to concentrate on studies which would play a dominant role in determining his future. He aims to become a scientist and is very optimistic that with hard work and support of his parents and teachers he would surely attain his goal in life.

A. R. regards himself to be quite a social person. He loves interacting with people of various age groups. He loves organizing various events such as quizzes, debates, etc. both at home and in class.

Case study 2

A student of grade ten at the Tagore International School, Student M.M. (Sl.No.13) is the eldest of two children. He is a young boy of great hope and high dreams. At such a young age he is well aware of his duties and responsibilities. However, this quality had acted as a pressurizing factor on certain occasions in his life. As a small child he had always felt the intense pressure of living up to the high parental expectations both socially as well as personally. This constantly subjected him to strict discipline which at times curtailed his personal freedom. Despite high parental expectations and pressures, he proudly proclaimed that his parents love him a lot. They spend quality time with him and his little sister going for picnics, playing games and watching television. He held that his father helps him with the academics while his mother looks after his social grooming.

M.M. had been in the school since his grade one. He recalled of being an average student in his initial grades. At school he had always been a shy and reserved person and restricted himself to academic activities. Moreover, his short height further lowered his confidence. He felt that others were much better to look at and hence their company was more preferred. However with continuous encouragement from his teachers and peers both his performance and personality showed a remarkable improvement over the years. He mentioned that his teachers had to face great difficulties in getting him to overcome his limitations and his shy nature. They often forced him to participate in classroom discussions, give up additional assignments and even conducted additional teaching sessions after usual class hours. His peers have also been of great assistance. They always encouraged him to go out with them, participate in various school activities. Despite such encouragement and support, M.M. still feels sad on the issue that though his academic performance has improved considerably but he fails to participate and perform well in other activities in the school.

Socially, he prefers interacting with very few people and generally loves staying indoors. M.M. desires to become a teacher in the future and hopes that he would be able to carry out his responsibilities in the best of manner. He also cherishes the secret hope that he would undergo certain changes in his physical appearance such as increase in his height, so that he can feel good looking as others.

Case study 3

Student P.S. (Sl.No.26) is an eleventh grade student at the Upras School. He is the youngest of two children and belongs to an upper middle class family. At the very outset, he greatly praised his family members whom he regards to be extremely supportive. According to him, he owes whoever he is at present to them. During his early years P.S. had been a shy and introvert person. He generally preferred being on his own and interacted with only his family members. This worried his parents who thought that attending school would eventually help him overcome this nature. With this objective in view, he was admitted to school at an early age. Exposure to the school opened out a totally new world for him. However during the initial stages, P.S. faced numerous problems in adjusting to the new environment and received innumerable complaints from the teachers and other school staff such as continuous crying, not participating in class activities, not interacting, etc. Soon these changed onto a more positive note with constant assistance of his parents, teachers as well as his friends. He recalled that under such instance though his parents showered him with great affection they also became a little stern subjecting him to certain disciplinary measures such as doing independent work, scolding on committing mistakes, etc.

Besides home, the school is P.S.'s favourite place and he is greatly attached to everything associated with it. He regularly attends his classes and is particular about his assignments. He loves studying Science and Mathematics. With constant encouragement from his parents and teachers he is sincere towards school work and more to the joy of others actively participates in other co-curricular activities such as elocution, debates, etc. Today he is widely appreciated by the school authorities for his participation and good manners.

P.S. regards himself to be quite a social person who enjoys the company of limited but dependable people. He does not consider himself to be a very social person and generally maintains a low profile regarding friends. Despite this he feels people of all age groups specially the younger ones enjoy his company. They also approach him for consultation if they have any problems. He is most comfortable with his parents and elder sister. He however loves sharing his secrets and problems with his family members. He also loves going to movies and swimming with his best friend Ayush. He aims to become an engineer though he feels it might undergo changes with better career options approaching him.

Case study 4

Student M.K. (Sl.No.38) studies in grade twelve at the Tagore International School. He is the youngest of three children and belongs to an upper middle class family. Recalling his childhood days he mentioned that all his needs were always met with great affection by his parents. He regards his parents to be the 'best' parents in the world, who not only love and respect his feelings, shower him with affection but also subject him to certain disciplinary measures. This has greatly helped him in growing up as a responsible person. They always encouraged him for independent work and experimentation. This has fostered in him a spirit of enquiry and adventure. He loves sharing and discussing whatever information he gathers with his father.

The school had been turning point in M.K.'s life. He has been a dedicated and serious student since his early years. He made conscious efforts to perform well in his class. He actively participates in class discussions and tries to be regular at his work. Though he loves studying Mathematics and Science, he generally avoids and doesn't enjoy studying English and Hindi. According to him, these two subjects generally lowers his aggregate. Regarding his performance, he widely appreciated the support of his teachers. The teachers always encouraged him to explore and experiment on new directions.

Though good in his studies, M.K. sincerely believes that only work and no play makes a person dull. By nature he had also been quite sociable enjoying the company of people. Today his social circle is quite large comprising of people of diverse age groups. He loves going out to various places, playing cricket and video games with his friends. When enquired if his company was preferred by others, he stated that they always involved him in their activities. However according to him, his short height at times makes him feel a little embarrassed in comparison to his friends though they never made any reference to it. He shyly mentioned that he hopes from the core of his heart that he can increase a few more inches in his height. This would be quite beneficial for future as he aspires to become a police officer when he grows up.

(d) Sighted students from non-integrated schools

Case study 1

Student F.A. (Sl.No.9) is a student of grade nine at the Tagore International School. He is the only child in a family of three members. From his childhood he has been a very active child taking great interest in studies as well as in social activities. He regards his childhood to be the best days of his life. Being the only child he was always showered with affection and care. His parents understood his feelings and always gave due importance to his viewpoints. This had a great influence on his life as it made him more responsible. Though he remembered certain instances of getting scolded but accepts that it contributed to his welfare. His parents assisted him in his studies and other school related activities. In this, his father played a more dominant role. Even today his father spends long hours after his office to look into his studies and at times they also have personal discussions.

Socially, F.A. is outgoing in nature and loves interacting with people from diverse groups. Throughout his childhood till his present age he had been liked by many for his good behaviour and helpful nature. Today he has a huge social circle comprising of people from diverse age group in his neighbourhood who are his good friends. They share great moments together such as playing and watching cricket, listening to new Hindi movie songs and even in playing pranks on others.

F.A. had always been a dedicated student at school. The teachers and peers praised him for his academic performance as well as social nature. The teachers regard him as a bright student full of life and enthusiasm to do new and diverse activities. They feel provided the right motivation and opportunity he would surely grow up to be a good person and have a bright career.

F.A. feels that besides the assistance of his father, he owes a lot to his teachers for his good performance. They have also played a great role in moulding his personality giving him the much needed confidence to do things independently. Science,

Mathematics and Computers are some of his favourite subjects. Referring to Computers, he mentioned that he can spend hours working on it. At school he also enjoys participating in activities such as debates and quiz but more of cricket. He regards Sachin Tendulkar as his role model and even makes attempts to play like him. F.A. dreams of becoming an engineer when he grows up and build huge bridges and more safe houses for the people.

Case study 2

Life for Student S.A. (Sl.No.17) has been a mixed experience. A student of grade ten at the Government Co-education Senior Secondary School and eldest of two children he lives with his father. Having lost his mother at the age of three, he always felt deprived of maternal love. Moreover, being the eldest of the two put added responsibilities on to his shoulders at an early age. As a child, S.A. had been a shy child who took long time to open up and interact with people except with his little sister. He recalled of many instances when his father would scold him to go ahead and interact with others and do things on his own. He holds that his father loves him and his sister a lot and despite his busy work schedule always manages to give them adequate attention and love. He assists them in their studies as well as plays and goes for outings. Despite such encouragement he still continues to be shy and introvert in nature. He interacts with only a small group of people and mostly prefers staying home.

Unfolding the varied dimensions of his personality, S.A. mentioned that on most occasions he lacks the confidence to undertake certain responsibilities for the fear of failure. He revealed that even in case of certain activities he undertook he felt unsure whether to persist ahead with them or not. He is aware that this quality could be harmful for his future and hopes one day he will be able to overcome this. He loves being at home, enjoys working on his computer and playing games with his little sister.

Though at present S.A. maintains a record of good performance, he recalls of himself being a below average student in his early grades. He feels sad that during that phase though his parents did not compare him to the other bright children in their family their relatives did. His performance was always scrutinized by them and he felt embarrassed. However, his parents encouraged him to work according to his own abilities. Today he fares well in class and enjoys studying Mathematics and Science.

The teachers referred to him as a quiet but a well disciplined child. According to them, he remains confined to himself and his academic activities. He does not interact much with the other students and also hesitates to participate in other school activities. However, he participates in class related activities and possesses a sharp mind. He is quick in solving mathematical problems and is inquisitive about new scientific knowledge. When enquired about his future he aspires to become a good doctor and serve people.

Case study 3

Student G.P. (Sl.No.22) a grade eleven student at the Upras School recalls of having always being a quite and reserved person. He is the youngest of two siblings and lives with his elder sister, mother and father. They originally hail from Pune but later shifted to Delhi when he was two years old. Since his childhood he had been a reserved person and did not interact much with others. This cautioned his parents who made all attempts to help him move of his "shell" and mingle with others. However, till date he remains the same person but hopes one day he would become more open to social interaction.

Since his early years G.P. preferred doing things on his own and availing of others, assistance only on occasions. He greatly praised his mother and sister for inculcating this quality in him. They always encouraged him to engage in independent work and to experiment with new ideas and things. They made all efforts to meet his essential requirements and look after his comforts. However, he pointed out that in doing so they never subjected him to any sort of overcare or protection. He coyly recalled some instances of being scolded for making mistakes so that he learnt not to repeat them. On looking back at those experiences he acknowledges the efforts of his parents which have helped him immensely in growing up as a responsible human being. According to him, all the members of the family share a close bondage amongst themselves by way of spending adequate time, sharing experiences, going for outings, watching movies, etc. His parents really understands him well and give due weightage to his viewpoints. His sister is extremely helpful and though ten years older than him is his best friend. G.P. did not report of having the company of a big social circle. He has a group of three friends with whom he shares his secrets and problems.

Revealing more about his own self, G.P. demurely mentioned that like most boys of his age group he is not flawless. He creates mistakes in his academics (getting low scores), watches too much of television, etc. On most occasions he accepts his mistakes. His parents, friends and teachers hold that this nature makes G.P. popular among others.

At school G.P. was found to be a good student. He performed well in his studies although his participation in the classroom and co-curricular activities was found to be limited. He diligently attends all the classes and observes the instructions given by his teachers. Though not much interactive in the class, G.P. is quite popular among his classmates for his hard work, sincerity and helpful nature. He loves studying English and Computers but really fears from Science and Mathematics. He feels that though these are not difficult subjects but he lacks confidence in performing well in them.

G.P. holds his teachers in high esteem greatly appreciating their efforts and for the motivation provided by them. He has experienced both the praises of the teachers for his good work and also their scolding for his setbacks. The teachers regard him as a good student who can perform far better provided with suitable opportunities. They also feel that at times his reserved nature restricts him from giving expressions to his capabilities. According to them, engaging in more fruitful interactions with others can prove to be more beneficial for him.

Enquired about his future goals, G.P. at present appears to be apprehensive of what he specifically wants to become but feels that he could be a good doctor. He hopes that with his growing years and more experiences he would become more focussed and would work more persistently towards his goals.

Case study 4

Student V.M. (Sl.No.36) is a student of grade twelve at the Government Senior Secondary Co-education School. He is the youngest of two siblings. Since his childhood he had been active and social in nature. He loved interacting with people from diverse age groups. He was always very talkative in nature for which he received scolding from his parents and teachers. Referring to his parents he mentioned of them being quite supportive but not that understanding. Both his parents are doctors by profession which left them with little time for their children. They at times failed to understand his true feelings that hurt him. On those occasions, he even felt like leaving home. However, his elder sister loves him a lot and takes great care of him. Besides his family, V.M. shares an extremely close rapport with his group of four friends whom he referred to as his "second family". He happily recalled all the great moments of happiness and agony they shared together. He regards them as "excellent" company who really understand his true feelings, assist him in his various endeavours and likes him just as he is. They spend most of the time playing cricket, watching movies and on occasions studying together.

At school teachers consider V.M. as a naughty child playing pranks on others and an average student. However, they feel that though a bright child he fails to perform well due to his "attention being devoted to other activities". He is however regular to his classes and completes work given on time. He loves studying Science, English and Computers but avoids

Mathematics since he finds it "numerical", "difficult and "boring". For him participation in co-curricular activities such as sports particularly cricket and basketball, elocution and debate constitutes the most exciting part of his school life. He reported of having won several medals in various events. His schoolmates also hold him in high esteem owing to his performance in these activities.

Enquired about his future plans, he aims to take up Graphic Designing though not completely sure of the requirements of the profession. Among his other dreams he also hopes that one day his parents would be able to give him his due attention and time.

Bibliography

Abadzi, H. (1985). Ability grouping effects on academic achievement and self-esteem in a south-western school district. *Psychological Abstract*, 72, 1, 266.

Abberley, P. (1987). The concept of oppression and the development of social theory of disability. *Disability, Handicap and Society*, 12, 1, 5-9.

Ainscow, M. (1991). *Effective Schools for All*. London: David Fulton.

Albrecht, G. L. (1992). *The Disability Business: Rehabilitation of America*. Volume 190, New Delhi: Sage Library of Social Research, Sage Publications.

Ames, C. (1992). Classrooms: Goals, Structures and student motivation. *Journal of Educational Psychology*, 84, 261-271.

Anderman, E. M. (2002). School Effects on Psychological Outcomes during Adolescence. *Journal of Educational Psychology*, 94, 4, 795-809.

Anderson, M., & Hughes, H. M. (1990). Parenting attitudes and the Self-esteem of young children. *Psychological Abstract*, 77, 6, 1431.

Armstrong, R. W., Rosenbaum, P. L., & King, S. (1992). Self-perceived social function among disabled children in regular classrooms. *Psychological Abstracts*, 79, 6, 2599.

Atkin, K. (1991). Health, illness, disability and black minorities: A speculative critique of present day discourse. *Disability, Handicap and Society*, 6, 37-47.

Bachman, J. G., & O'Malley, P. M. (1977). Self-esteem in young men: A longitudinal analysis of the impact of educational and occupational attainment. *Journal of Personality and Social Psychology*, 35, 365-380.

Bailey, J. (1998). Medical and Psychological Models in Special Needs Education. In C. Clark & A. Millwood, *Theorising Special Education*. London: Routledge.

Baine, D. (1986). *Testing and Teaching Handicapped Children and Youth in Developing Countries*. UNESCO.

Baine, D. (1988). *Handicapped Children in Developing Countries: Assessment, Curriculum and Instruction*. Edmonton: Vector Press.

Baker, K., & Donelly, M. (2001). The Social Experiences of Children with disability and the influence of environment: A framework for intervention. *Disability and Society*, 16, 1, 71-85.

Baker, L. D., & Reitz, H. J. (1978). Altruism toward the blind: Effects of sex of helper and dependency of victim. *Journal of Social Psychology*, 104, 19-28.

Bala, M. (1985). A comparative study of the mental make-up and educational facilities for the physical handicapped and normal children. In M. B. Buch, *Fourth Survey of Research in Education, Vol. 2.* NCERT, 1983-1988.

Baldwin, S. A., & Hoffmann, J. P. (2002). The Dynamics of Self-esteem: A Growth-Curve Analysis. *Journal of Youth and Adolescence*, 31, 2, 101-113.

Banerjee, G. (2004). *Legal Rights of Persons with Disabilities*. New Delhi: Rehabilitation Council of India.

Barber, B. K., & Olsen, J. A. (1997). Socialization in Context: Connection, regulation and autonomy in family, school and neighbourhood. *Journal of Adolescent Research*, 12, 287-315.

Barnes, C. (1991). *Disabled People in Britain and Discrimination: A case for anti-discrimination legislation*. London: Hurst and Co.

Barnes, C. (1999, December). *A Working Social Model? Disability and Work in the 21st Century*. Paper presented at the Disability Studies Conference and Seminar, Apex International Hotel, Edinburgh.

Bartle, E., Anderson, S. & Sabatelli, R. (1989). A model of parenting style: Adolescent individuation and adolescent self-esteem, *Journal of Adolescent Research*, 4, 283-298.

Barton, L., & Tomlinson, S. (1984). *Special Education and Social Interests*. London: Cromwell Publishers.

Bateman, B. (1962). Sighted Children's perceptions of blind children's abilities. *Exceptional Children*, 29, 1, 42-46.

Battistich, V., Solomon, D., Watson, M., & Schaps, E. (1997). Caring School Communities. *Educational Psychologist*, 32, 137-151.

Battle, P., & Blowers, K. (1982). A longitudinal comparative study of the self-esteem of students in regular and special education classes. *Psychological Abstracts*, 61, 1, 233.

Bauman, M. K. (1950). A comparative study of personality factors in blind, handicapped and non-handicapped individuals. *American Psychologist*, 5, 340-341.

Baumgardner, A. H. (1990). To know oneself is to like oneself: Self-certainty and Self-affect. *Journal of Personality and Social Psychology*, 58, 1062-1072.

Baumrind, D. (1991). The influence of parenting style on adolescent competence and substance use. *Journal of Early Adolescence*, 11, 56-94.

Bayliss, P. (1995). Segregation, integration, exclusion, inclusion: Frameworks and rationales. *Special Education Gent*, 7, 4-26.

Beach, J. D., Robinet, J. M. & Hakim-Larson, J. (1995). Self-esteem and Independent Living Skills of Adults with Visual Impairment. *Journal of Visual Impairment and Blindness*, 89, 6, 531-540.

Bear, G. G., Proctor, W. A., & Waldron, N. L. (1991). Evaluation Report: Integrating Students with Disabilities in the Least Restrictive Environment in Responses to Questions, Teachers and Administrators Frequently Ask About Inclusive School Programmes. *Phi Delta Kappan*, 78, 2, 150-157.

Beaty, L. A. (1993). Adolescents self-perception as a function of Vision Loss. *Psychological Abstracts*, 80, 2, 768.

Beck, A. T. (1976). *Cognitive therapy and the emotional disorder*. New York: International Universities Press.

Behl, D. D., Akers, J. F., Boyce, G. C., & Taylor, M. J. (1996). Do mothers interact differently with children who are visually impaired? *Journal of Visual Impairment and Blindness*, 90, 501-511.

Belgrave, F. Z. (1991). Psychosocial predictors of adjustment to disability in African Americans. *Journal of Rehabilitation*, 57, 37-40.

Bennett, N. (1991). The quality of classroom learning experiences for children with special educational needs. In M. Ainscow (Ed.), *Effective Schools for All*. London: David Fulton.

Berk, L. E. (2003). *Child Development* (6th ed.). Delhi: Pearson Education.

Berndt, T. J. (1996). Exploring the effects of friendship quality on social development. In W. M. Bukowski., A. F. Newcomb & W. W. Hartup (Eds.), *The Company to Keep: Friendships and the developmental significance*. New York: Cambridge University Press.

Berndt, T., & Hawkins, J. (1985). *The effects of friendships on students' adjustment after the transition to high school*. Paper presented at the meeting of the American Educational Research Association, Chicago.

Berzonsky, M. D., & Kirk, L. S. (2000). Identity status, identity processing style: A transition to University. *Journal of Adolescence*, 15, 81-98.

Bharadwaj, P. (1995). Personality factors among handicapped and non-handicapped. In M.B. Buch, *Sixth All India Educational Survey, Vol. 2*. Delhi: NCERT.

Biklen, D., Ferguson, D., & Ford, A. (1989). *Schooling and Disability II*. University of Chicago Press.

Bina, M.J. (1993). Do Myths Associated with Schools for Students Who are Blind Negatively Affect Placement Decisions? *Journal of Visual Impairment and Blindness*, 87, 6, 213-215.

Bissa, S., Singh, B. G. & Helode, R. D. (1993). Self-concept: A comparison between blind and normal students. *Perspectives in Psychological Researchers*, 16, 58-60.

Bishop, V. (1986). Identifying the components of success in the mainstream. *Journal of Visual Impairment and Blindness*, 80, 939-946.

Blackhurst, A. E., & Berdine, W. H. (1993). *An Introduction to Special Education* (3rd ed.). New York: Harper Collins College Publishers.

Blumenfeld, P. C., Pintrich, P. R., Meece, J., & Wessels, K. (1982). The formation and role of self-perceptions of ability in elementary school. *Elementary School Journal*, 82, 401-420.

Booth, T. (1991). Integration, disability and commitment: A response to Marten Soder. *European Journal of Special Needs Education*, 6, 1, 1-15.

Bossert, S. T. (1979). *Tasks and Social Relationships in Classrooms: A study of instructional organization and its consequences*. New York: Cambridge University Press.

Bowden, J., & Thornburn, J. (1993). Including a student with Multiple Disabilities and Visual Impairment in Her Neighbourhood School. *Journal of Visual Impairment and Blindness*, 87, 6, 268-272.

Bowe, F. (1980). *Rehabilitating Americans Towards Independence for Disabled and Elderly People*. New York: Harper and Row.

Bowman, J. T. (1987). Attitudes towards Disabled Persons: Social Distance and Work Competence. *Journal of Rehabilitation*, 53, 1, 41-49.

Brinker, R. P., & Thorpe, M. E. (1985). Integration of severely handicapped students and the proportion of IEP objectives achieved. *Psychological Abstracts*, 72, 3, 886.

Bronfenbrenner, U. (1979). *The Ecology of Human Development*. MA: Harvard University Press.

Bronfenbrenner, U. (1986). Ecology of the family as a context for human development: Research perspectives. *Developmental Psychology*, 22, 723-742.

Bronfenbrenner, U. (1989). Ecological systems theory. *Annals of Child Development*, 6, 189-249.

Brown, B. B., & Lohr, M. J. (1987). Peer-Group Affiliation and Adolescent Self-esteem: An Integration of Ego-Identity and Symbolic-Interaction Theories. *Journal of Personality and Social Psychology*, 52, 1, 47-55.

Buch, M. B. (1988). *Sixth All India Educational Survey, Vol. 2.* Delhi: NCERT.

Burgdorf, R. L. (Ed.). (1980). *The Legal Rights of Handicapped Persons: Cases, Materials and Texts.* Baltimore: Paul. H. Brookes Publishers.

Buunk, B. P., Collins, R. L., & Taylor, S. E. (1990). The affect consequences of social comparison: Either direction has its ups and downs. *Journal of Personality and Social Psychology*, 59, 1238-1249.

Byrd, E., Byrd, P. D., & Allen, C. M. (1977). Television programming and disability. *Journal of Applied Rehabilitation Counselling*, 8, 1, 28-32.

Cambra, C. (1996). A comparative study of personality descriptors attributed to the Deaf, the blind and individuals with no sensory disability. In S. Satapathy & S. Singhal, Mental Health of Visually and Hearing Impaired Adolescents. *Journal of Personality and Clinical Studies*, 16, 2, 119-127.

Camilleri, J. M. (1999). Disability: A Personal Odyssey. *Disability and Society*, 14, 5.

Campbell, J. D. (1990). Self-esteem and Clarity of the Self-concept. *Journal of Personality and Social Psychology*, 59, 3, 538-549.

Campbell, J. D., Chew, B., & Scratchy, L. S. (1991). Cognitive and emotional reactions of daily events: The effects of self-esteem and self-complexity. *Journal of Personality*, 59, 473-505.

Canton, H., & Rankin, E. (1980). Variability in Age and Experience among Blind Students using Basal Reading Materials. *Journal of Visual Impairment and Blindness*, 95, 5, 261-271.

Chadwick, A. (1996). Knowledge, Power and the Disability Discrimination Bill. *Disability and Society*, 11, 25-40.

Chang, S. C., & Schaller, J. (2000). Perspectives of Adolescents with Visual Impairments on Social Support from their Parents. *Journal of Visual Impairment and Blindness*, 84, 69-84.

Christensen, C. (1993). Deviant, disabled or different: the politics of labelling. *Australian Disability Review*, 3, 5-12.

Cobb, A. (1977). Blindness as Inconvenience: How Unwelcome Truth Becomes 'Myth'. *Journal of Visual Impairment and Blindness*, 71, 406-410.

Cohen, L. H., Burt, C. E., & Bjork, J. P. (1987). Life stress and adjustment: Effects of life events experienced by young adolescents and their parents. *Developmental Psychology*, 23, 583-592.

Cohen, S. (1977). Special People. In B. Lawerence, Self-Concept Formation and Physical Handicap: Some educational implementations for integration. *Disability, Handicap and Society*, 1991, 6, 2, 139-146.

Cole, S., & Lejeune, R. (1972). Illness and Legitimation of Failure. *American Sociological Review*, 37, 347-356.

Coleman, M. (1983). Handicapped labels and instructional segregation: Influences on children's self-concepts versus the perceptions of others. *Learning Disability Quarterly*, 6, 3-11.

Connell, J. P., Spencer, M. B., & Aber, J. L. (1994). Education risk and resilience in African-American youth: Context, self, action and outcomes in school. *Child Development*, 65, 493-506.

Connors, J. L., & Donnellan, A. M. (1993). Citizenship and culture: The role of disabled people in Navajo society. *Disability, Handicap and Society*, 8, 256-280.

Coopersmith, S. (1967). *The Antecedents of Self-esteem*. CA: Freeman.

Coopersmith, S. (1984). *Coopersmith Self-esteem Inventory*. CA: Consulting Psychologists Press.

Covington, M. V. (1989). Self-esteem and failure in school: Analysis and Policy implications. In M. A. Mecca., N. J. Smelser & J. Vasconcellos (Eds.), *The Social importance of Self-esteem*. Berkley: University of California Press.

Crocker, J., & Major, B. (1989). Social Stigma and Self-esteem: The Self-protective Properties of Stigma. *Psychological Review*, 96, 4, 608-630.

Cruickshank, W. M. & Johnson, G. O. (1975). *Education of Exceptional Children and Youth*. New Jersey: Prentice-Hall, Inc.

Cutsforth, T. D. (1951). The blind in school and society: A psychological study. In D. Hudson, Causes of Emotional and Psychological Reactions to Adventitious Blindness. *Journal of Visual Impairment and Blindness,* 88, 6, 499-503.

Dash, A., & Mohanty, K. (1981, November). *Some studies on perceptual socio-emotional and curiosity abilities of deaf and blind children*. U.G.C. Symposium on Physically Handicapped, Department of Experimental Psychology, Pune University.

Dash, M. (2000). *Education of Exceptional Children*. New Delhi: Atlantic Publishers.

Deci, E., & Ryan, R. (1985). *Intrinsic motivation and self-determination in human behaviour*. New York: Academic Press.

Degerner, T., & Koster-Dreese, Y. (Eds.). (1995). Human Rights and Disabled Persons: Essays and Relevant Human Rights Instruments. In G. N. Karna, *United Nations and Rights of Disabled Persons: A Study in Indian Perspective*. New Delhi: A. P. H. Publishing Corporation.

Dewsbury, G., Clarke, K., Randall, D., Rouncefield, M., & Sommerville, I. (2004). The anti-social model of disability. *Disability and Society*, 19, 2, 145-158.

Dillon, C., Byrd, K., & Byrd, D. (1980). Television and Disability. *Journal of Rehabilitation*, 46, 4, 67-69.

Dimigen, G., Roy, A. W. N., Horn, J. & Swan, M. (2001). Integration of Visually Impaired Students into Mainstream Education: Two Case Studies. *Journal of Visual Impairment and Blindness*, 95, 3, 161-164.

Dishion, T. J. (1999). The family ecology of boys' peer relations in middle childhood. *Child Development*, 61, 874-892.

Dodds, A. (1993). *Rehabilitating Blind and Visually Impaired People: A Psychological Approach*. London: Chapman and Hall.

Dodds, A. G., Ferguson, E. P., Ng, L., Flannigan, H., Haubs, G., & Yates, L. (1994). The concept of adjustment: A structural model. *Journal of Visual Impairment and Blindness*, 88, 487-497.

Dols, M. (1987). Insanity and its treatment in Islamic society. *Medical History*, 31, 1-14.

Donaldson, J. (1981). The visibility and image of handicapped people on television. *Exceptional Children*, 47, 413-416.

Donoghue, C. (2003). Challenging the Authority of the Medical Definition of Disability: An analysis of the resistance to the social constructionist paradigm. *Disability and Society*, 18, 2, 199-208.

Doob, A., & Ecker, B. P. (1970). Stigma and Compliance. *Journal of Personality and Social Psychology*, 14, 302-304.

Dornbusch, S., Ritter, P., Leiderman, P., Roberts, D., & Fraleigh, M. (1987). The relation of parenting style to adolescent school performance. *Child Development*, 58, 1244-1257.

Dote-Kwan, J., & Hughes, M. (1994). The home environment of young blind children. *Journal of Visual Impairment and Blindness*, 86, 31-42.

Dowling, M., & Dolan, L. (2001). Families with Children with Disabilities, Inequalities and the Social Model. *Disability and Society,* 16, 1, 21-35.

Dubois, D. L., Bull, C. A., Sherman, M. D., & Roberts, M.

(1998). Self-esteem and adjustment in early adolescence: A social contextual perspective. *Journal of Youth and Adolescence*, 27, 5, 557-582.

Dumont, M., & Provost, M. A. (1999). Resilience in adolescence: Protective role of social support, coping strategies, self-esteem and social activities on experience of stress and depression. *Journal of Youth Adolescence*, 28, 343-363.

Eagelstein, S. (1975). The social acceptance of blind high school students in an integrated school. In W.S. Keilbaugh, Attitudes of Classroom Teachers Towards Their Visually Handicapped Children. *Journal of Visual Impairment and Blindness*, 71, 10, 430-434.

Eccles, J., & Wigfield, A. (1985). Teacher expectations and student motivation, In J. Dusek (Ed.), *Teacher expectations*. NJ: Lawrence Erlbaum.

Elliot, T. R., & Byrd, E. K. (1982). Media and Disability. *Rehabilitation Literature*, 43, 348-355.

Elliot, T. R., & Byrd, E. K. (1984). Video Depictions of Blindness and Attitudes Towards Disability. *Journal of Rehabilitation*, 50, 1, 49-52.

Epperson, D. C. (1963). Some interpersonal and performance correlates of classroom alienation. *School Review*, 71, 360-376.

Epstein, J. L., & McPartland, J. M. (1976). The concept and measurement of the quality of school life. *American Educational Research Journal*, 13, 15-30.

Erikson, E. H. (1959). *Identity and the Life Cycle*. New York: Norton.

Erin, J. N., Corn, A. L., & Wolffe, K. (1993). Learning and study strategies of secondary school students with visual impairments. *Journal of Visual Impairment and Blindness*, 87, 7, 263-267.

Erwin, E. J. (1993). Social Participation of Young Children with Visual Impairments in Specialized and Integrated Environments. *Journal of Visual Impairment and Blindness*, 87, 5, 138-142.

Fazelhoy, R. S. (1989). Integrated Education in India: Benefits and Problems. *Journal of Visual Impairment and Blindness*, 83, 1, 47-50.

Festinger, L. (1954). A Theory of Social comparison processes. *Human Relations*, 7, 117-140.

Fine, M., & Asch, A. (1988). Disability Beyond Stigma: Social Interaction, Discrimination, and Activism. *Journal of Social Issues*, 44, 1, 3-21.

Finkelstein, V. (1990). Disability: An Administrative Challenge? In M. Oliver, *Social Work: Disabling People and Disabling Environments*. London: Jessica Kingsley Publisher.

Finkelstein, V. (1997). Emancipating Disabling Studies. In T. Shakespeare (Ed.), *The Disability Reader: Social Sciences Perspectives*. London: Cassell.

Finkelstein, V. (1998, June). *The Biodynamics of Disablement? Disability and Rehabilitation Systems Research*. Paper presented at Harare, Zimbabwe.

Finkelstein, V. (2001, December). *The Social Model of Disability Repossessed*. Paper presented at Manchaster Coalition of Disabled People.

Fordham, K., & Stevenson-Hinde, J. (1999). Shyness, friendship quality and adjustment during middle childhood. *Journal of Clinical Psychology and Psychiatry*, 40, 5, 757-768.

Foucault, M. (1971). Madness and Civilisation: A history of insanity in the age of London, In D. Reeve, Negotiating Psycho-Emotional Dimensions of Disability and their Influence on Identity Constructions. *Disability and Society*, 7, 5, 493-508.

Fox, N. J. (1993). *Post-modernism, Sociology and Health*. Buckingham: Open University Press.

French, S. (1993). "Can You See the Rainbow? The Roots of Denial", In J. Swain, V. Finkelstein, S. French and M. Oliver, *Disability Barriers, Enabling Environment*, Milton Keynes, U.K. Open University Press.

French, S. (1999). "The Wind Gets in My Way", In M. Corker and S. French (Eds.), *Disability Discourse*, Milton Keynes, U.K: Open University Press.

French, S., Gillman, M., & Swain, J. (1997). From a Different Viewpoint: the lives and experiences of visual impaired people. In T. Cook, J. Swain and S. French, Voices from Segregated Schooling: towards an inclusive education system. *Disability and Society*, 16, 2, 293-310.

Gardener, L. (1982). Understanding and Helping Parents of Blind Children,*Journal of Visual Impairment and Blindness*, 76, 3, 81-85.

Gartner, A., & Lipsky, D. K. (1987). Beyond Special Education: toward a quality system for all students. *Harvard Educational Review*, 57, 43, 367-395.

Gecas, V. (1972). Parental Behaviour and Contextual Variations in Adolescent Self-esteem. *Sociometry*, 35, 2, 332-345.

Gecas, V., & Schwalbe, M. L. (1983). Beyond the Looking Glass Self: Social Structure and Efficacy-based Self-esteem. *Social Psychology Quarterly*, 46, 2, 77-88.

Ghai, A. (2000). Towards Understanding Disability. *Psychological Studies*, 45, 3, 145-149.

Gilson, S. F., & Depoy, E. (2000). Multiculturalism and Disability: a critical perspective. *Disability and Society*, 15, 2, 207-218.

Goel, S. K., & Sen, A. K. (1985). Research in Personality dimensions on the visually handicapped. In A. Sen (Ed.), *Psycho-Social Integration of the Handicapped: Challenge to the Society*. Delhi: Mittal Publications.

Goffman, E. (1963). *Stigma: Notes on the management of spoiled identity*. Englewood Cliffs: N.J. Prentice-Hall.

Gordon, M. (1973). Role Theory and Illness. In G.L. Albrecht, *The Disability Business: Rehabilitation of America* (*Vol. 190*). New Delhi: Sage Library of Social Research, Sage Publications.

Gottlieb, J. (1981). Mainstreaming: fulfilling the promise? *American Journal of Mental Deficiency*, 86, 115-126.

Government of India. (1964). *Education and National Development: Report of the Education Commission 1964-66*. New Delhi: Ministry of Human Resource Development.

Government of India. (1990). *Towards an Enlightened and Humane Society: National Policy of Education, 1986—A Review-Part 1*. New Delhi.

Government of India (1992). *National Policy on Education 1986: With modifications undertaken in 1992.* New Delhi: Ministry of Human Resource Development.

Government of India. (1992). *Scheme of Integrated Education for the Disabled Children*. New Delhi: Ministry of Human Resource Development.

Government of India. (1995). *The Persons With Disabilities (Equal Opportunities, Protection of Rights and Full Participation) Act, 1995.* New Delhi: Ministry of Human Resource Development.

Government of India. (1995). *The Rehabilitation Council of India Act: Act No.34.* New Delhi: Ministry of Welfare.

Green, K. D., Forehand, R., Beck, S. J., & Vosk, B. (1980). An assessment of the relationships among measures of children's social competence and children's academic achievement. *Child Development*, 5, 1149-1156.

Griffin-Shirley, N., & Nes, S. L. (2005). Self-esteem and Empathy in Sighted and Visually Impaired adolescents. *Journal of Visual Impairment and Blindness*, 99, 5, 276-285.

Gronmo, S. J., & Augestad, L. B. (1999). Physical Activity, Self-concept and Global Self-worth of Blind Youths in Norway and France. *Journal of Visual Impairment and Blindness*, 94, 8, 522-526.

Gwaltney, J. (1983). *Blindness as a cultural problem*. Wenner-Gren Foundation Working Papers in Anthropology, New York.

Haber, L. A., & Smith, R. T. (1971). Disability and Deviance: Normative Adaptations of Role Behaviour. *American Sociological Review*, 36, 87-97.

Hahn, H. (1982). Disability and Rehabilitation Policy: Is paternalistic neglect really benign. *Public Administration Review*, 42, 4, 385-392.

Hahn, H. (1982). The Politics of Physical Differences: Disability and Discrimination. *Journal of Social Issues*, 44, 1, 39-47.

Haider, S. I. (1990). *A Comparative Study of some Psychological Characteristics and Academic Achievement of Visually Handicapped Children in Special Schools and in Integrated Settings*. Doctoral Dissertation, Jamia Millia Islamia University, New Delhi.

Haider, S. I. (1998). *Visually Handicapped Children*. New Delhi: Rawat Publications.

Hales, G. (1996). *Beyond Disability: Towards Enabling Society*. New Delhi: Sage Publications.

Hallahan, D. P., & Kauffman, J. M. (1978). *Exceptional Children: Introduction to Special Education*. Englewood Cliffs, N. J. Prentice-Hall Inc.

Hallinan, M. T., & Sorensen, A. B. (1985). Ability grouping and student friendships. *American Educational Research Journal*, 22, 485-489.

Harley, R. K., Garcia, M., & Williams, M. F. (1989). The Educational Placement of Visually Impaired Children. *Journal of Visual Impairment and Blindness*, 83, 10, 512-517.

Harris, P. (1995). Who am I? Concepts of disability and their implications for people with learning difficulties. *Disability and Society*, 10, 3, 341-351.

Hart, L. A. (1989). Social Acknowledgements for Children with Disabilities: Effects of Service Dogs. *Child Development*, 60, 6, 1529-1534.

Harter, S. (1983).'Developmental Perspectives on the Self-Systems'. In P.H.Mussen, *Handbook of Child Psychology, Vol 4*. New York : Wiley.

Harter, S. (1990). Issues in the assessment of the self-concept of children and adolescents. In L. E. Berk (Ed.), *Child Development*, (6th ed.). Delhi: Pearson Education.

Harter, S. (1999). *The construction of self-developmental perspective*. New York: Guilford.

Harvey, D. H. (1985). Mainstreaming: Teachers' attitudes when they have no choice about the matter. *Psychological Abstract*, 73, 9, 2491.

Hasan, Q., Khan, S. R., & Khan, M. W. (1983). Living without eyesight. *Indian Journal of Clinical Psychology*, 10, 251-256.

Hastings, H. K. (1947). An investigation on some aspects of the personality of the blind. In A. Sen (Ed.), *Psycho-Social Integration of the Handicapped: Challenge to the Society*. Delhi: Mittal Publications.

Hatcher, M., & Rasch, J. (1980). Deinstitutionalization and Community Based Treatment Alternatives. *Journal of Rehabilitation*, 46, 3, 64-67.

Havill, S. (1970). The sociometric status of visually handicapped students in public schools. In M. Hoben., & V. Lindstrom, *Evidence of Isolation in the Mainstream. Journal of Visual Impairment and Blindness*, 74, 8, 289-292.

Hayes, A. (1994). Families and Disability. In A. Ashman and J. Elkins (Eds.), *Educating Children with Special Needs*. New York.

Hegarty, S., & Alur, M. (2002). *Education with Children with Special Needs: From Segregation to Inclusion*. New Delhi: Sage Publications.

Hegarty, S., Pocklington, K., & Lucas, D. (1982). Integration in Action. In P. Bayliss, Segregation, integration, exclusion, inclusion: Frameworks and rationales. *Special Education Gent*, 7, 4-26.

Heinemann, A. W., & Shontz, F. C. (1982). Acceptance of disability, self-esteem, sex role identity and reading aptitude in deaf adolescents. *Rehabilitation Counselling Bulletin*, 25, 197-203.

Helldin, R. (2000). Special Education Knowledge Seen as a Social Problem. *Disability and Society*, 15, 2, 247-270.

Hewett, F. M., & Forness, S. R. (1984). *Education of*

Exceptional Learners. Massachussetts: Allyn and Bacon Inc.

Higgins, N. (2000). 'The Orientation and Mobility in my Life': Perceptions of people who are blind and their parents. *Psychological Abstracts*, 87, 2, 691.

Hirsch, B. J., & Rapkin, B. D. (1987). The Transition to Junior High School: A Longitudinal Study of Self-esteem, Psychological Symptomatology, School Life and Social Support. *Child Development*, 58, 1235-1243.

Hoben, M. (1980). Towards integration in the mainstream. *Exceptional Children*, 47, 2, 100-105.

Hoben, M., & Lindstrom, V. (1980). Evidence of Isolation in the Mainstream. *Journal of Visual Impairment and Blindness*, 74, 8, 289-292.

Hodapp, R.M. (1998). *Development and Disabilities: Intellectual, Sensory and Motor Impairments*. New York: Cambridge University Press.

Hoffman, E. (1975). The American public school and the deviant child: The origins of their involvement. *Journal of Special Education*, 9, 415-423.

Hoge, R. D., Smith, K. E., & Hanson, L. S. (1990). School experiences predicting changes in self-esteem of sixth and seventh grade students. *Journal of Educational Psychology*, 82, 1, 117-127.

Hornby, G. (1994). *Counselling in Child Disability Skills for Working with Parents*. London: Chapman and Hall.

Horton, J.K. (1988). *Guides for Special Education, No. 6: Education of Visually Impaired Pupils in Ordinary School*. UNESCO: Hellen Keller International.

Howell, K. (1976). *Inside Special Education*. New York: Charles. E. Merill Co.

Hubbard, I. S. (1988). An objective study of the personality of the blind. In A. Sen (Ed.), *Psycho-Social Integration of the Handicapped: Challenge to the Society*. Delhi: Mittal Publications.

Hudson, D. (1994). Self-esteem and visual impairment. In J.

D. Beach, J. M. Robinet, & J. Hakim-Larson, Self-esteem and Independent Living skills of Adults with Visual Impairment. *Journal of Visual Impairment and Blindness*, 89, 6, 531-540.

Hughes, B. (1999). The Constitution of Impairment: Modernity and the aesthetic of oppression. *Disability and Society*, 14, 2, 155-172.

Hughes, H. M., & Paterson, M. (1997). The Social Model of Disability and Disappearing Body: towards a social model of impairment. *Disability and Society*, 12, 3, 325-340.

Hull, J. (1990). Touching the Rock. In A. Dodds (Ed.), *Rehabilitating Blind and Visually Impaired People: A Psychological Approach*. London: Chapman and Hall.

Hurt, J. (1988). *Outside the Mainstream: A history of special education*. London: Batsford.

Husain, M. G. (1984). *Problems and Potentials of the Handicapped*. New Delhi: Atlantic Publishers.

Husen, T., & Posethelwaite, T. N. (1994). *The International Encyclopedia of Education*. Oxford: Pergamon Press.

Huure, T. M., Komulainen, E. J., & Aro, H. M. (1999). Social Support and Self-esteem among Adolescents with Visual Impairment. *Journal of Visual Impairment and Blindness*, 93, 1, 26-37.

India Today. (1987, November). *The burdened child*, pp. 11-24.

Jahoda, A., Markova, I., & Cattermole, M. (1988). Stigma and the self-concept of people with a mental handicap. *Journal of Mental Deficiency Research*, 32, 103-115.

Jangira, N. K. (1987). Education for Rehabilitation of the Disabled. *Indian Journal of Disability and Rehabilitation*, 1, 9-12.

Jangira, N.K. (1987). *Small group work choices of visually impaired and other children in integrated settings*. New Delhi: DTESEES, NCERT.

Jangira, N. K., & Mani, M. N. G. (1990). *Integrated Education for Visually Handicapped: Management Perspective*. Delhi: Academic Press.

Jernigan, K. (1965). *Blindness—Concepts and Misconceptions*. Baltimore: National Federation of the Blind.

Jindal-Snape., Kato. M., & Maekawa, H. (1998). Using self-evaluation procedures to maintain social skills in a child who is blind. *Journal of Visual Impairment and Blindness*, 92, 362-366.

Johnson, W. D., & Johnson, T. R. (1990). Integrating Handicapped Students into the Mainstream. *Exceptional Children*, 47, 2, 90-99.

Joiner, J. G., Lovett, P. S., & Goodwin, L. K. (1989). Positive Assertion and Acceptance among Persons with Disabilities. *Journal of Rehabilitation*, 55, 3, 22-29.

Jones, E., Farina, A., Hastorf, A. H., Markus, H., Miller, D. T., & Scott, R. A. (1984). *Social Stigma: The psychology of marked relationships*. New York: Freeman.

Juni, S., & Roth, M. (1981). Sexism and handicapism in interpersonal helping. *Journal of Social Psychology*, 115, 175-181.

Kairie, M. W. (2004). Education of Students with Visual Impairments in Kenya: Trends and Issues. *International Journal of Special Education*, 19, 2, 16-22.

Kalyanpur, M. (1996). The Influence of Western Special Education on Community-based Services in India. *Disability and Society*, 11, 2, 249-270.

Karna, G.N. (1999). *United Nations and Rights of Disabled Persons: A Study in Indian Perspective*. New Delhi: A. P. H. Publishing Corporation.

Karna, G.N. (2001). *Disability Studies in India: Retrospect and Prospects*. New Delhi: Gyan Publishing House.

Kassebaum, G. C., & Bauman, B. O. (1965). Dimensions of the Sick Role in Chronic Illness. *Journal of Health and Human Behaviour*, 6, 16-20.

Katz, I., & Glass, D. C. (1979). An ambivalence theory of behaviour towards the stigmatized. In C. J. Taylor, Factors Affecting Behaviour Towards People With Disabilities, *The Journal of Social Psychology*, 138, 6, 766-771.

Kauffman, J. M., & Hallahan, D. P. (1981). *Handbook of Special Education*. New Delhi: Prentice-Hall.

Kauffman, M. J., Gottlieb, J., Agard, J. A., & Kukic, M. B. (1975). Mainstreaming: Towards an explication of the construct. *Focus on Exceptional Children*, 7, 1-12.

Kef, S. (2004). The role of parental and peer support in adolescents well-being: A comparison of adolescents with and without a visual impairment. *Journal of Adolescence*, 27, 4, 453-466.

Kekelis, F., & Anderson, E. (1984). Family Communication styles and language. *Journal of Visual Impairment and Blindness*, 78, 54-65.

Kernis, M. H., Brown, A. C., & Brody, G. H. (2000). Fragile self-esteem in children and its associations with perceived patterns of parent child communication. *Psychological Abstract*, 87, 2171.

Khalil, F. I. (1993). The effect of rehabilitation with microcomputer access on blind people's locus-of-control, self-efficacy and self-esteem. *Dissertation Abstract International*, 53, 9, 3170.

Kirk, S. A., & Gallagher. (1979). *Educating Exceptional Children*. Boston: Houghton Mifflin Co.

Kirk, S. A., &. Weiner, B. B. (1963). *Behavioural Research on Exceptional Children*. Washington. D C.: NEA.

Kleck, R., Buck, P. L., Goller, W. L., London, R.S., Pfeiffer, J.R., & Vukcevic, D.P. (1968). Effect of stigmatizing conditions of the use of personal space. *Psychological Reports*, 23, 111-118.

Kleck, R., Ono, H., & Hastorf, A. H. (1966). The effects of physical deviance on face-to-face interaction. *Human Relations*, 19, 425-436.

Kleege, G. (1999). *Sight Unseen*, New Haven, CT: Yale University Press.

Kling, K. C., Hyde, J. S., Showers, C. J., & Buswell, B. N. (1999). Gender differences in self-esteem: A meta analysis. *Psychological Bulletin*, 125, 153-161.

Konarska, J. (2003). Childhood Experiences and Self-acceptance of Teenagers with Visual Impairment. *International Journal of Special Education*, 18, 2, 52-56.

Kroger, J. (1989). *Identity in Adolescence: The Balance between Self and Other*. New York: Routledge.

Kroger, J. (1995). The differentiation of "firm" and "developmental" foreclosure identity statuses: A longitudinal study. *Journal of Adolescent Research*, 10, 317-337.

Kroger, J. E. (1980). Residential mobility and self-concept in adolescence. *Adolescence*, 15, 967-977.

Kundu, C. L. (2000). *Status of Disability in India 2000*. New Delhi: Rehabilitation Council of India.

Laird, E. (1992). Personal Communicated. In M. J. Bina, Do Myths Associated with Schools for Students Who are Blind Negatively affect Placement Decisions?. *Journal of Visual Impairment and Blindness*, 87, 6, 213-215.

Lalkhen, Y., & Norwich, B. (1990). The Self-concept and Self-esteem of Adolescents with Physical Impairments in Integrated and Special School Settings. *European Journal of Special Needs Education*, 5, 1, 1-12.

Lambert, N. M. (1972). Intellectual and non-intellectual predictors of high school status. *Journal of Special Education*, 6, 247-259.

Land, S., & Vineberg, S. (1965). Locus of control in blind children. *Exceptional Children*, 31, 257-260.

Landua, E. D., Epstein, S. L., & Stone, A. P. (1978). *The Exceptional Child through Literature*. New Jersey: Prentice-Hall Inc.

Large, T. (1982). The Effects of Attitudes Upon the Blind: A Re-examination. *Journal of Rehabilitation*, 42, 2, 33-34.

Lawerence, B. (1991). Self-concept Formation and Physical Handicap: Some educational implications for integration. *Disability and Society*, 6, 2, 139-146.

Leicester, M. (1999). Disability Voice: Towards an enabling

education. In T. Cook, J. Swain and S. French, Voices from Segregated Schooling: Towards an inclusive education system. *Disability and Society*, 16, 2, 293-310.

Leonard, B.D. (1978). Impaired view: Television portrayal of handicapped people. *Dissertation Abstracts International*, 39, 2603A-2604A.

Levi, D. (1941). The evil eye and the lucky hunchback. In M. Miles, Disability in an Eastern Religious Context: Historical perspectives, *Disability and Society*, 10, 1, 49-65.

Li, L., & Moore, D. (1998). Acceptance of Disability and its correlates. *Journal of Social Psychology*, 138, 1, 13-25.

Libert, R.M. (1975). Television and Attitudes. In C. Dillon; K. Byrd & D. Byrd, Television and Disability. *Journal of Rehabilitation*, 46, 4, 67-69.

Linkowski, D. C. (1998). The Acceptance of Disability Scale: An update 1969-1983. In L. Li & D. Moore, Acceptance of Disability and its correlates. *Journal of Social Psychology*, 138, 1, 13-25.

Linkowski, D. C., & Dunn, M. A. (1974). Self-concept and acceptance of disability. *Rehabilitation Counselling Bulletin*, 17, 28-32.

Lipsky, D. K., & Gartner, A. (1987). Capable of Achievement and Worthy of Respect: Education for Handicapped Students as if they were full-fledged Human Beings. *Exceptional Children*, 54, 1, 69-74.

Llewwllyn, A., & Hogan, K. (2000). The Use and Abuse of Models of Disability. *Disability and Society*, 15, 1, 157-165.

Lockwood, R. (1983). The influence of animals on social perception. In B. Mader & L. A. Hart, Social Acknowledgements for Children with Disabilities: Effects of Service Dogs. *Child Development*, 60, 6, 1529-1534.

Long, B. H., Henderson, E. H., & Ziller, R. C. (1967). Developmental changes in the self-concept during middle childhood. *Merrill-Palmer Quarterly*, 10, 201-215.

Lopez-Justicia, M. D., Pichardo, M. C., Amezcua, J. A., &

Fernandez, E. (2001). The Self-concepts of Spanish Children and Adolescents with Low Vision and Their Sighted Peers. *Journal of Visual Impairment and Blindness*, 95, 3, 150-160.

Lowenfeld, B. (1963). The Visually Handicapped. *Review of Educational Research*, 33, 1, 38-47.

Luthra, P. N. (1974). Role of Department of Social Welfare in the Rehabilitation of the Handicapped. *Journal of Rehabilitation in Asia*, 15, 9-19.

MacIver, D. (1987). Classroom Factors and Student Characteristics Predicting Students' Use of Achievement Standards during Ability Self-Assessment. *Child Development*, 58, 1258-1271.

Mader, B., & Hart, L. A. (1989). Social Acknowledgements for Children with Disabilities: Effects of Service Dogs. *Child Development*, 60, 6, 1529-1534.

Maehr, M. L., & Midgley, C. (1991). Enhancing student motivation: A school-wide approach. *Educational Psychologist*, 26, 39-427.

Mallory, B. L., Nichols, R. W., Charlton, J. I., & Marfo, K. (1993). Traditional and Changing Views of Disability in Developing Societies, in M. Miles, Disability in an Eastern Religious Context: historical perspectives,. *Disability and Society*, 10, 1, 1995, 49-69.

Mani, D. R. (1988). *The Physically Handicapped in India: Policy and Programme*. New Delhi: Ashish Publications.

Marchant, G. J., Paulson, S. E., & Rothlisberg, B. A. (1995, April). *The road to school success: Students' perceptions of parenting, teaching, and school*. Paper presented at the American Educational Research Association, San Francisco, CA.

Marcia, J. E. (1966). Development and validation of ego identity status. *Journal of Personality and Social Psychology*, 3, 551-558.

Marcia, J. E., Waterman, A. S., Matteson, D. R., & Orlofsky, J. L. (1990). *Ego identity: A handbook for psycho-social research*. New York: Springer-Verlag.

Marks, D. (1999). Dimensions of Oppression: theorizing the

embodied subject, Disability in an Eastern Religious Context: Historical Perspectives. *Disability and Society*, 14, 5, 611-626.

Marsh, H. W. (1990). The structure of academic self-concept: The Marsh/Shavelson model. *Journal of Educational Psychology*, 82, 623-636.

Marsh, H. W., Parker, J.W., & Barnes, J. (1985). Multidimensional adolescent self-concepts: Their relationship to age, sex and academic measures. *American Research Educational Council*, 22, 422-444.

Marsh, H. W., Smith, T. D., & Barnes, J. (1985). Multidimensional self-concepts: Relations with sex and academic achievement. *Journal of Personality and Social Psychology*, 77, 5, 581-596.

Marshall, H. H., & Weinstein, R. S. (1984). Classroom factors affecting students' self-evaluations: An interactional model. *Review of Educational Research*, 54, 301-325.

Martinez, R., & Sewell, K. W. (1996). Self-concept of Adults with Visual Impairments. *Journal of Rehabilitation*, 62, 2, 55-58.

Martinot, D., & Monteil, J. M. (1995). The academic self-schema: An experimental illustration. *Learning and Instruction*, 5, 63-76.

Martinot, D., & Monteil, J. M. (2000). Use of the Self-concept in Forming Preferences by French Student of Different Levels of Academic Achievement. *Journal of Personality and Social Psychology*, 140, 1, 119-131.

McCarthy, J. D., & Hoge, D. R. (1982). Analysis of Age Effects in Longitudinal Studies of Adolescent Self-esteem. *Developmental Psychology*, 18, 3, 372-379.

McDaniel, J. (1976). *Physical disability and human behaviour*. Elmsford, NY: Pergamon Press.

McGaha, C. G., & Farran, D. C. (2001). Interactions in an Inclusive Classroom. *Journal of Visual Impairment and Blindness*, 95. 2, 80-94.

Mead, G.H. (1934). *Mind, Self and Society*. Chicago: University of Chicago Press.

Merell, K. W., Cedeno, C. J., & Johnson, E. R. (1993). The

relationship between Social behaviour and Self-concept in school settings. *Psychology in Schools*, 30, 293-298.

Messent, P. (1984). Correlates and effects of pet ownership. In B. Mader & L. A. Hart (1989). Social Acknowledgements for Children with Disabilities: Effects of Service Dogs. *Child Development*, 60, 6, 1529-134.

Michalko, R. (1998). *Mystery of the Eye and the Shadow of Blindness*, Toronto: University of Toronto Press.

Miles, C. (1991). Mobilising skills for special education in Pakistan: A personal cross-cultural experience. *International Journal of Special Education*, 6, 201-212.

Miles, M. (1995). Disability in an Eastern Religious Context: Historical perspectives. *Disability and Society*, 10, 1, 49-65.

Mittler, P., Mittler, H., & McConachie, H. (1986). *Guides for Special Education, No. 2: Working Together: Guidelines for partnership between professionals and parents of children and young people with disabilities*. UNESCO.

Moore, J.P. (1991). Occupational Self-efficacy, Career Beliefs and Self-esteem of Visually Impaired Students. *Dissertation Abstract International*, 54, 4, 1243.

Moos, R. (1978). A typology of junior high school classrooms. *American Educational Research Journal*, 15, 53-66.

Morris, J. (1994). 'Prejudice'. In S. French (Ed.) *On Equal Terms Working with Disabled People*. Oxford: Butterworth-Heinemann Ltd.

Morrison, J. M., & Ursprung, A. W. (1987). Children's Attitudes Toward People with Disabilities: A Review of the Literature. *Journal of Rehabilitation*, 53, 1, 45-49.

Narasimhan, M. C., and Mukherjee, A. K. (1986). *Disability: A continuing challenge*. New Delhi: Wiley Eastern Ltd.

Nathan, R. (1991). After me, what?. *Times of India*, October, p. 3.

NCERT. (2000). *First Regional Workshop: Assessment of Needs for Inclusive Education*. International Centre for

Special Needs Education, NCERT: New Delhi.

Neidenthal, P. M., Cantor, N., & Kihlstrom, J. F. (1985). Self to prototype matching: A strategy for social decision-making. *Journal of Personality and Social Psychology*, 48, 575-584.

Newman, B. M., Lohman, B. J., Newman, P. R., Myers, M. C., & Smith, V. L. (2000). Experiences of urban youth navigating the transition to ninth grade. *Youth and Society*, 31, 387-416.

Newman, P. R., & Newman, B. M. (1976). Early adolescence and its conflict: Group identity vs. alienation. In B. B. Brown and M. J. Lohr, Peer-Group Affiliation and Adolescent Self-esteem: An Integration of Ego-Identity and Symbolic-Interaction Theories. *Journal of Personality and Social Psychology*, 52, 1, 47-55.

Nurmi, J. E., & Pullianien, H. (1991). The changing parent child relationship, self-esteem and intelligence as determinants of orientation to the future during early adolescence. *Psychological Abstract*, 78, 10, 2719.

O'Moore, M. (1980). Social acceptance of the physically handicapped child in the ordinary school. *Child Care, Health and Development*, 6, 6, 317-328.

O'Toole, B. J. (1991). *Guide to Community-based Rehabilitation Services*. UNESCO.

Obeyeskere, G. (1977). The theory and practice of psychological medicine in the Ayurvedic tradition. In M. Miles, Disability in an Eastern Religious Context: historical perspectives. *Disability and Society*, 10, 1, 1995.

Obiakor, F. E., & Stile, S. S. (1990). The Self-concepts of Visually Impaired and normally sighted middle Children. *Journal of Psychology*, 124, 2, 199-206.

Oliver, M. (1983). *Social Work with Disabled People*. London: The Macmillan Press Ltd.

Oliver, C. (1986). Self-concept Assessment: A Case study. *Mental Handicap*, 14, 24-25.

Oliver, M. (1990). *The Politics of Disablement*. London:

Macmillan Press.

Oliver, M., & Zarb, G. (1989). The Politics of Disability: A new approach. *Disability, Handicap and Society*, 4, 3, 221-239.

Orkan-Lecka, M. (1980). Blind adolescents' adjustment to disability in two different settings. *Psychological Abstracts*, 64, 3, 705.

Pal, G. (2000). Education of the Disabled: The Shifting Paradigms. *Perspectives in Education*, 18, 1, 31-42.

Parish, T., Baker, S., Arheart, K., & Adamchak, P. (1980). Normal and exceptional children's' attitudes towards themselves and one another. *Journal of Psychology*, 104, 2, 249-253.

Paulson, S. E., Marchant, G. J., & Rothlisberg, B. A. (1998). Early Adolescents' Perceptions of Patterns of Parenting, Teaching, and School Atmosphere. *Journal of Early Adolescence*, 18, 1, 5-26.

Perez, M. I. M., & Lopez, R. L. C. (2000, July). *The Influence of Variable Psycho-social Self-concept in the School Performance of the Blind and/or Visually Impaired*. Paper presented at International Council for Education of People with Visual Impairment (ICEVI, European Conference), Cracow-Poland.

Peters, S. (1996). The Politics of disability identity. In L. Barton (Ed.). *Disability and Society: emerging issues and insights*. London: Longman.

Pfeiffer, D. (1998). The ICIDH and Need for its Revision, Disability in an Eastern Religious Context: Historical perspectives. *Disability and Society*, 13, 4, 503-523.

Pierce, J.W., & Wardle, J. (1996). Body size, parental appraisal and self-esteem in blind children. *Journal of Child Psychology and Psychiatry*, 37, 205-212.

Piers, E., & Harris, D. (1964). Age and other correlates of self-concept. *Journal of Educational Psychology*, 55, 91-95.

Pijl, S. J., & Meyer, C. J. W. (1991). Does Integration count for much? An analysis of the practice of integration in eight countries. *European Journal of Special Needs Education*, 6, 2, 100-110.

Pijl, S. J., Meyer, C. J. W., & Hegarty, S. (1997). *A Global Agenda*. London: Routledge.

Priestley, M. (1998). Constructions and Creations: Idealism, materialism and disability theory. *Disability and Society*, 13, 1, 75-94.

Proctor, T. B., & Choi, H. S. (1994). Effects of Transition from Elementary School to Junior High School on Early Adolescents' Self-esteem and Perceived Competence. *Psychology in the Schools*, 31, 319-327.

Quay, H. C. (1973). Special Education: Assumptions, Techniques Evaluative Criteria. *Exceptional Children*, 40, 3, 165-170.

Quinn, G. (1995). The International Convention on Civil and Political Rights and Disability: A conceptual framework. In G. N. Karna, *United Nations and Rights of Disabled Persons: A Study in Indian Perspective*. New Delhi: A. P. H. Publishing Corporation.

Quinn, P. (1998). *Understanding Disability: A Life Approach*. New Delhi: Sage Publications.

Reddy, N. Y. (1997). Personality correlates of coping behaviour in the physically handicapped students, *Disabilities and Impairments*, 11, 24-32.

Reeve, D. (2002). Negotiating Psycho-emotional Dimensions of Disability and their Influence on Identity Constructions. *Disability and Society*, 17, 5, 493-508.

Reiber, R .W., & Carton, A. S. (1993). (Eds.). *The Collected Works of L. S. Vygotsky, Volume 2: The Fundamentals of Defectology*. New York.

Reindal, S. M. (1995). Discussing Disability: An investigation into theories of Disability. *European Journal of Special Needs Education*, 10, 1, 58-69.

Reitzes, C. D., & Multran, E. (1980). Factors influencing

educational expectations and academic performance. In S. Satapathy, *Psycho-Social Dynamics of Academic Performance of Sensory Impaired Adolescents*, Doctoral Thesis, JNU, New Delhi, 2000.

Renick, M. J., & Harter, S. (1989). Impact of social comparisons on the developing self-perceptions of learning disabled students. *Journal of Educational Psychology*, 81, 4, 631-638.

Reynolds, M. C., & Wang, M. C. (1983). Restructuring 'special' education school programmes: A position paper. *Policy Studies Review*, 2, 1, 189-212.

Reynolds, M. C., Wang, M. C., & Walberg, H. J. (1987). The Necessary Restructuring of Special and Regular Education. *Exceptional Children*, 53, 5, 391-398.

Richardson, S. A., Hastroff, A. H., & Dornsbuch, S. M. (1964). Effects of disability on a Child's Description of Himself. *Child Development*, 35, 893-907.

Roberts, A., Seidman, E., Pedersen, S., Chesir-Teran, D., & Allen, L. L. (2000). Perceived Family and Peer Transactions and Self-esteem among Urban Early Adolescents. *Journal of Early Adolescence*, 20, 1, 68-92.

Roberts, R. E. L., & Bengston, V. L. (1996). Affective ties to parents in early adulthood and self-esteem across 20 years. *Social Psychology Quarterly*, 59, 96-106.

Roeser, R. W., Midgley, C., & Urdan, T. C. (1996). Perceptions of the School Psychological Environment and Early Adolescent's Psychological and Behavioural Functioning in School: The Mediating Role of Goals and Belonging. *Journal of Educational Psychology*, 88, 408-422.

Roeser, R. Wolf, K.van der., & Strobel, K. R. (2001). On the Relation between Social-emotional and School Functioning During Early Adolescence: Preliminary Findings from Dutch and American Samples. *Journal of School Psychology*, 39, 2, 111-139.

Rosenberg, M. (1965). *Society and the Adolescent Self-*

Image. NJ: Princeton University Press.

Rosenberg, M. (1985). Self-concept and psychological well-being in adolescence. In R. L. Leahy (Ed.), *The Development of Self*. FL: Academic Press.

Rosenblum, L. P. (2000). Perceptions of the Impact of Visual Impairment on the Lives of Adolescents. *Journal of Visual Impairment and Blindness*, 94, 7, 434-445.

Rosenholtz, S. J., & Simpson, C. (1984a). Classroom organization and student stratification. *Elementary School Journal*, 85, 21-37.

Rosenholtz, S. J., & Simpson, C. (1984b). The formation of ability conceptions: Developmental trend or social comparison. *Review of Educational Research*, 54, 31-63.

Rossman, A. (1962). Social structure and acculturation among the Kanuri of Northern Nigeria. In J. Scheer and N. Groce, Impairment: A Human Constant: Cross-cultural and Historical Perspective on Variation, *Journal of Social Issues*, 44, 1, 23-27.

Roy, A. W. N., & MacKay, G. F. (2002). Self-perception and Locus of Control in Visually Impaired College Students with Different Types of Vision Loss. *Journal of Visual Impairment and Blindness*, 96, 254-266.

Rutter, M. (1983). School effects on pupil progress: Research findings and policy implications. *Child Development*, 54, 1-29.

Ryan, R. M., & Grolnick, W. S. (1986). Origins and Pawns in the classroom: Self-report and projective assessments of individual differences in children's perceptions. *Journal of Personality and Social Psychology*, 50, 550-558.

Ryan, R. M., Stiller, J. D., & Lynch, J. H. (1994). Representations of relationships to teachers, parents, and friends as predictors of academic motivation and self-esteem. *Journal of Early Adolescence*, 14, 226-249.

Saez, P. E. (1989). Integration of Blind and Visually Impaired Children: The Philosophy. *Journal of Visual Impairment and Blindness*, 83, 1, 54-58.

Salend, S. (1994). Factors contributing to the development of successful mainstreaming programmes. *Exceptional Children*, 50, 409-415.

Samerotte, G., & Harris, M. (1976). Some factors influencing helping: The effects of a handicap, responsibility and requesting help. *Journal of Social Psychology*, 39, 883-886.

Sartre, J. P. (1958). *Being and Nothingness: An essay on phenomenological ontology*, translated by H. E. Barnes. London: Metheun and Co.

Sartre, J. P. (1982). Critique of Dialectical Reasoning. In B. Hughes, The Constitution of Impairment: Modernity and aesthetic oppression. *Disability and Society*, 14, 2, 155-172.

Satapathy, S., & Singhal, S. (2000). Mental Health of Visually and Hearing Impaired Individuals. *Personality and Clinical Studies*, 16, 2, 119-127.

Satapathy, S., & Singhal, S. (2001). Predicting Social-Emotional Adjustment of the Sensory Impaired Adolescents. *Journal of Personality and Clinical Studies,* 17, 2, 85-93.

Saxena, R. R. (1981). *Third All-India Educational Survey: Institutions for Physically Handicapped Persons*. Delhi: NCERT.

Scheer, J., & Groce, N. (1988). Impairment : A Human Constant: Cross-Cultural and Historical Perspective on Variation. *Journal of Social Issues*, 44, 1, 23-27.

Schneider, C.R., & Anderson, W. (1980). Attitudes toward the Stigmatized: Some insights from recent research. *Rehabilitation Counselling Bulletin*, 23, 299-313.

Scott, R. A. (1969). The making of blind men. In D.Hudson, Causes of Emotional and Psychological Reactions to Adventitious Blindness. *Journal of Visual Impairment and Blindness*, 88, 6, 498-503.

Seetharam, M. (1982). *Study of the Centrally Sponsored Scheme of Integrated Education for Handicapped*

Children in Normal Schools in Delhi. New Delhi: Council for Social Development.

Seighart, P. (1985). *The Lawful Rights of Mankind: An Introduction into the International Legal Code of Human Rights.* Oxford.

Shakespeare, T. (1994). Cultural Representation of disabled People: dustbins or disapproval? *Disability and Society*, 9, 3, 283-301.

Shakespeare, T. (1997, December). 'Researching Disabled Sexuality'. In C. Barnes, *A Working Social Model? Disability and Work in the 21st Century.* Paper presented at the Disability Studies Conference and Seminar, Edinburgh.

Sharma, N. (2001). *Cognitive Styles and Language Comprehension of the Blind.* New Delhi: Rawat Publications.

Sharma, S. (1988). Mainstreaming the Visually Handicapped. *Indian Educational Review*, 23, 4, 30-41.

Sharma, S., Sigafoos, J., & Carroll, A. (2000). Social Skills assessment of Indian children with visual impairments. *Journal of Visual Impairment and Blindness*, 94, 3, 172-176.

Sherill, C., Hinson, M., Gench, B., Kennedy, S., & Low, L. (1990). Self-concepts of disabled youth athletes. *Perceptual and Motor Skills*, 70, 1093-1098.

Shrauger, J. S., & Shoeneman, T. J. (1979). Symbolic Interactionist View of Self-concept: Through the Looking Glass Darkly. *Psychological Bulletin*, 86, 3, 549-573.

Sieber, R. T. (1979). Classmates as workmates: Informal peer activity in the elementary school. In K. R. Wentzel, Relations between Social Competence and Academic Achievement in Early Adolescence. *Child Development*, 62, 1066-1078.

Simmons, R., Rosenberg, F., & Rosenberg, M. (1973). Disturbance in the self-image at adolescence. *American Sociological Review*, 38, 553-568.

Simmons, R. G., Blyth, D. A., Van Cleave, E. F., & Bush,

D. M. (1979). Entry into early adolescence: The impact of school structure, puberty, and early dating on self-esteem. *American Sociological Review*, 44, 948-967.

Simmons, R. G., Rosenberg, M., & Rosenberg, F. (1973). Disturbance in the Self-Image at Adolescence. *American Sociological Review*, 38, 553-568.

Singh, V. P., & Akhtar, S. N. (1971). A comparative study of the self-concept of visually handicapped and non-handicapped children. *Indian Journal of Psychology*, 8, 2, 53-55.

Singh. J. P. (2004, March). *Education for Persons with Disabilities, HRD Needs and the Role of Social Scientists.* Paper presented at International Conference on Education and the Social Science Paradigms, New Delhi: JNU.

Sinha, S. P. (1982). Personality adjustment of the blind students. Indian *Journal of Psychometry and Education*, 13, 37-42.

Slee, R. (1993). The Politics of Integration—New sites for old practices?. *Disability, Handicap and Society*, 8, 4, 351-360.

Smith, S. M., & Petty, R. E. (1995). Personality moderators of mood congruency effects on cognition: The role of self-esteem and negative mood regulators. *Journal of Personality and Social Psychology*, 68, 1092-1107.

Soder, M. (1980). School Integration of the mentally retarded. In P. Bayliss, Segregation, integration, exclusion, inclusion: Frameworks and rationales. *Special Education Gent*, 7, 4-26.

Soder, M. (1989). Disability as a social construct: The labelling approach revisited. *European Journal of Special Needs Education*, 4, 2, 117-129.

Soder, M. (1991). Theory, ideology and research: A response to Tony Booth. *European Journal of Special Needs Education*, 6, 1, 17-23.

Sommers, V. S. (1944). The influence of parental attitudes and social environment on the personality development of the adolescent blind. In L. Gardner, Understanding and Helping Parents of Blind Children. *Journal of Visual Impairment and Blindness*, 76, 3, 81-85.

Spungin, S. J. (1989). Trends and issues : International Education Programmes for Visually Handicapped Children. *Journal of Visual Impairment and Blindness*, 83, 1, 41-43.

Stangvik, G. (1997). Beyond Schooling: Integration in a Policy Perspective. In S. Pijl, C. J. W. Meyer, & S. Hegarty, S. *A Global Agenda*. London: Routledge.

Starr, P., & Heiserman, K. (1977). Acceptance of disability by teenagers with oral-facial clefts. *Rehabilitation Counselling Bulletin*, 20, 198-201.

Steinberg, L., Elmen, J. D., & Mounts, N. S. (1989). Authoritarian Parenting, Psycho-social Maturity and Academic Success among Adolescents. *Child Development*, 60, 1424-1436.

Stone, E., & Priestley, M. (1996). Parasites, pawns and partners: disability research and the role of non-disabled researchers. *International Journal of Sociology*, 47, 4, 699-716.

Swann, W. B. Jr. (1983). Self-verification: Bringing social reality into harmony with the self. *Journal of Personality and Social Psychology*, 53, 1038-1051.

Swann, W. B., Hixan, J. G., Stein-Seroussi, A., & Gilbert, D. T. (1990). The fleeting gleam of praise: Cognitive processes underlying behavioural reactions to self-relevant feedback. *Journal of Personality and Social Psychology*, 59, 17-26.

Szivas-Bach, S. E. (1993). Social Comparisons, stigma and mainstreaming: the self-esteem of young adults with a mild mental handicap. *Mental Handicap Research*, 6, 217-236.

Tajfel, H. (1978). *Differentiation between social groups: Studies in the social psychology of intergroup relations.*

London: Academic Press.

Taylor, C. J. (1998). Factors Affecting Behaviour Towards People with Disabilities. *Journal of Social Psychology*, 138, 6, 766-771.

Taylor, S. E., & Brown, J. D. (1988). Illusions and well-being: A social psychological perspective of self-concept: Specificity to depression symptoms and relation to positive and negative affectivity. *Volta Review*, 73, 80-105.

Taylor, S. E., & Brown, J. D. (1988). Illusions and well-being: A social psychological perspective of mental health. *Psychological Bulletin*, 103, 193-210.

Taylor, W. W., & Taylor, I. W. (1970). *Services for the Handicapped in India*. New York: International Society for Rehabilitation of the Disabled.

Teare, F. J. (1985). Behavioural adjustment as a function of cognitive functioning and visual functioning. *Psychological Abstracts*, 72, 3, 889.

Telford, C. W., & Sawrey, J. M. (1977). *The Exceptional Individual*. New Jersey: Prentice-Hall Inc.

The Hindu. (2001). Inclusive Learning in Schools, October 9.

The Salamanca Statement and Framework for Action on Special Needs Education; Adopted by World Conference in Special Needs Education: Access and Quality. Salamanca, Spain; 7-10 June, 1994.

Thomas, D. (1985). The determinants of teachers? Attitude to integrating the intellectually handicapped. *British Journal of Educational Psychology*, 52, 251-263.

Tomlinson, S. (1982). *A Sociology of Special Education*. London: Routledge and Kegan Paul.

Tregaskis, C. (2002). Social Model Theory: the story so far… *Disability and Society*, 17, 4, 457-470.

Tuttle, D.W. (1987). The Role of the Special Educators, Teacher-Counsellor in Meeting Students' Self-esteem Needs. *Journal of Visual Impairment and Blindness*,

81, 4, 156-161.

Tuttle, D. W., & Tuttle, N. R. (2004). Self-esteem and adjusting with blindness. In N. Griffin- Shirley & S. L. Nes, Self-esteem and Empathy in Sighted and Visually Impaired Adolescents. *Journal of Visual Impairment and Blindness*, 99, 5, 276-285, 2005.

UNESCO (1999). *Salamanca Five Years On: A Review of UNESCO Activities in the Light of the Salamanca Statement Framework of Action of Special Needs Education*. Paris: UNESCO.

Van, H., Vincent, B., Kazdin, A. E., & Hersen, M. (1987). Assessment of problem behaviour in Visually Handicapped Adolescents. *Psychological Abstract*, 74, 4, 1223.

Varma, V. P. (1991). Social Rehabilitation of the Blind. In T. N. Kitchlu, *A Century of Blind Welfare in India*. Delhi: Penman Publishers.

Vosk, B., Forehand, R., Parker, J. B., & Richard, K. (1982). A multimethod comparison of popular and unpopular children. *Developmental Psychology*, 18, 571-575.

Vygotsky, L. S. (1927/1993). Defect and Compensation. In R. W. Reiber & A. S. Carton, (Eds.). *The Collected Works of L. S. Vygotsky, Volume 2: The Fundamentals of Defectology*. New York.

Wagner, G. (1956). The Bantu of North Kavirond. In J. Scheer and N. Groce, Impairment a Human Constant: Cross-cultural and Historical Perspective on Variation. *Journal of Social Issues*, 44, 1, 23-27.

Ward, J., & Center, Y. (1987). Attitudes to integration of disabled into regular classes: A factor analysis of functional characteristics. *British Journal of Educational Psychology*, 57, 22-24.

Warnock Report. (1978). *Report of the Committee of Enquiry into the Education of Handicapped Children and Young People*. London: HMSO.

Warren, D. H. (1994). Blindness and children: An individual difference approach. In N. Griffin-Shirley & S. L. Nes, Self-esteem and Empathy in Sighted and Visually Impaired adolescents. *Journal of Visual Impairment and Blindness*,

99, 5, 276-285, 2005.

Waschull, S. B., & Kernis, M. H. (1996). Level and stability of self-esteem as predictors of children's motivation and reasons for anger. *Journal of Personality and Social Psychology*, 22, 4-13.

Weiner, B. (1985). An attributional theory of achievement motivation and emotion. *Psychological Review*, 92, 548-573.

Weinlader, H. G. (1991). Psychological factors with impact on orientation and mobility in blind children. *European Journal of Special Needs Education*, 6, 3, 210-208.

Wentzel, K. R. (1991). Relations between Social Competence and Academic Achievement in Early Adolescence. *Child Development*, 62, 1066-1078.

Wenz-Goss, M., & Siperstein, N. G. (1993). Importance of social support in the adjustment of children with learning problems. *Exceptional Children*, 63, 2, 183-193.

Wenz-Gross, M., Siperstein, G. N., & Untch, A. S. (1997). Stress, Social Support, and Adjustment of Adolescents in Middle School. *Journal of Early Adolescence*, 17, 2, 129-151.

Werner, H. (1959/1978). Significance of general experimental psychology for the understanding of abnormal behaviour and its correction and prevention. In R. M. Hodapp, *Development and Disabilities: Intellectual, Sensory and Motor Impairments*. New York: Cambridge University Press.

Westbrook, M. T., Ledge, V., & Pennay, M. (1993). Attitudes towards disabilities in a multicultural society. *Social Science and Medicine*, 36, 615-623.

Woo, T. A., & Frank, N. (2000). Academic Performance and Perceived Validity of Grades: An Additional Case of Self-enhancement. *The Journal of Social Psychology*, 140, 2, 218-226.

Wright, B. A. (1960). *Physical Disability: A Psychological Approach*. New York: Harper and Row.

Wylie, R. (1979). *The Self-concept: Theory and Research on*

Selected Topics (*Vol.2*). London: University of Nebraska Press.

Wylie, R. C. (1979). *The Self-concept* (*Vol.1*). Lincoln: University of Nebraska Press.

Yabiku, S. T., Axinn, W. G., & Thornton, A. (1999). Family integration and children's' self-esteem. *American Journal of Sociology*, 104, 1494-1524.

Yelsma, P., & Yelsma, J. (1998). Self-esteem and Social Respect within the High School. *The Journal of Social Psychology*, 138, 4, 431-441.

Yoshikawa, H. (1994). Prevention of cumulative protection: Effects of early family support and education on chronic delinquency and its risks. *Psychological Bulletin*, 115, 28-54.

Youngs, G. A., Jr. Rathge, R., Mullis, R., & Mullis, A. (1990). Adolescent stress and self-esteem. *Adolescence*, 25, 333-341.

Yuhker, H. E. (1965). Attitudes as determinants of behaviour. *Journal of Rehabilitation*, 31, 6, 15-16.

Zigler, E., Balla, D., & Watson, N. (1972). Developmental and experimental determinants of self-image disparity in institutionalized and non-institutionalized retarded and normal children. *Journal of Personality and Social Psychology*, 23, 81-87.

Index